This special edition of

THE AMAZING CRIME
AND TRIAL OF
LEOPOLD AND LOEB

By MAUREEN McKERNAN

has been privately printed
for the members of
The Notable Trials Library

Special Edition Copyright © 1989
THE NOTABLE TRIALS LIBRARY
Division of Gryphon Editions, Inc.
P.O. Box 76108, Birmingham, Alabama 35253
Printed in the United States of America

THE AMAZING CRIME

AND TRIAL OF

LEOPOLD AND LOEB

INTRODUCTION

BY ALAN M. DERSHOWITZ

IT WAS CALLED "the murder of the century." The defense attorney was "the lawyer of the century." And this would be "the trial of the century"—the second or third in Clarence Darrow's distinguished career.

The crime was the stuff of films and novels. Indeed, two movies—one called *The Rope* by Alfred Hitchcock, the other *Compulsion* starring Orson Wells—were based on the infamous Leopold-Loeb case. Numerous books were written about it. This contemporaneous account is the richest in documentation, containing substantial portions of the legal proceedings, psychiatric reports and confessions. Best of all, it contains one of the most remarkable legal arguments in the history of advocacy—Clarence Darrow's successful plea for the lives of his teenage clients, Nathan Leopold, Jr. and Richard Loeb. No lawyer, indeed no civilized person, should go through life without reading—if only there were a tape recording!—Darrow's eloquent defense of young human life.

The crime itself was indefensible. The brilliant, spoiled and bored sons of two of Chicago's wealthiest families planned to commit the perfect crime both for the thrill of it and to prove their perverse misunderstanding of Friedrich Nietzsche's philosophy of the "superman," who was above all law so long as he made no mistake. Their plan, worked out over several months, was to kidnap and immediately kill one of their younger neighbors and hide his body. They would then demand and collect a ransom. The body would never be discovered, the crime would never be solved and only they would know that they had prevailed over ordinary human beings and their simple-minded legal system.

But far from being the "perfect crime," the murder of 14-year-old Bobby Franks turned out to be amateurishly botched. Before any ransom could be paid, the boy's body was discovered in a culvert near where Nathan Leopold often went bird-watching. A pair of telltale glasses was found adjacent to the body. They were easily traced to Leopold who first came up with a paper-thin alibi and soon thereafter confessed to the crime. His fellow murderer likewise confessed. Each of the "superboys" placed the blame for the actual killing on the other.

The famous Clarence Darrow—who generally defended working-class people—was called into this rich-boy case. There was no hope for a factual defense, since virtually every detail of the confessions had been corroborated by hard evidence. Nor was an insanity defense a realistic prospect, since the boys did not meet the rigorous "right-wrong" test then applicable in Illinois. Their crime had been carefully planned and the young criminals were fully cognizant that what they were planning was wrong, as a matter of conventional morality and legality. The fact that they regarded themselves as above such bourgeois constraints would not make for a compelling insanity defense.

But it was clear to Darrow that whether or not they qualified for an insanity defense, these kids were emotionally disturbed. He determined therefore to present a plea for enlightened compassion based on their youth, their emotional makeup and the irrationality of the crime itself. He waived a jury trial, pleaded his clients guilty and presented his case for mitigation to a judge. In support of his argument, he offered the testimony of three of the nation's leading psychiatrists. Their reports are quite informative, if not completely convincing.

What *is* convincing is Darrow's eloquence. His reasoning is as relevant today as it was in 1924. We are still debating whether to execute teenagers, and Darrow's combination of philosophy, psychology and compassion remains among the most compelling arguments on the side of life.

Darrow's brilliance lies in the obviousness of his arguments. He makes it easy for the listener to agree with him. He never asks for long logical or moral leaps. He appeals to common sense, to everyday experience and to moral consensus. As you read his words, you begin to nod your head in agreement with his premises. Before long, he has you agreeing with his conclusion. By the time you finish, you wonder whether any fair-minded judge could impose the death penalty on these two confused boys.

Darrow thought that if he could save these two young killers, he would help put an end to what he considered the barbarity of executing children:

> I am not pleading so much for these boys as I am for the infinite number of others to follow, those who perhaps cannot be as well defended as these have been, those who may go down in the storm, and the tempest, without aid. It is of them I am thinking, and for them I am begging of this court not to turn backward toward the barbarous and cruel past.

> . . . .

> . . . I know your Honor stands between the future and the past. I know the future is with me, and what I stand for here; not merely for the lives of these two unfortunate lads, but for all boys and all girls; for all of the young, and as far as possible, for all of the old. I am pleading for life, understanding, charity, kindness, and the infinite mercy that considers all. I am pleading that we overcome cruelty with kindness and hatred with love. I know the future is on my side.

Darrow succeeded in saving "these two unfortunate lives." But his impact on the "future" remains to be seen. I wonder if we would still be executing "boys and girls," if we had a Clarence Darrow today who could appeal with his eloquence to the evolving historical conscience of our Constitution, and not just to its dry words.

Alan M. Dershowitz

CAMBRIDGE, MASSACHUSETTS
FEBRUARY 17, 1989

Nathan Leopold, Jr., and Richard Loeb, self-confessed slayers of 14-year-old Robert Franks, with their guards, in Judge Caverly's courtroom

THE AMAZING CRIME
AND TRIAL OF
LEOPOLD AND LOEB

By

MAUREEN McKERNAN

WITH AN INTRODUCTION BY

CLARENCE DARROW AND WALTER BACHRACH

CHICAGO
THE PLYMOUTH COURT PRESS
1924

CONTENTS

FOREWORD

The object of this volume is to present fully, accurately and disinterestedly the facts in connection with the unique crime and trial of Leopold and Loeb, which has stirred the entire English speaking world as no other in modern times.

The author was given access to the entire official record of the trial as well as all original documentary evidence, and throughout the preparation of this volume was assisted by Lewis A. Stebbins, LL. B., one of the foremost attorneys of Chicago, especially in presentation and discussion of the questions of law involved.

The author acknowledges indebtedness to State's Attorney Robert E. Crowe, Clarence Darrow, Benjamin C. Bachrach and Walter Bachrach for their valuable co-operation and material embodied in this volume.

THE AUTHOR.

Introduction

On July 23rd, 1924, there began in the Criminal Court of Cook County, Illinois, before his Honor, Judge John R. Caverly, Chief Justice of that court, a hearing in the case of People of the State of Illinois against Nathan F. Leopold, Jr., and Richard A. Loeb, in which for the first time in a court of justice an opportunity was presented to determine the mental condition of persons accused of crime, according to the dictates of science and modern psychiatry, without arbitrary and unscientific limitations imposed by archaic rules of law.

The civilized world had been startled out of its routine complacency on May 31st, 1924, by the amazing confession of these two youths of nineteen and eighteen years, respectively, of the kidnapping and murder of a young neighbor and acquaintance of Richard Loeb, fourteen-year-old Bobby Franks, purely for the thrill and adventure involved in their deed.

The wealth of the three families, their prominence in the community of Chicago, the bizarre and apparently motiveless homicide, and the instantaneous newspaper notoriety which was given to the crime from every conceivable angle aroused public interest throughout the entire civilized world in the fate to be meted out to the young murderers.

The obviously irrational character of the crime directed the minds of everyone immediately into speculation as to the mental condition of the two boys, and forecast a defense on the ground of legal insanity, at the same time that the unusual—and in the case of Leopold, extraordinary—intellects of both boys presented the difficulty of successfully maintaining such a defense.

Under the statutes of the State of Illinois the crime of murder is punishable by imprisonment for a term of not less than fourteen years in the state penitentiary, or for life, or by death, and under a plea of guilty to the crime of murder the judge is required to hear evidence in aggravation and mitigation of the offense. Although, with their unusual intellects, both boys appeared readily to know the difference between a right act and a wrong act and to have the power to choose between the two, which is the archaic test of legal sanity in a criminal case, the defense counsel soon ascertained that both boys were suffering from extensive derangements of their emotional life or affectivity, which derangements entered into and caused the commission of the crime, and which, therefore, in a court of justice, would most naturally be a circumstance mitigating the offense.

The world was again startled, therefore, when, on July 21st, 1924, the defendants appeared in court with their lawyers and, having obtained leave to withdraw their pleas of not guilty, pleaded guilty. The public, being prepared for and expecting a highly technical effort to be made to obtain the acquittal of these defendants by their wealthy families, was entirely unprepared for this most natural and simple procedure, whereby an effort could be made to mitigate the offense and thereby obtain the imposition of a sentence of life imprisonment in the penitentiary, resulting in the defendants' escaping the extreme penalty of the law, and at the same time resulting in a protection of society from the danger incident to their freedom.

When the pleas of guilty were entered it was made clear to the Court and to the public that the families of the defendants were interested only in securing an impartial consideration of the mental condition of the defendants, and sought by a demonstration of their mental illnesses to obtain from the Court, at the very most, and at the same time the very least, their confinement in the penitentiary for life.

The backbone of the defense being an investigation into the mental condition, counsel immediately applied themselves to the building up of the medical phase of the case. They obtained the services of two psychiatrists and endocrinologists, Doctors Karl M. Bowman, Chief of Staff of the Boston (Mass.) Psychopathic Hospital, and Harold S. Hulbert, of Chicago, Associate in Neurology and formerly Instructor in Nervous and Mental Diseases at the University of Illinois, to make a thorough investigation of the mental condition and a personality study of the two boys and draw up an extensive report, in which would be embodied their findings in detail, without any conclusions therein contained as to the mental condition of the defendants. This would furnish a starting point for the subsequent investigations and examinations of Doctor William A. White, Superintendent of St. Elizabeth's Hospital (the Government Hospital for the Insane) at Washington, D. C.; Doctor William Healy, Director of the Judge Baker Foundation of Boston, an organization devoted to research in the subject of juvenile delinquency, co-operating in its work with the various courts of Boston, Mass., and Doctor Bernard A. Glueck, formerly psychiatrist at Sing Sing penitentiary at Ossining, New York, three of the most distinguished psychiatrists in the United States.

Extended and repeated examinations and observations of both defendants, extending over a period of two weeks, by Doctors Bowman and Hulbert, with the entire co-operation of the jail authorities, the defense counsel and the two defendants, resulted in the Bowman-Hulbert report, subsequently offered in evidence in the cause.

After repeated examinations and observations of both boys, under the most favorable conditions, and a consideration of the Bowman-Hulbert report, each doctor concluded that each boy was suffering from a mental disease, characterized by disturbance of his emotional life, which, when the two boys were brought into association with each other, resulted in the murder of young Robert Franks.

The prosecution made extended arguments, lasting several days, attacking the competency and admissibility of such evidence in mitigation of the offense; but the novelty of this character of proceeding rendered inapplicable the precedents cited by the prosecution in this effort, and the duty of the judge to hear evidence in mitigation under the statute being mandatory, Judge Caverly permitted the defense to offer its medical testimony. He imposed no limitation whatsoever upon either the substance of the evidence introduced or the method of its introduction, thereby making possible for the first time in the history of medical jurisprudence a completely scientific investigation in a court of law of the mental condition of persons accused of crime. This case, therefore, makes an epoch in the advance of the administration of the criminal law, demonstrating the possibility of the utilization by our criminal courts of modern medical knowledge on the subject of mental disorders.

The propriety of such an investigation, the high plane of professional dignity maintained by the psychiatrists, and the importance of this step in the progress of the enlightened administration of the law find their demonstration on practically every succeeding page of this volume.

Parents and teachers as well as persons whose professions bring them into frequent contact with juvenile delinquency will find in this volume rich material throwing light upon hitherto unrevealed problems of adolescence and the causes of crime.

Lawyers will undoubtedly find much to interest them because of the opportunity to study the forensic method of presentation of the results obtained from a mental examination of accused persons, by the application of the principles of modern psychology and psychiatry.   CLARENCE DARROW.

WALTER BACHRACH.

The Crime Startles Chicago

Early morning mists still lay in the hollows of an open bit of prairie south of Chicago, when at about eight o'clock on May 22nd, 1924, some workmen decided to cut across the waste land along a dim, forgotten trail. It's a lonely tract. A few workmen traverse it each week. Almost the only other people who go there are students of bird life, who find in that wild bit of unused land birds in every thicket, living undisturbed in the fringes of the factories.

Little ponds scatter its acres and low bushes break the even stretches of grass and marsh. It was only by a whim of chance that the workmen that morning passed that way. The path runs past the open end of a culvert that drains beneath a railroad track, and by another chance of fortune one of the workmen was attracted by a flash of white through the shrubs that grew about the open culvert's mouth.

The flash of white, when they parted the bushes, proved to be the feet of a child, just showing above the surface of the murky pool of water in the drain. Standing in the water above their knees, they pulled, from where it had been wedged down into the culvert's mouth, the naked body of a boy. He had been dead, they saw, for several hours.

Thinking that it might be some child who had braved a swim too early in the season, they laid the body upon the grass and looked about for his clothes.

All that they could find was one woolen golf stocking. A few feet away, presently, one of them found a pair of horn-rimmed spectacles. Studying the body, they saw two welts on its forehead, small scratches on the shoulders and the breasts, and a cut in the scalp. A few stains marred the even white of the boy's face about the mouth. They knew from the boy's soft hair, from the smooth texture of his skin, and from his clean little hands that this was no homeless waif.

So, in the early morning, on the fog-drenched Hegewich wastes, these workmen gazed in puzzled speculation upon the body of the fourteen-year-old Robert Franks, whose death for days was to puzzle Chicago, the mystery of whose murder was to turn into amateur detectives every man and woman who could read the meager details of the killing of the son of Jacob Franks. So unexpectedly did these men discover the corpus of a homicide unrivaled in the annals of crime.

At about the time the workmen were lifting the body of Robert Franks from the Hegewich ditch, Jacob Franks, the boy's father, was pacing the floor in his home. The Franks home, large and comfortable, is typical of the homes of Hyde Park, where some of the most prosperous people of Chicago have lived for many years.

On the table rested a cigar box, containing Ten Thousand Dollars in old bills. Jacob Franks was waiting for a telephone call that would tell him what to do with that sealed cigar box.

The night before Robert Franks had not come home to dinner. He was a child of regular habits, and his family became alarmed. They called the Harvard School, two blocks north, where Robert, with the other sons of the rich men of the neighborhood, attended school. Mrs. Franks called several of her friends on the telephone and Jacob Franks looked in the yards of several neighbors.

Later, growing really frightened, Jacob Franks called an old friend, Samuel Ettelson, an attorney, and asked him if he had seen Robert about. Then they called the police and asked them to look for a fourteen-year-old boy.

All they could tell the police was that the boy had last been seen leaving the grounds of the private school he attended about five o'clock. Several playmates had seen him then. They knew when he had left the playground at the back of the school, because he had been umpiring a baseball game, but had deserted it to go home. The last that anyone had seen of him was in front of the school, walking slowly south toward his home, along the sun-dappled walk in the pleasant late May afternoon.

They were hoping to hear soon from some friend where the boy might have stopped to visit, when the telephone rang, about ten-thirty o'clock. Mrs. Franks answered the call. A man's voice, soft and well modulated, said, "Your son has been kidnapped. He is all right. Further news in the morning." Mrs. Franks, stunned, held to the receiver and asked, "Who is it?" The man answered, "Johnson," and hung up.

With that the family had to be content until the next morning, when a special delivery letter, which had been mailed at the Hyde Park postal station, was delivered. The letter had been written on linen paper of good quality. Its words were well chosen. The phraseology even suggested that someone with a smattering of legal knowledge might have written it.

The letter said:

"Dear Sir:

"As you no doubt know by this time, you son has been kidnapped. Allow us to assure you that he is at present well and safe. You need fear no physical harm for him, providing you live up carefully to the following instructions, and such others as you will receive by future communications. Should you, however, disobey any of our instructions, even slightly, death will be the penalty.

"1: For obvious reasons, make absolutely no attempt to communicate with either the police authorities or any private agency.

Should you already have communicated with the police, allow them to continue their investigations, but do not mention this letter.

"2: Secure, before noon to-day, $10,000.00. This money must be composed entirely of old bills, of the following denominations: $2,000.00 in $20.00 bills; $8,000.00 in $50.00 bills. The money must be old. Any attempt to include new or marked bills will render the entire venture futile. The money should be placed in a large cigar box, or, if such is impossible, in a heavy cardboard box, securely closed and wrapped in white paper. The wrapping paper should be sealed at all openings with sealing wax.

"3: Have the money thus prepared as directed above, and remain home after one o'clock P. M. See that the telephone is not in use.

"You will receive further communication instructing you as to your future course. As a final word of warning, this is a strictly commercial proposition, and we are prepared to put our threats into execution, should we have reasonable ground to believe that you have committed an infraction of the above instructions. However, should you carefully follow out our instructions to the letter, we can assure you that your son will be safely returned to you within six hours of our receipt of the money.

"Yours truly,

"GEORGE JOHNSON."

With no intention of disobeying the letter's instruction, Franks prepared the cigar box as he was told, sealed it as the letter directed, and then from early morning waited for further instructions.

Fearing to arouse the ire of "Mr. Johnson," the father did not consult further with the police. It was thought best to follow the instructions of the letter. So anxious were both Mr. and

Mrs. Franks for the safety of their son, that they were willing to follow the kidnapper's instructions to the letter.

As Jacob Franks paced the floor of his home, the money ready, there ran through his mind the question continually, "Who would kidnap his son?" The ransom asked was a small one to ask of a man of Franks' wealth. He had piled up a fortune in Chicago real estate, starting years ago, lending money in the days when Chicago was "wide open" and gambling houses had been common. He had loaned money to gamblers, to rich men, poor men, beggar men, thieves—and from his dealings with them all he had earned the name of "Honest Jake" Franks, a square man, who loaned ninety-five cents on the dollar.

Could it be that some enemy of those old days, for some real or fancied wrong, sought to strike at the father through his son? Such were the thoughts that tortured Jacob Franks as he waited with his wife, his friend, and even the servants of the household hanging breathless for the jingle of the telephone.

Finally the call came. "A taxi cab will be at your door." Then Franks was instructed to take with him the money, enter the taxi and ride to a certain drug store on Sixty-third Street. So excited was the man that he misunderstood the name of the store, but when he tried to recall "Mr. Johnson" the latter had hung up. The taxicab came, but while it was waiting a second telephone call came.

This time it was the police. A little boy's body had just been found far south in a marshy waste of ground. It probably wasn't the Franks boy, the father was assured, for this child wore horn-rimmed glasses. At least a pair had been found near the culvert where the body had been discovered. It would do no harm to see the body, though.

So Jacob Franks learned a few hours later that his son was dead. He learned, too, from the Coroner, that the child had been dead probably before "Mr. Johnson" had called the night before. The country undertaker, where the body had been taken, had placed the spectacles on the child's face, but they were too narrow.

So the glasses, the slender clew by which the mystery was to be unraveled, were laid aside.

The Coroner said death had come from strangulation, and from blows upon the head with some dull instrument. The blows had not been heavy ones—scarcely heavy enough to break the skin, but heavy enough to kill. Swellings of the tongue and the throat indicated that the child had been strangled, too. There were scratches on the body that might have been made in many ways, though probably occurred when the body was pushed into the drain, it was agreed.

So there Jacob Franks and the detective force, which already had come to his assistance, were faced with only two clews to the person or persons who had killed the boy, a pair of horn-rimmed glasses and a typewritten letter—nothing else; a typewritten letter, with no outstanding characteristics, and a pair of glasses, such as thousands of people wear.

Slender threads, indeed, to follow:

For days Chicago was torn with the mystery. The rest of the country began to take an interest in the death of this obscure little boy in Chicago. Who had murdered Bobby Franks? Why had they done it? Why had they killed him before they even asked for a ransom?

Wild rumors swept the town. Almost every detective on the police force was assigned to the case. Every newspaper in town assigned its best reporters to the story. No clew was too unimportant to follow. Every one turned detective. Friends of the Franks family flocked to its aid and, for the time being, became amateur sleuths.

The detective bureau of Chicago was flooded with a thousand and one clews. Every man named Johnson was investigated.

From the narrow width of the horn-rimmed spectacles, from the well-modulated voice of the telephone, and from the impression left by the ransom letter, that it had been written by an educated man, there was constructed an image of "Mr. Johnson." A tall, thin-faced individual, perhaps, well educated and sorely pressed for money.

A little boy living near the Harvard School said he had seen a gray Winton car sweep down the street just after Bobby left the school grounds. Every Winton car owner in the city had to account for himself on the afternoon of May twenty-first. Winton cars in towns about Chicago were seized. The "Mr. Johnsons" who drove Winton cars found themselves forced to answer many insistent questions.

But, most interested were the youths of the neighborhood, themselves sons of wealthy men. Hyde Park, the prosperous district that lies adjacent to the University of Chicago campus, extending from Grand Boulevard to the pleasant shore of Lake Michigan, was combed from end to end by reporters, detectives and friends of the Franks family for any possible clew to the kidnaping and killing of the Franks boy.

Among these young men there was none more interested than Richard Loeb, eighteen-year-old son of one of the most prominent men in Chicago. The boy was a distant cousin of Robert Franks. His father, Albert Loeb, Vice-President of Sears, Roebuck & Co., had long been known for his philanthropy and patronage of the arts.

The Loeb home was one of the finest in that district of fine homes. Robert Franks had often played tennis with Richard Loeb on the Loeb tennis courts. Indeed, that was one of the first places his father had searched for his son the night he had failed to return from school.

Handsome, popular at college, Richard Loeb was one of the most prominent figures in his social set, for his own winning personality as well as for the prominent standing of his parents. He had been graduated, at seventeen, from the University of Michigan—the youngest graduate of that school. He was marked in his classes at the University of Chicago, where in the spring of 1924 he was a special student, for the brilliancy of his mind.

"A nice kid," his companions all called him. Traveling with a set several years his seniors, because he was in their classes at school, he was a lovable mixture of little boy grown old too fast and sophisticated man of the world. He had attended the Harvard School, and before that had been taught at home for many years by a private governess.

He new the teachers of the Harvard School well. So when he offered his services to some young newspaper reporters he knew they were glad to get his suggestions about the students at the school. They were glad to have him help sift this neighborhood in which he had grown up for traces of someone who might have seen Robert Franks after he reached the sidewalk in front of his school on the afternoon of May twenty-first.

"Let me go with you," Loeb had said to James Mulroy, a reporter on the Daily News, "where they left this boy's body. I knew him well."

"What kind of a kid was he?" Mulroy asked. "Well, if you were going to pick out some kid to kidnap, Bobby was just about the cocky sort of a little chap you'd pick out." So interested was Loeb that he took all the time anyone wanted, telling about the characteristics of the teachers at the school, about the employes, about the place and the habits of the students.

His own younger brother was then a student at Harvard School, but so alarmed was Mrs. Albert Loeb that she rushed the child away to the family estate at Charlevoix, in upper Michigan, where he would be safe from kidnapers.

Fear of more kidnapings at this time seized all the parents of children and more than one youngster was rushed away on a visit to distant relatives or friends or sent to summer estates.

A constant detail of detectives was kept at the Franks home, for fear the kidnapers might try to harm other members of the family. Mrs. Franks was too ill to see even her closest friends. Mr. Franks spent all his time giving what help he could to detectives on the case. Notes, palpably imitations of the ransom letter, but written by other people with the probable purpose of frightening the family, were received by Jacob Franks.

It was a fine holiday for cranks and amateur detectives, and anyone's guess was as good as another's.

Almost at once the first arrests were made. Three teachers at the Harvard School were taken to detective headquarters for questioning. They were held and grilled for hours. Mr. Franks and his friend, Mr. Ettelson, had suggested that, perhaps, the teachers at the school, or someone connected with the school, might know about the kidnaping. It was thought, in the hopelessness of solution, which the case presented those first three or four days, that possibly some teacher, hard pressed for money and tempted by the signs of wealth, which they saw about them continually, might be guilty of the crime. Within reason, it seemed then, that some teacher, tired of the meager existence afforded by a school master's salary, envious of the private cars and chauffeurs of their students, had been tempted to make a strike for an easy relief from pressing debts.

It was then that Richard Loeb's suggestions were most eagerly sought by reporters and even detectives. Knowing the Harvard School and its whole personnel so well that he might be able to give some valuable suggestion. Pitifully, steadfastly, the harassed teachers insisted their innocence, but still they were held.

Some of them admitted a knowledge of the Hegewich prairie. They had taken students there to study birds. The tract of land, with its little lakes and its plentiful bird life, had always been a favorite with the Harvard nature study classes. The students, most of whom owned automobiles, found its distance from the city of no moment and often visited the place on picnicking and nature study expeditions.

Though interest centered in the Harvard School, many detectives still sought the mythical "Mr. Johnson," the writer of the letter, the sender of the phone call, upon whom every one looked as the slayer of Robert Franks. It had been agreed that the glasses were his—lost as he hid the body in that lonely waste land where he thought it would never be found.

Men who looked like him were questioned. One poor, unfortunate drug clerk, his job gone, without funds and ill, in some remote part of the city, had acted in a manner to arouse the suspicions of his acquaintances. His name was given to the police. Horribly harassed with his own troubles, his mind none too well balanced, he became so frightened at his resemblance to the fancied "Mr. Johnson" that he fled to Kentucky and there committed suicide on the very night the solution of the crime was reached by the State's Attorney.

The town was still raining suggestions upon the detectives, with the State's Attorney's office seemingly still in a maze when the horn-rimmed glasses took their proper place in the scheme of things—the only real clew to the person or persons who had thrust Bobby Franks' body into the open culvert.

This was because, by very sensible investigation, a group of detectives from the Detective Bureau of the Chicago Police Department had traced the glasses to a certain oculist. Looking back through his files, he found that those glasses had been sold to a nineteen-year-old boy, Nathan F. Leopold, Jr., a student at the University of Chicago.

This was nine days after the murder of Robert Franks. A nine days' wonder before the keystone of the edifice of mystery was hit upon. From then on events moved rapidly.

With the teachers of the Harvard School still in custody, though not under arrest, a squad of detectives was sent to Leopold's home to ask him to come down and explain to the Chief of Detectives how his glasses, if they were his, happened to be in the Hegewich marsh.

Nathan Leopold was one of the youngest honor students at the University of Chicago. His father, Nathan F. Leopold, is a millionaire box manufacturer and head of large lake shipping interests. The Leopold home was only three blocks from the Franks home. Visiting Leopold when the detectives called was Richard Loeb.

Taken to the La Salle Hotel, Joseph P. Savage, of the State's Attorney's Office, asked Nathan Leopold if he was not familiar with the scene where the body was found. He said he was very familiar with it—that he had been out there, perhaps, one hundred and fifty or two hundred times studying birds. He said he knew the exact spot where the body was found, because the Saturday or Sunday before the murder he had been out there and had run over the mouth of the culvert in an attempt to shoot some birds.

He was asked if he had read the ransom letter and he said he had. "What is your opinion of the man who wrote the letter?" he was asked. "Well, he must have been a man of some education, either a high school man, or probably a high school graduate. I was unable to find errors of any sort in that letter except possibly the word 'kidnapped.' It is spelled with one or two 'p's.' I don't know which. Either, I think, is proper."

When he was shown the pair of glasses found by the workmen on the marsh, he put them on and said: "If I were not positive that my glasses are at home, I would say these are mine." But a search of his home by the boy and a detective failed to locate his own glasses.

In the meantime, the detectives were paying little attention to

Richard Loeb. He had been brought along with Leopold, but no one thought he knew more than he had already told. All the attention was centered on Leopold and the glasses. One other thing was not forgotten—that was the typewritten note.

Leopold was a friend of Samuel Ettelson, who was representing the Franks family. Nathan Leopold located him on the telephone from the State's Attorney's Office at the Franks home. The State's Attorney was assured that this boy came of a perfectly respectable family and that it was ridiculous to suppose that he might have any knowledge of the crime, even if the glasses were his—even if he had visited the Hegewich marsh.

At first Leopold could not remember what he had done on the day of the murder. Then he remembered that he and Dick Loeb had spent the afternoon in Lincoln Park, in the north part of the city, looking for a rare species of bird.

Leopold, at nineteen, had already gained for himself no little fame as a student of bird life. He had lectured before scientific bodies about the rare Kirtland Warbler, whose life habits were little known until Leopold made a study of the bird and took motion pictures of it feeding its young in the northern woods.

According to his statement, they had spent the afternoon, after luncheon in the loop, studying birds in Lincoln Park and drinking gin—drinking too much gin to go home for dinner. They went to the Cocoanut Grove, on Sixty-third Street, for dinner, and after dinner driving in Nathan's maroon Willys-Knight car up and down Sixty-third Street, looking for some girls with nothing to do. They found the girls, Nathan said, and took them out to the wooded island in Jackson Park. The girls, however, did not agree with the boys on methods of spending the evening, and so they were told to get out and walk home, so the boys drove home alone. That was their story. Later Richard told it, too. Not a flaw—both told the same plausible story—simply, willingly and smilingly.

The second day the boys were held, their fathers and Jacob Loeb, Richard's uncle, came to see if they were receiving proper treatment. "We merely wanted to assure ourselves that the boys were not being abused," the men said. "If the boys are in Mr. Crowe's own custody, we want them to remain as long as possible and give any assistance they can. Mr. Crowe must become satisfied, and we must be satisfied that they know nothing that may have a bearing or help in the solution of this crime."

So the boys were sent a change of linen and fresh suits. But the questioning continued. Such nice, well-bred, patient boys they were—smiling and willing to talk; willing to discuss anything with the detectives and the State's Attorney's staff, and willing to tell over and over just what they had done that sunny May afternoon.

Around and around the story of their activities of the afternoon of May twenty-first, Robert E. Crowe, the State's Attorney for Cook County, looked for a break—for some opening. There were no flaws in the story—and yet! There were Leopold's glasses—the State's Attorney was not satisfied. Somewhere there was a flaw—and finally they found it in the impersonal typewritten letter of "Mr. Johnson."

"What kind of a typewriter do you use?" he had been asked. "A Hammond" had been the safe reply. The ransom note had been written on an Underwood—a portable type, revealed by a study of the characters in the letter.

James Mulroy, a former student at the University of Chicago, and, at the time of the murder, a reporter on the Daily News, learned that during the winter Leopold had four of his classmates working with him preparing for an examination. A typewriter in Leopold's home had been used. The students showed Mulroy their copies of the outlines that had been prepared on Leopold's typewriter. They undoubtedly had been written on the same machine that had written the ransom note.

So, there they had the flaw in the wall. There Crowe found the tiny break for which he had hunted so tirelessly. Against the whole police force these two boys had stood adamant, unbroken, smiling, with their story down pat, and no one believing, in spite of the glasses that were Leopold's, that the boys could have had any hand in the crime. To Dick Loeb, scarcely any attention was paid—except that Crowe did not forget, while Leopold's story was under fire, that Dick had said they had been together all that day.

Leopold denied he had ever owned an Underwood typewriter —or a portable Underwood. When told that his four fellow students said he had had one in February, he said, "Well, if that is the case, one of them must have brought it with him. It certainly did not belong to me."

When confronted by these boys, he persisted in denying the possession or ownership of such a machine. He was asked "If these boys did not own it, who else could have?" And he answered "Leon Mandel, the second." But Leon Mandel was in Europe, over a month. If he had not taken it away from Leopold's home before he sailed, the machine would still be at Leopold's house.

With detectives, the boy looked through his home for the machine as he had looked for the glasses. It was not there. But a servant told a detective that the machine had been there two weeks ago. Then Mandel had not taken it with him. But the machine was not to be found. So, he agreed that the machine had not belonged to Mandel.

Now to Dick Loeb, the boy who had come along to be in on the fun—not to miss anything. Everyone who knew Loeb believed that the State's Attorney was wasting his time holding such a nice kid, and such a mouthy one too. Anything he might have known would have been told long ago—and such a nice boy could not be implicated in such a crime.

Leopold was not so well known, nor was he so popular with his acquaintances. There were fewer voices raised to champion Nathan, but every one was for Dick Loeb.

Things stood at a seeming deadlock, and the newspaper men, sitting in the outer offices of the State's Attorney's suite, were wondering when they dared go home—or praying that something definite would happen.

About midnight, Dick Loeb sent for the State's Attorney and said he wanted to talk with him. "What are you holding me for?" he asked. The State's Attorney asked, "You realize you are in custody, do you?" Up to that time it had all been just a friendly conference to see if the boys might be able to throw some light on some clew—perhaps some light on the school teachers, who were still in custody.

"You haven't anything on me—you are not asking me about this, so what are you holding me for?" Mr. Crowe told the boy that they were paying no attention to him at all. "We're paying all our attention to tightening the web about Leopold," was the answer. "But that makes a web about me," must have been the boy's thought.

The flaw was widening. The long prayed for was about to happen. And then, it did happen—after all those cruel days of suspense, suspicion, fear, baffling mystery and false clews.

Sven Englund, chauffeur of the Leopold family, came into the room where Dick Loeb sat. Out over the town, many detectives were still wondering if some good clew had been overlooked. Sven Englund walked into the office of Mr. Crowe and touched the keystone of that baffling wall of mystery. The wall began to crumble.

"The evidence we have against Nathan indicates that he killed this boy," said Mr. Crowe. Loeb listened, gulped, and then stammered, "My God! Give me a drink of water." He was given the drink. Sven Englund, the chauffeur, had come

to Mr. Crowe and told him a simple thing—that the maroon
car of Nathan's had been in the garage from morning until
about ten-thirty o'clock the evening of May twenty-first. He
knew because he had repaired the car and cleaned it. The boys
must have driven some other car.

This, Mr. Crowe told Dick. The boy paled, stammered and
asked for a drink. "Well, I'll tell you the entire truth." So
the wall began to crumble, taking with it in its wreck the
happiness of two self-respecting honored families. Taking with
it the faith of friends and the lives of the boys.

Out of the lips of Dick Loeb, who had come along to be in
on the fun, from the lips of the amateur sleuth who had helped
the reporters, came the story of the crime, detail by detail, and
with it the most amazing motive for a killing that the world
has known since mediaeval days when kings killed for pastime.

They had killed Robert Franks, because they wanted the
excitement of committing a perfect, detection-defying crime.

A crime, which, except for the horn-rimmed glasses, might
have remained the thing the boy had planned and dreamed of—
the perfect crime!

While he was telling his story in one room to John Sbarbaro,
Assistant State's Attorney, Nathan Leopold sent for Joseph
Savage, another Assistant to Mr. Crowe and Mr. Crowe, him-
self.

The wall was crumbling faster!

"I'm going to charge you with this murder, Nathan," he was
told. "Why, you haven't anything on me except the flimsiest
circumstances, you will never do that." "You don't know that
your pal, your best friend, is telling the details of this murder,
do you?" "No! My God! He would never do that! He
would stand until hell freezes over." Then, Mr. Crowe mentioned details of the plot the boys had formed—mentioned details of the plan of Bobby Franks' murder. "If Loeb did not

tell me that, who did?" "Well, if Loeb is talking, I will tell you the *real* truth," said Nathan F. Leopold, Jr., placing his hand to the crumbling wall.

Both boys put their hands to the wall of mystery that had baffled the world, and pushed it over upon themselves. Told how they had wanted some excitement—how they were surfeited with the ease and comfort of their lives as rich men's sons and wanted a real thrill. Told of their inability to find zest in any pastime and so they had turned to the plotting of a master crime. Like children, they told it, and, as they told it, found zest in the telling.

One had wanted all his life to be a feared and terrifying criminal—had even dreamed of such a life back in his nursery days and during the growing days when, sheltered and shut in from other boys of his own age by a devoted governess, he had fashioned a world of his own from the books he read. It was an amazing confession of a friendship of two boys in which they decided to practice some of the theories they had assimilated from reading with immature minds, facts of life and the world which were meant only for age and discretion.

Before dawn, the whole story was in the hands of the State's Attorney. The boys had agreed on everything except who actually killed Bobby Franks. Each maintained the other had done it. Placed face to face, their friendship was broken and two frightened boys, scared out of their sophistication and polished manners, cried and accused each other. Little boys, each of them, not polished men at all, crying from beneath the ruins of the wall they had pushed over upon themselves.

Let it be said for them, in passing, that the breach in their friendship, which had lasted from the year they were fifteen, was soon healed and the accusations forgotten.

More interesting than their manners and their poise, at that moment, however, is the story of their confession.

The Confession

"Now, Nathan, I just want you to go on in your own way and tell us the story from the beginning, tell us the whole thing."

"When we planned a general thing of this sort was as long ago as last November I guess at least, and we started on the process of how to get the money which was the most difficult problem. We had several dozen different plans, all of which were not so good for one reason or other. Finally we hit upon the plan of having money thrown from a moving train, after the train had passed a given landmark. The landmark we finally chose was the factory of the Champion Manufacturing Company at 74th Street and the I. C. Railroad tracks. The next problem was the system of notification to the father. We originally planned a number of relays, in other words the man was to receive a special delivery letter telling him his son had been kidnapped and was being held for ransom, then to secure ten thousand dollars in denominations as follows: Eight thousand dollars in fifty dollar bills and two thousand dollars in twenty dollar bills. He was to get old, unmarked bills whose numbers were not in sequence, and these he was to place in a cigar box, securely tied, wrapped in white paper, the ends were to be sealed with sealing wax. The reason for this was to give the impression that the box would be delivered personally to a messenger of the real executives of the plan. He was then to receive a phone call at about one or two o'clock in the afternoon instructing him to proceed to a 'Help Keep the City Clean' box whose location was to be definitely given. Then he was to find another note which would instruct him to proceed to a drug store which had a public phone booth. He was to be called at this phone booth, the drug store being very near the I. C. track, and given only just enough time to rush out, buy a ticket and board a through train without allowing him enough time to instruct detectives or police as to where he was going. In the train he was to proceed to the rear car, look in the box left for telegraph blanks for another letter. This letter instructed him to go to the rear platform of the car, face east and look for the first large red brick factory adjacent to the tracks which had a black water tower bearing a white inscription 'Champion.' He was to count two or three after that and then throw the box as far to the east as he could. The next problem was getting the victim to kill. This was left undecided until the day we decided to pick the most likely-looking subject that came our way. The particular case happened to be Robert Franks. Richard was acquainted with Robert and asked him to come over to our car for a moment. This occurred near 49th and Ellis Avenue. Robert came over to the car, was introduced to me and Richard asked him if he did not want to help him."

"Richard who?"

"Richard Loeb. He replied no, but Richard said, well, come in a minute. I want to ask you about a certain tennis racket. After he had gotten in, I stepped on the gas, proceeded south on Ellis Avenue to 50th Street. In the meantime Richard asked Robert if he minded if we took him around the block, to which Robert said, no. As soon as we turned the corner, Richard placed his one hand over Robert's mouth to stifle his outcry, with his right beating him on the head several times with a chisel, especially prepared for the purpose. The boy did not succumb as readily as we had believed so for fear of being observed Richard seized him, and pulled him into the back seat. Here he forced a cloth into his mouth. Apparently the boy died instantly by suffocation shortly thereafter. We proceeded out to Calumet Boulevard in Indiana, drove along this road that leads to Gary, being a rather deserted place. We even stopped to buy a couple of sandwiches and some drinks for supper."

"Where?"

"On Calumet Boulevard at I guess 132nd Street, the body was covered by an automobile robe which we had brought along for the purpose. We drove up and down this road until dark, then proceeded over the path which leads out towards Hegewisch, from 108th and Avenue F to the prearranged spot for the disposal of the body. We had previously removed the shoes, trousers and stockings of the boy, leaving the shoes and the belt by the side of the road concealed in the grass. Having arrived at our destination we placed the body in the robe, carried it to the culvert where it was found. Here we completed the disrobing, then in an attempt to render identification more difficult we poured hydrochloric acid over the face and body. Then we placed the body into the drain pipe and pushed it as far as we could. We gathered up all the clothes, placed them in the robe and apparently at this point the glasses fell from my pocket. I carried the robe containing the clothes back to the automobile, a distance of some 300 yards, and one of the socks apparently dropped from the bundle. We then proceeded north to 104th and Ewing Avenue from where I telephoned my folks telling them I should be a trifle late in arriving home. We drove to 47th and Woodlawn and from there I telephoned Franks' home. I spoke to Mrs. Franks and told her that my name was George Johnson, that her boy had been kidnapped but was safe, and that further instructions would follow. In passing 55th Street we had mailed a special delivery letter which had been completed except for the address which I printed on it. After taking my aunt and uncle home I returned to my home and after my father had retired, Richard and I proceeded to his home where we burned the remaining clothes. Hid the robe and washed the more obvious blood stains from the automobile. Then I parked the automobile near my home. The next day at 2:30 Central time or 3:30 Chicago time we were down at the Illinois Central station at 12th Street. Here Richard bought a ticket to Michigan City on the three o'clock train, entered the train, and deposited the letter in the telegraph blank box. In the meantime I called the Franks' home and told Mr. Franks to proceed immediately to the drug store at 1465 East 63rd Street and to wait at the easterly of the two public phone booths for a telephone call. I told him a Yellow cab would be at his door to take him. I repeated the number twice and he asked if he couldn't have a little more time, to which I replied no, it must be immediately. About the time I was phoning, Richard had returned from the train and we started out south intending to call the drug store from Walgreen's store, 67th and Stony Island. We chanced to see a newspaper lying on the stand with headlines "Unidentified boy found in swamp." We deliberated a few moments as to what to do, Dick thinking that the game was up. I, however, insisted that it could do no harm to call the drug store. This I did, but was told that no Mr. Franks was in the building. We then went to 68th and Stony Island, another drug store, and again telephoned, we met with the same reply. Then we gave it up as a bad job and returned the car to a place where it had been rented. Our original plan had included a relay which was to send Mr. Franks to a 'Help Keep the City Clean' box at the corner of Vincennes and Pershing but we had difficulty in making the envelope stick as we intended, and hence decided to eliminate this relay. Thursday, immediately after dinner, we drove the car to our garage and started to clean up the rest of the blood stains. Our chauffeur, Sven Englund, noticed us and came out to help. Whereupon Richard told him it was merely some red wine which had been spilled.

"Who did clean it up?"

"Dick did most of it and I helped him."

"Is there anything else you can think of at this time?"

"No."

"Your original plan when you were thinking it out as late as last November, Nathan, did you have anyone at that time that was to be the victim?"

"Nobody in particular. We had considered Mr. Clarence Coleman, also Mr. Walter Baer, Walter Baer, Jr., as the victim, and Clarence Coleman's son."

"When was the plan finally effected whereby you considered the Franks boy?"

"When we saw him on the 9th by pure accident."

"At that time were you waiting for some one else?"

"We had been cruising around watching several groups of boys playing, waiting for somebody to start home."

"You had been doing that for how long, Nathan?"

"From about three o'clock in the evening until about five."

"And you did not have any boys prior to that time?"

"No."

"This day in particular you stayed out with the idea in mind of getting the boy that day, is that it?"

"Yes, sir."

"What time did you meet Richard Loeb that day, Wednesday, May 21st, 1924?"

"At eleven o'clock."

"Where did you meet him?"

"At the university."

"What did you do after that?"

"Drove down in my car to the Rent-a-Car people.

"Where is that?"

"That is at 1408 or 10 Michigan Avenue."

"Then what did you do?"

"Rent a Willys-Knight."

"At that time?"

"Yes."

"Under what name."

"Morton D. Ballard."

"Had you ever rented a car there before?"

"Yes, sir."

"Under what name?"

"The same."

"When did you rent a car there?"

"About three weeks previously."

"And you used it for what purpose?"

"Merely so we would have no difficulty in getting the car the next time."

"Is that the letter you typed?"

"Yes."

"Will you look at that, Nathan?"

"Is that the letter you addressed?"

"Yes."

"They handle Willys-Knights and Fords?"

"Willys-Knights and Fords."

"Willys-Knights and Fords exclusively, is that right?"

"Yes, sir."

"What did you pay over there?"

"Seventeen cents a mile for Willys-Knights and 15 cents a mile for Fords."

"You could keep the car over night?"

"Yes, we made that arrangement Wednesday."

"After you got the car what time did you get the car down there that day?"

"At 11:30."

"Do you remember who you talked to there, Nathan?"

"It was one of two men, I don't remember."

"Can you remember the names?"

"No."

"You would know them if you saw them?"

"Yes."

"If I came over there for a car would they require any security?"

"Yes. The first time they made me deposit fifty dollars and the last time thirty-five. I was supposed to have an identification card of some sort but I never received it, so I had to look up my old lease number and give that as reference."

"What address did you give, Nathan?"

"Originally the Morrison Hotel, went down and rented a room and left a suitcase in it, and sent some mail there for the purpose of having mail addressed to that address. When we went down to get out mail on the subsequent day the suitcase had been taken. Apparently the fact the beds had not been used was noticed and some suspicion occurred. The suitcase had been apparently confiscated and I therefore telephoned the Rent-A-Car people we had changed our address to Oakwood and Grand."

"You phoned over immediately that that was your new address?"

"Yes, sir."

"Did you ever get your suitcase, Nathan, from the Morrison Hotel?"

"No."

"Did you register at the Morrison Hotel?"

"I did not; Richard did."

"Under the name of?"

"Morton D. Ballard."

"What day was that, do you remember, Nathan?"

"That was just prior to us getting the first car, I would say two or three weeks before."

"Whose suitcase was it?"

"Dick's."

"You never applied for the suitcase after that?"

"No, I figured the suitcase was worth less than we owed."

"What kind of a suitcase was it?"

"It was a dilapidated suitcase, I could not describe it very well."

"Did you have anything in it?"

"I think there were some library books in it."

"You went then to this—what is the name of that hotel?"

"The Trenier Hotel. I had expected to stop there, but changed my plans and asked them to hold mail coming for Morton D. Ballard. I stopped there on a number of occasions after that, I would say as much as half a dozen times, and never did get any mail from there. This seemed very peculiar inasmuch as Richard addressed two letters to the Trenier Hotel."

"Did you get the letters back?"

"No, no return address on them."

"Went in the dead letter office?"

"I do not see why they should have. We followed them up two days afterwards."

"You say you did stop there several times after that?"

"Yes, sir, a number of times."

"You stopped, went over for the mail?"

"Yes."

"You did not register there?"

"No."

"At no time you registered there?"

"No."

"Did you ever register in any other hotel, Nathan, during this period?"

"No. I further opened a bank account in the Hyde Park State Bank at the corner of 53rd and Lake Park."

"Under the name of Morton D. Ballard?"

"Yes, sir."

"How much money did you deposit there?"

"One hundred dollars."

"Have you drawn that out since that time?"

"Yes."

"Was it a checking account?"

"Checking account."

"And you have no balance in the bank now?"

"No, sir."

"That was opened up there during your negotiations with the deal on Michigan Avenue?"

"Yes, sir."

"What was that name again?"

"Rent-a-Car."

"That was for the purpose of —— ?"

"Having a good identification."

"This day you went down there for the car, who drove it?"

"I did."

"Where was your car at that time?"

"Dick had my car just east of Michigan Boulevard."

"When you left there what did you do?"

"We drove up together, or rather we each one—we each drove one car up to Kramer's restaurant at 35th and Cottage."

"Kramer's restaurant at 35th and Cottage Grove?"

"Yes, sir."

"That was on Wednesday, the 21st?"

"Wednesday, the 21st."

"May 21st, 1924?"

"Yes."

"Kramer's restaurant is where?"

"35th and Cottage Grove Avenue."

"What did you do at that time?"

"Had lunch there and put up the side curtains on the rented car."

"About what time was that?"

"I imagine we got there about 12:15."

"What time did you leave there?"

"It must have been one or a little later."

"When did you put up the side curtains?"

"Just before coming, before coming into there to eat."

"After you came out, what time did you come out of there?"

"We left after one."

"Then what did you do?"

"We drove to my home and I put my car in the garage, then we drove over to Ingleside Avenue just south of a blind alley south of 47th Street."

"What time did you put your car in the garage that day?"

"I should say at about one-twenty or one-thirty."

"In the afternoon?"

"Yes."

"And where was the other when you put your car in the garage?"

"The other car was right in back of mine because we wanted to fill it with gas."

"In the driveway?"

"Yes."

"You brought that in and filled it with gas, did you?"

"Yes."

"And left your car there?"

"Yes, sir."

"Then what did you do?"

"Then we drove over to Ingleside Avenue, which is south of the alley, south of 47th Street."

"While you were filling the car up with gas, did you see anyone around the garage there?"

"I don't remember if Sven came down then or not."

"Did you see Mr. Sven or Mrs. Sven there?"

"Mr. and Mrs. Englund, I am under the impression that Mr. Englund was there, I am not sure."

"You talk about the brakes being bad on that car?"

"Yes, on my car. It was on that occasion that they squeaked, and he put on oil and he warned me about going out after they had been oiled."

"After you filled the car with gas what did you do?"

"I drove to this spot on Ingleside Avenue."

"About what time?"

"It must have been about a quarter to two."

"Then what did you do—you drove where you say?"

"To a point just south of the alley, south of 47th Street, Ingleside."

"You drove to a point which is south of the alley, south of 47th Street?"

"Yes. I waited in the car."

"On Ingleside?"

"On Ingleside."

"What is there, anything?"

"Apartment buildings. I waited in the car there while Dick went through the alley to a place where he could either command a view of Harvard School, or if he saw any likely looking children he could start playing with them. After some time, I should say around three, several of the groups of boys playing in the afternoon with the so-called tutors had left for a vacant lot on 49th and Drexel. We followed them up there, I having made a stop at home for my field glasses in the meantime."

"And what time was that?"

"Around three or three-fifteen and we parked on the opposite side of Drexel Boulevard, that is on the west side of Drexel Boulevard and watched these children at play. We also sneaked around on foot to the front, behind a lot, where we could observe without being seen. We also had another group of boys spotted in a lot just across the street from my home, 48th and Greenwood. We waited around until about a quarter of five, when the gangs broke up, but one of the boys had run down the alley, as we thought merely in play, and would be back. Apparently they had greatly disappointed us. We missed our opportunity of following any of them home. We then went down Lake Park to 41st Avenue, where an acquaintance of Richard Loeb's had a son who might be expected home at that time."

"Do you remember the name?"

"Levinson."

"Do you know the address?"

"No, it is Sol Levinson, a lawyer, 41st and Lake Park. We repassed the lot on Greenwood, 48th and Greenwood, came over 48th Street to Ellis—no, we came over 49th Street to Ellis, it was 48th Street to Ellis, and here Dick spied Robert Franks. He was at that time north of 48th Street on Ellis Avenue, on the west side of the street."

"You are sure it was on the west side of the street?"

"Positively, walking south on the west side of the street."

"Then you were where at that time?"

"We were at 48th and Ellis."

"On 48th or Ellis?"

"On 48th."

"Facing what direction?"

"West."

"On what side of the street would that be, on the east side?"

"We were driving down there, we immediately turned around and about the time that we had turned around and given Robert a chance to get a sufficient distance from another pedestrian on the street he was almost at 49th Street. It was here that we picked him up."

"You turned your car and started South on Ellis Avenue, is that it?"

"Yes, south on Ellis Avenue."

"On the west side of the street?"

"On the west side of the street."

"Robert Franks was at 49th?"

"He was almost at 49th."

"On Ellis?"

"Yes."

"Was he on the northwest corner, approximately?"

"Not quite."

"You hadn't had a chance to cross?"

"No."

"And you drove up alongside of where he was?"

"Yes."

"And what happened?"

"Then Dick opened the front door and yelled, 'Hey, Bob.' He came over to the car and Dick asked him if he couldn't give him a lift home. He declined, but Dick said, 'Come in a minute, I want to talk to you about a tennis racket.'"

"That was the time he got into the car."

"Yes."

"Where were you sitting at that time?"

"I was sitting at the driver's wheel, Dick was in the rear seat."

"What time was it, approximately, Nathan?"

"Between five and five-fifteen."

"That was when you proceeded on your journey?"

"Yes."

"You went south then to 50th Street?"

"South to 50th."

"And east on 50th?"

"East on 50th to I believe, Dorchester or Blackstone."

The mother of the victim, Mrs. Jacob Franks, at the funeral. Photograph of little "Bobby" Franks and casket containing his body leaving the Franks home

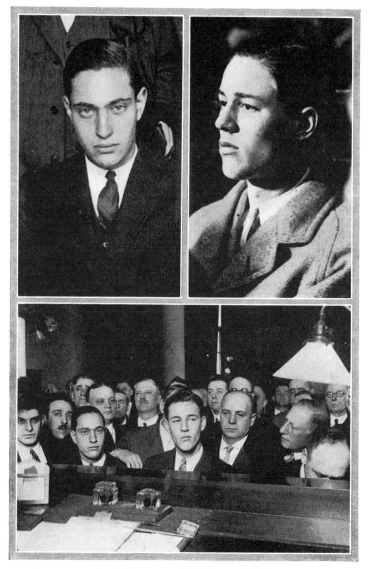

Character study of the two youthful slayers, "Babe" Leopold and "Dickie" Loeb. Below, they plead "not guilty" at their arraignment before Judge Caverly

"When was the first time that Richard struck Robert with a chisel, do you know?"

"Between Ellis and Greenwood on 50th."

"Had he become suspicious of anything when you returned for him at that time?"

"No, because Richard asked him if he minded if we took him around the block, to which he replied no."

"That was the original plan, to take him so no one would see him?"

"Yes, sir."

"And after you made this trip out in the country and came back, what time did you get back?"

"Get back to where?"

"To your home?"

"Ten-thirty."

"You still had the car that you had rented from the Rent-a-Car Company?"

"Yes, sir."

"Was that the car that you drove your folks home in?"

"No."

"What did you do with the rented car?"

"I parked it on Greenwood Avenue just north of our drive-way."

"On Greenwood Avenue?"

"On Greenwood Avenue."

"And you had your car in the garage?"

"I got my own car in the garage and drove around to the side it was."

"Then what did you do with your other car when you came back?"

"When I took Dick home—let me see. God, I think they were in my car, because that chisel was thrown from my car, wasn't it? How could that have been accomplished? I am not quite clear on that point.   But what he must have done was take the bundle—no, we didn't do that either, because I remember washing the other car."

"That was the car that you rented?"

"Yes, we must have taken the rented car."

"You must have taken the rented car and driven out 50th Street?   In other words, that was after you came back?"

"Yes, I was around there until one o'clock."

"That was after you got back?"

"Yes.   I was around there until one o'clock."

"Where did Richard wait for you?"

"At my home."

"What did you do with the rented car then?"

"Washed it fairly thoroughly there."

"When, that night?"

"One-thirty, yes."

"Whereabouts?"

"On 50th Street, at the gate to Loeb's."

"What did you wash it with?"

"We found a bucket with some water and a brush and some soap."

"Where?"

"In Loeb's basement."

"Then you came out and washed it?"

"Yes, sir."

"You were unable to get all the stains off?"

"Well, it was at night and we didn't want to be monkeying around too much."

"Where did you take your car to get some of the blood stains off?"

"No place."

"You drove the car in some place to get some of the blood stains off?"

"No, that was the next day in our garage. It was still Wednesday night you see."

"What did you do with the rented car that night?"

"I drove it back to the place previously occupied, which is just north of our driveway, and stood it in front of an apartment house."

"That was at one-thirty?"

"One-thirty."

"After you drove your aunt and uncle home in your car and came back what did you do in the house then? Richard Loeb was in the house?"

"Went in and had a few drinks, sat and talked with Dad."

"About what time was that?"

"That must have been about eleven o'clock."

"Then what did you do?"

"Dad retired about eleven-thirty or twelve, and we had a few more drinks and left about one o'clock."

"Did you play cards while you were there?"

"Yes, sir, I think we played two games of casino for fun."

"Well, what did you do after that?"

"We went over to Dick's house with the clothes."

"The clothes in the rented car?"

"Yes, sir."

"And those were out in the rented car all the time?"

"Yes."

"In a robe?"

"In a robe."

"When you got to Dick's house what did you do?"

"We went in the basement and burned the clothes. We intended burning the robe, but it was too large to fit in and would have caused an awful stench. Right after making that phone call to Franks, we were in the rented car, we drove over to Loeb's then in the rented car, burned the clothes, washed the blood stains, then took the rented car to my house and left it there, then I got my car out and took the folks home in that. Then after I got back to my house I still had that car, when I took Dick home it was in that car, and it was then we threw the chisel out."

"When you took Dick home you took the rented car, or your car?"

"My own car."

"What actually happened when you came in the first time?"

"We had disposed of the clothes."

"You had disposed of the clothes in the car?"

"Yes, sir."

"And left the robe hidden in the car?"

"No, I had left the robe hidden in some brush there."

"You mean outside?"

"Outdoors, yes."

"And Dick had the chisel in his possession?"

"Yes, sir."

"And when you changed cars he just took it from one car to another car?"

"Yes."

"Did he leave that in the car or not?"

"I don't believe so, no."

"Where did he throw the chisel out at?"

"It was over there between 48th and—or between 49th and 50th I think, on Greenwood."

"After you left Richard there and came back, you put your car in the garage, did you?"

"Yes, sir."

"Then what did you do?"

"I turned off the parking light on the parked car and went to bed."

"Then what did you do?"

The next morning I got up and went to school as usual at eight o'clock. I met Dick at eleven.

"Where?"

"At the University."

"You had made arrangements the night before to meet the next day?"

"Yes, sir, we drove down to my house, and it was then that we drove the rented car to the garage to clean it up more thoroughly."

"In your garage?"

"Outside of my garage, but in my driveway."

"What did you clean it up with?"

"With soap and water and some gasoline and a brush."

"Did anyone help you clean it up."

"Sven tried to, but we told him it was all right, that we were all through."

"Was there any remark made then with reference to the blood stains in the car?"

"Yes, Dick was afraid that possibly Sven had seen these blood stains and he said it was some red wine."

"He told the chauffeur that?"

"Yes, sir."

"Who drove the rented car downtown?"

"I drove the rented car downtown."

"And Dick drove your car, did he?"

"Dick drove my car."

"Then you went down, and how much did you pay, do you remember, for the use of the car?"

"This was Thursday, was it?"

"Yes."

"Wait just a moment. We cleaned the car out. I have forgotten where we ate, we stopped some place for lunch and we didn't have my car until we both drove the rented car."

"You didn't have your car at all?"

"No, my car was in the garage and we drove down to the 12th Street Illinois Central Station, and the rest of the account is contained in the previous part."

"With the rented car?"

"Yes, sir."

"When did you return the rented car?"

"We returned the rented car about five or five-thirty."

"How much money?"

"Twenty-five dollars and some cents on it."

"And he gave you the balance of your deposit back."

"Yes, sir."

"You drove the rented car, both of you, to the I. C. Station?"

"Yes, and then drove back south. After we had found that Mr. Franks was not at the drug store we drove to my house, got my car, and Dick drove my car down, while I drove the rented car down. Dick parked on Wabash Avenue just south of 14th Street while I returned the car."

"About what time was that?"

"Between five-fifteen and five-thirty. When we returned we stopped to get a soda at the drug store."

"Whereabouts?"

"47th and Ellis. I met Mr. Mitchell at that time."

"You had a conversation with him?"

"I had a conversation with him. I took Dick home and on the way back stopped and bought a paper at 48th and Ellis which told about the fact that this boy was Franks and went home."

"Then what happened?"

"I got supper. I stayed at home studying law."

"Did you see Dick the next day?"

"The next day was Friday, yes."

"Was that the time you had the conversation of what you would say in the event you were called in?"

"I am not sure if it was then or not. We discussed that a number of times."

"Prior to the happening or after the happening?"

"Possibly after that, I couldn't be sure."

"You discovered there was a pair of glasses found out there, Nathan?"

"Yes."

"You learned that through a newspaper?"

"Yes."

"Then you and Richard Loeb had some conversation about the glasses and so forth?"

"Yes, sir."

"You contemplated at that time that you would be called in and asked about it?"

"Yes, sir."

"In the event they were found. You never thought they would find the owner of the glasses, did you?"

"No, sir, I did not."

"You were called in by ——"

"Captain Wolf."

"What did Captain Wolf ask you?"

"Captain Wolf wanted to know whether I had visited the particular area frequently, whether there were many ornithologists whom I knew, or fishermen, particularly among the members of the Harvard School, or its faculty. Also whether the Franks boy had been interested."

"You gave him the information?"

"Yes."

"Did you mention the fact to him at that time that you had worn glasses?"

"Yes."

"He never asked you to produce your glasses?"

"No."

"Were you able to remove all those blood stains?"

"Almost entirely."

"Enough so that it was not noticeable?"

"Yes."

"What time was it, Nathan, now, you saw the newspapers announcing that?"

"About six o'clock."

"This chisel that was thrown out of the car by Richard that you told about, Nathan, that had what kind of tape on it?"

"Zinc oxide."

"Where did you get that tape from, from home?"

"In the bathroom."

"This was the tape you were telling me about that your brother had in the bathroom when you walked in?"

"Yes."

"Did you take the whole roll of it?"

"Yes."

"Where did you leave the rest of it?"

"We had discussed that, Dick and I, and we think it must have been in the car."

"Did you put tape on near the sharp end or the blunt end?"

"The sharp end."

"Using the head of the chisel, or the blunt end I guess you would call it, for the purpose of ——"

"Striking."

"Which end did Richard strike with, do you know? Did he strike with the sharp end or the other end?"

"He struck with the other end. That is why I cannot explain the blood stains. Well, probably the blood was rather effusive."

"You don't know whether it was the other end or not, do you?"

"Yes, I know."

"You know it was the blunt end he was struck with?"

"Yes, sir."

"Where did the chisel come from?"

"From a hardware store between 45th and 46th on Cottage Grove Avenue."

"Who bought the chisel?"

"Dick."

"That same day?"

"No, I think he bought that a few days previously."

"For that purpose?"

"Yes."

"At a hardware store where?"

"At 45th and 46th on Cottage."

"Do you remember what you paid for it?"

"I think it was seventy-five cents."

"Which one of you bought it?"

"Dick."

"You bought that two or three days before?"

"I think so, yes."

"How did you carry it around with you?"

"As I recollect, we put it in the pocket of the rented car. I think we bought that on the very day, on Wednesday the 21st, I am almost sure of that now."

"The same day?"

"Yes, sir."

"That was the day you went in and got the tape in the house?"

"Yes."

"Now the time you first started to wear glasses was when, Nathan?"

"In October or November, 1923."

"And who was your doctor that prescribed the glasses?"

"Emil Deutsch."

"And he is located where?"

"30 North Michigan."

"And the one who filled the prescription?"

"Almer Coe."

"How long did you wear the glasses, Nathan, afterward?"

"Until February or March."

"1924?"

"1924."

"Then you sort of discontinued wearing them, is that it?"

"Yes, sir. They had actually remained in the pocket of the suit which happened to be this suit."

"The suit that you have got on now is the suit you wore the night you placed the body there, is that it?"

"Yes, sir."

"After you started out there, Nathan, did you remove your clothes at all while you were placing the body?"

"My coat, yes."

"Just how did you place the body in the drain pipe, just explain how you placed the body there?"

"I think it was head first. I had a pair of rubber boots."

"Where did you get the rubber boots?"

"My own."

"Did you take them from your home?"

"Yes, sir."

"That day in this rented car, did you?"

"Yes, put them on right at the culvert where I stepped into the water, took the feet of the body while Dick took the head end and the hands, and when it struck the water, pushed it in, gave it a shove as far as I could."

"Was it much of a job, Nathan, to push the body in?"

"At first I thought it was rather doubtful whether it would fit at all, but after it once started it was not hard at all."

"Then after you pushed it in as far as you could with your hands, Nathan, you used your feet and pushed it up further?"

"Yes."

"Had rigor mortis set in at that time?"

"Yes."

"At the time you had taken your coat off did you lay it on the ground some place?"

"Yes, right by my shoes."

"That is not the time you lost your glasses?"

"No, that is not the time. Dick had run across the railroad track to see if anybody could be seen from the other end, and I went up to the top of the railroad track, for some reason or other, to put on my shoes, and he brought my coat to me. I think we struck a match—no, we had a flashlight with us, and it must have been at that time that the glasses fell out."

"What time was it, again, that you put the body in the drain?"

"About nine-thirty or nine-twenty."

"Dick brought your coat up to you where you were putting on your shoes?"

"Yes."

"Now this letter, Nathan, that you had already prepared in an envelope without any address on it, you had prepared that letter some time prior to that time?"

"Yes."

"Just when did you prepare that letter?"

"Four or five days ahead of time."

"No one, definitely, as to whom you were going to send it to?"

"No, just 'dear sir.'"

"But the address you placed on later on?"

"Yes. It was not addressed inside, it was just 'dear sir.'"

Dick Loeb has already made his confession, which was virtually that of Leopold. The latter's is more concise and so the text of Loeb's is not given. After both confessions were given the boys were brought together and the text of their conversation is here given. In it they discuss the point where they differed—namely, who struck the blows which killed Robert Franks. Each boy, it must be remembered, blamed the other for the actual deed.

LOEB: "There are certain corrections that Leopold has made in mine that are not important, such as 14th Street, and the boots being his, instead of his brother's, which don't amount to a damn, I mean it don't make any difference, they are not important, and don't affect the case. However, I would like to say this:

"In the first place he says that that chisel was wrapped by me. It was wrapped by him, and wrapped by him in Jackson Park. He brought it in and put it in the car and he wrapped that chisel while waiting there in Jackson Park in that little nine-hole golf course. All right.

"In the second place he mentioned that the idea of the thing, that the main thing was to get the place and the means of throwing that package, and he stuck on that thing in the train, and it was his idea. But he doesn't mention the method of the killing, that he had that very well conceived and planned out, as evidenced by the ether in the car, which was absolutely the notion that he followed through. The boy was to be etherized to death, and he was supposed to do that, because I don't know a damn thing about it and he does. He had a number of times chloroformed birds and things like that, and he knows ornithology. I don't know a damn thing about that.

"He said the time was November when the idea was first conceived. Well now, I don't know exactly, I believe I said two months in my statement. I know right well it was not November. It may have been a little bit longer than two months, it might have been two and a half months, but it certainly was not any longer than that.

"There are one or two other minor things that he mentioned.

For instance, he said he drove the red car downtown. No, he says he drove the rented car downtown. I don't know, I got that mixed up. Which did you say? When you left your home on Tuesday afternoon were you driving the red car?"

LEOPOLD: "The rented car."

LOEB: "Well, you were not, you were driving the red car. I will show you why you were, because I didn't know exactly where that place was on Michigan Boulevard. I don't to this day. If I was to drive down Wabash, I don't know the streets. You know exactly where it was. You drove the red car, you went ahead of me and I followed you, and where you parked the red car I stopped up alongside of you in the red car and picked you up, you just got out of your car into my car. I stopped next to you, I was following you all the time in the rented car. You had the red car and drove the red car and parked it there. So there are one or two other things. In the first place I never touched that body after the hydrochloric acid was poured on that body. After the hydrochloric acid was poured on that body you stepped into that culvert with your boots on and you took hold of the feet and gave the body a push and the body splashed in there and it splashed on your pants too, and you worried about it."

STATE'S ATTORNEY CROWE: "Who hit him with a chisel?"

LOEB: "He did."

MR. CROWE: "Who is 'he'?"

LOEB: "Nathan Leopold, Junior. He was sitting up in the front seat. I said he was sitting up in the front seat. I mean I was sitting up in the front seat. This is obviously a mistake, I am getting excited. This Franks boy got up in the front seat. Now he was a boy that I knew. If I was sitting in the back seat he would have gotten into the back seat with me. He was a boy I knew, and I would have opened the door and motioned him in that way. As it was, he got in the front seat with me because I knew the boy and I opened the front door. He didn't see Babe until he was inside the car. He stood at the same place. I introduced him to this Franks boy and then took him into the car. I took him into the car and when he got in the car I said, 'you know Babe? This is Bobbie Franks.'

"And then one thing I wish to point out. I have been made a fish right along here. Now this story that you speak of in your testimony, this story of the finding of all this alibi, all these women, and being drunk in the Cocoanut Grove and everything, we planned that definitely. It was definitely decided that the story was not to go after Wednesday noon, which would be a week after the crime. We were to protect our story. We were to just say that we didn't know what we were doing, and there was no evidence. We felt that you were safe with your glasses after a week had passed, that your glasses being out there would not necessitate an air-tight alibi, because we didn't figure anything else, and we figured that you would be safe enough after a week not to know exactly where you were on that particular Wednesday afternoon."

MR. CROWE: "Who felt that?"

LEOPOLD: "I told the same story exactly here to Mr. Savage."

MR. CROWE: "All right."

LOEB: "When you came down Thursday and you told another story which you had agreed not to tell, I came down to Mr. Crowe and he questioned me, and questioned me about my actions and everything else, and I denied ever being drunk, I denied being with you, Leopold, and I denied being up at the Cocoanut Grove, and those things being put together made me absolutely certain that you had told the stories you shouldn't have told.

"Then he started to talk about the Park, about being out at Lincoln Park. He mentioned parks. He brought it around, but I knew what he was driving at. That was Lincoln Park, and when he did that I stepped in to try to help you out.

"I think it is a damned sight more than you would have done for me. I tried to help you out because I thought that you at least, if the worst comes to the worst, would admit what you had done and not try to drag me into the thing in that manner. Well now, that is all I have got to say."

MR. SAVAGE: "Have you got anything to say to that?"

LEOPOLD: "Yes, I have."

MR. SAVAGE: "Nathan wants to say a word."

LEOPOLD: "His correction about what car I was driving down I think is correct. Those are all absurd, dirty lies. He is trying to get out of this mess. I can explain to you myself exactly how I opened the door to let the Franks boy in, and he got up from the back seat, leaned over forward and spoke to the boy from the back. I was driving the car, I am absolutely positive. The reason for changing that story was, as you remember, when you first questioned me as to my actions I was very indefinite, and I was urged to remember, quite strongly, what I had been doing, and I am sorry that you were made a fish of and stepped into everything and broke down and all that, I am sorry, but it isn't my fault. All the rest of the corrections he made, with the exception of that one of the car, are lies."

MR. CROWE: "Now listen, boys?"

LEOPOLD: "Yes."

MR. CROWE: "You have both been treated decently by me?"

LEOPOLD: "Absolutely."

MR. CROWE: "No brutality or no roughness?"

LEOPOLD: "No, sir."

MR. CROWE: "Every consideration shown to both?"

LEOPOLD: "Yes, sir."

MR. CROWE: "Not one of you have a complaint to make, have you?"

LEOPOLD: "No, sir."

MR. CROWE: "Have you, Loeb?"

LOEB: "No."

Spot on the shore of Lake Michigan where Leopold and Loeb buried the burned, blood-stained robe. Below, culvert where the victim's body was found

Slayers' relatives attend court session. Left to right, Nathan Leopold, Sr., Foreman Leopold, brother, Jacob Loeb, uncle of "Dickie," and Allan Loeb, brother. Below, the slayers after confessing

Through the Eyes of Friends

So much for the bare story of the crime. The story of how the boys helped the police collect all the evidence to substantiate their confessions; how they proved conclusively the truth of their amazing first accusations, all moves very rapidly, but before that is related there must be presented a picture of these boys themselves, a view of them through the eyes of their friends and acquaintances, who had known them from childhood.

Not the view presented by medical experts. Not the view their defenders took of them, nor the picture painted by the State's Attorney in his prosecution of the boys. More interesting at this point is a picture of these two boys as their friends knew them— the story of Nathan F. Leopold, Jr., and Richard Loeb as they were up until that May afternoon when they rented a car, took their steel chisel and went adventuring between lunch and bedtime.

Nathan F. Leopold, Jr., is the youngest of his family. The nickname "Babe" was given to him in early childhood.

His grandparents came to America in the early nineteenth century. In Germany his father had been a young radical who had believed in democracy and fair play for the poor man. He was a youth of deep thought and real courage. America for him meant a land of promise.

He settled in Wisconsin. There his children were born. When his son, Nathan F. Leopold, was still a child, the family moved to Chicago. That son was, in turn, to become the father of young Nathan F. Leopold, Jr.

Coming to Chicago some twenty years after his migration to America, his children were educated here. The girls married into the best Jewish families in the city.

Either by marriage or by direct kinship, Nathan F. Leopold, Jr., is related to every branch of a little royalty of wealth which Chicago has long recognized. The women of that connection have married into the best families of Europe.

The baby of his family, Nathan F. Leopold, was precocious almost from birth.

He sat up at three months; he laughed when he was four months old; he began to walk when he was three months old, and between four and five months old he spoke his first words. He walked well when he was fourteen months old.

He started to school when he was less than six years old, and from the very first his academic record was above the average. It might almost be called precocious.

As a little youngster, "Babe" was bright and alert, but not strong and rugged. He had been frequently sick in infancy, and his family exercised constant care over his health. So, as a little chap, he felt an inferiority to his playmates—boys of his own age.

When he was nine years old his tonsils were removed, and he himself explained the result by saying, "Before I had my tonsils out I was a girl; after, I became like a little boy." He then had more energy for sports, but never did acquire much liking for them or much skill.

Rather his life from the very first was for books and study. The first two years the child went to a girls' school. It had been a co-educational school, but became a girls' school about the time he entered, and he and another lad were the only boy students.

He entered school when he was five years and eleven months old, so he knew only girls, met few children outside of school, being too frail for the ordinary sand lot activities of the other youngsters of the neighborhood.

Attended by nurses and governesses, and with his precocious taste even then for reading and studying, he was not like other little boys. Both because of the wealth of his parents and his own disposition, he missed that rough and tumble fighting life which so early comes to the average boy, giving him a sense of give and take. Shut in by the luxuries of his home, guarded because of his frail health and looked upon with wonder for his brilliancy, the child early began to live a life of his own.

When he was seven years old, he was tried out in the public school, but he did not get along well, and the family put him back in the girls' school for the rest of that year. A nurse always accompanied him to and from school until he was eleven years old.

When he was eight years of age, he entered a public school in the low third grade and was soon put in the high third grade. His progress continued ordinarily until he was in his fifth grade, and his teacher took such an interest in him, particularly because of his love of ornithology, that she arranged for him to skip a grade. He finished the public school in the middle of the year when he was eleven years old, and immediately entered the Harvard School by taking examinations, thus advancing himself another half year.

All during the time he was going to school he realized he was not like other children. Because he was not physically their equal, he consoled himself with his own mental superiority. He noticed early that his family was in better circumstances than most of his fellow students. He, alone, lived on Michigan Boulevard. A nurse always accompanied him to and from school. That gave him a feeling of superiority.

Entered in the Harvard School, he was a fair match for boys his own age physically, but was entered in a class with boys older than he.

While at the Harvard School he had a burning desire for Greek. Very early he developed a curiosity to know what common English words meant in other languages. His first experiment was in learning how to say "yes" in as many languages as possible.

At an age when most boys were interested in girls and football, to the exclusion of other things, he was studying Greek, and even took a year of Greek in school instead of French, as he should have done. He was always at the head of his class, but made very few close friends. He got along pleasantly enough with everybody, but, it may be interesting to note here, of all the people who knew him, when the story of his crime broke upon the world, there were few who could say that they really knew the boy intimately. A queer, reserved chap, living to himself among his books, substituting his studies for the normal active interests of boys his own age. It may be interesting to quote from the School Review of 1920, the annual Harvard School Student publication, a few comments on various members of his class. Here is one comment on Nathan Leopold, Jr.:

"The present junior class is, indeed, a good crowd. In the leadership of . . . ., as Class President, they have become distinctly a social crowd, not omitting the Great Nathan."

In another place this appears in quotations: "Of course, I am the Great Nathan. When I open my lips let no dog bark."

And in another place a poem speaks of the same person:

> "And so our list of juniors has,
> At least, been briefly told,
> With one exception only—it is
> It is the mighty Leopold."

In another place it referred to him as "Nathan Leopold, the crazy bird of the school, the member of the fifth class, who is forever harping on birds, their use, and their twitterings, known in all zoos, bird paradises and bipedal creature communities."

After Nathan left the Harvard School, he attended the Uni-

versity of Chicago for one year. Then he went to the University
of Michigan for a year, at Ann Arbor. The third year he returned to the University of Chicago and lived at home.

Although altogether he attended college only three and one-
half years, he received a Bachelor of Philosophy Degree and Phi
Beta Kappa at nineteen.

He then took one term of postgraduate work, and in the year
1923-4 was a student of law at the University of Chicago. His
major work in college was in languages, including English, German, French, Sanskrit, Russian, Latin, Greek, Modern Greek
and Umbrian.

His interest in girls had never been pronounced, although,
when the story of his disastrous spring afternoon adventure burst
like a bomb upon his friends, there were many girls who sprang
to his defense. He had danced a little, had taken girls about to
some extent, but his social interests were always secoondary to
the interest he took in his school and scientific studies, the greatest of which was the study of birds.

One of the rare permits to shoot birds in the Chicago parks
was given to "Babe" Leopold.

Many years ago he began a collection of stuffed birds, which
make his room seem more like a museum than the intimate home
of a boy. He had added to them until they made a collection
worthy of display in any museum or school.

He organized bird classes. Children of the neighborhood,
young men and many married women of his social set belonged
to his classes in bird lore.

So proud was his family of his mental attainments that he
was left very much to himself. With wealth, leisure, harmoni-
ous home life, he found himself very free to pursue any line of
interest which he fancied.

From infancy, Nathan had known the value of his father's
millions. In his boyhood, in the northern resorts, where he al-

ways spent his summers, he and his little friends fished in and out of season in the northern lakes. The little rich boy paid the fines. Father's money bought new outfits for them when they wanted them.

Then, Nathan wanted to shoot birds in the city parks. His record as a student of birds and his family influence got him a license, which other boys would never have been able to obtain. He had his father's chauffeur to drive him about where he would, and was given a monthly allowance of one hundred twenty-five dollars, just for spending money. From the time he was a little boy, he had luncheons at the best hotels, dinner at the most sophisticated dining places, a winter in Hawaii, and summers where he pleased, so at nineteen, life had never been hard for this heir to several millions.

His money, let it be said for him, never made him a sluggard. He gave remarkable application to scientific work and his studies.

His family's position in that circle of wealth, of which it was a part, gave him a wide acquaintance, but his birds and his books made him a solitary, but well enough liked boy, with few intimate friends.

Such is Nathan Leopold, Jr., as we find him with the interest of the world constantly centered upon him.

Little "Dick" Loeb, coming of a family as wealthy as Leopold's, grew up in much the same surroundings.

He was a weakly child until he was four and a half years old. Then his health improved, and by the time he was nine years old, he was strong and hardy.

As a youngster, he was placed under the care of a governess— a Canadian woman with very strong ideas of discipline and of punishment. She had the conventional ideas of rearing children. She read a great deal to him and it was largely due to her tutoring and reading that he advanced so rapidly in school.

As a child, he preferred her company to that of boys. It is

said that she intended to exclude from his life normal contacts with other boys.

The books she read to him were the better class of books, which could be read to children, such as Dickens, Ben Hur, Rise and Fall of the Dutch Republic, histories and others.

She was so strict in her punishments that he found it necessary, to evade the consequence of his misdemeanors, to lie and deceive her. He acquired a habit of lying to evade punishment, it is said, and this habit grew with him through life.

Richard was always a handsome, happy little youngster. He drew friends and gained their affection.

The Loeb family has a summer estate at Charlevoix, in northern Michigan. It is a show place of that part of the country—a house, which might well be called a palace, on a high bluff overlooking the miles and miles of wooded shores of Pine Lake. The happy little boy gathered about him a ring of devoted and admiring servants. His summers and most of his holidays were spent at Charlevoix. There is no one in town that does not know him—the banker, the doctor, the waitresses, the roustabouts around the docks, the boys and girls of the town. Even in the darkest days of his trouble, no one there would believe a word against him. Friendly, generous and kindly he seemed to them. He might almost be called the Bonny Young Prince of the place.

His father built him a boat house and landing on Pine Lake. A trusty, seaworthy little boat was bought for him, and in it, in the summer time, he and Nathan Leopold cruised all the pleasant waters of northern Michigan, even out upon Lake Michigan, then in and out the Straits of Mackinac.

There are fishermen on some small islands, where only mail boats touch, who know "Dick" Loeb. "A swell kid" they call him, "even if he is a millionaire's son, he is the most regular guy you ever knew."

He began to go with girls when he was fourteen years old, at the time he finished the Harvard School, and entered the University. Three, four and five years older were his classmates, but they liked the boy and made him one of them. It was about that time that he passed from the jurisdiction of his governess.

It may be interesting to note, at this point, the unfailing attraction "Dick" Loeb seems always to have had for girls of his own age. He says that, when he was fourteen and entered college, he wanted to be as near like his classmates as possible. Those classmates, it has already been pointed out, were on an average, three or four years older than Dick—at an age when girls are of the utmost importance. So Dick's love affairs at fourteen took on the intensity of the ordinary seventeen or eighteen year old boy.

When he was arrested, and the news of his crime became public, at least a half dozen girls in his own set were prostrated. Two or three of them went to pieces, hysterically informed his family and closest friends that "Dick" was the boy whom they cared for more than any other.

His pink cheeks, his soft brown eyes, his sweet ingratiating ways, endeared him to feminine hearts, old and young. He was irresistible to girls of his own age.

His tastes, too, in girls, extended through every walk of life. A millionaire's daughter, in his social set, was ill for days after he was arrested. A fisherman's daughter in a gingham dress, on a tiny island in the Straits of Mackinac, wept when she read in the newspapers that her Prince Charming, who had come sailing to see her in the summer time, was in trouble. From the top of society to the bottom, they wouldn't believe that "Dickie" Loeb could possibly be guilty of the murder to which he had confessed.

During these first feverish days, after his confession, every woman who had ever known the boy was a self appointed committee of defense for "Dick" Loeb.

It is interesting to note, in the light of revelations later, that every one who knew the boys, particularly during those first days, believed that "Dick" had been led into this mysterious affair by Nathan Leopold, Jr.

His friends remembered instances when he had tried to break his friendship with Leopold. Leopold, "Dick's" friends were sure, planned this murder plot. For some wild erotic reason of his own, Leopold had wanted to experiment in murder. "Dick," in his own boyish ignorance, and loyalty to his friend, had been led on against his will. Such was the judgment of all Loeb's family and associates. That Loeb could possibly have dreamed of such a thing himself, was never suggested.

The picture which Loeb himself gave to the astonished world of a young, plotting criminal, planning a death for the fun of it, was not the image his friends held of him when he disappeared from their gaze behind the jail house doors. "Dickie," the petted criminal—"Dickie," the murder plotter, is not the creature these women who loved him knew at all.

Leopold had never been popular enough among his own kind to be invited to join a college fraternity. Loeb, on the other hand, was one of the most popular and petted members of his chapter, both at Ann Arbor and the University of Chicago. Irresponsible, his fraternity brothers called him, but they loved him.

As an upper classman, Loeb was never considered staid enough to be placed in command over the freshmen and other members of the fraternity. Rather, he was a heedless, beloved member, on whom little responsibility was placed, but he was popular, well liked and much sought after.

In Charlevoix, in the large colony of wealthy families who own imposing summer homes, "Dick" was always welcome. He missed few dances in the summer, from the town free-for-alls to the most exclusive dances in the richest homes. Hostesses were always glad to welcome him. Any girl whom he chose to select in that exclusive summer colony was proud and pleased at his attention. His kindheartedness is the thing, even yet, that they talk about in Charlevoix.

They tell a story in Charlevoix to show the lad's unfailing sympathy and tender-heartedness. The summer he was fifteen years old, driving to a dance one evening at dusk, his automobile collided with a horse and buggy at a dark street corner. He had not yet turned on the automobile lights and the accident was said to be unavoidable. A woman was hurt and her grandson slightly injured. "Dick" helped take her to the hospital, but, once there, when he realized that she was injured, he wept and fainted. He had to be almost carried home. Every day, he visited the woman, taking her flowers and fruit, and the best of food. He persuaded his father, not only to pay all the hospital bills, but to pay off a mortgage on the woman's home, and to send her on a trip that winter to mend her shattered nerves.

She was another woman who cried when she heard that nice "Dickie" Loeb was quartered in jail.

Leopold often accompanied "Dickie" to the northern resort, but he was never so popular. He had no ingratiating ways, he had no cheery greeting for everybody. He was not the "mixer" that "Dickie" was, and so, when the news of their confession and arrest reached Charlevoix everybody said that it must have been the fault of that "unpleasant Leopold." "Dick" Loeb would not hurt a fly. "A kind of a crazy kid" they called him, "a little wild, a heavy drinker, a little noisy when he was happy, which was most of the time, but never a murderer—not 'Dickie' Loeb!"

So they stood in the eyes of their acquaintances, when their confessions burst like a bomb shell on the world, as "Dick," the good, sweet, irresponsible boy, and Leopold the Sinister. "Dick," with only friendship in his heart for all the world, dominated by Leopold, the silent plotter.

Quite a different picture from the one the boys themselves built, during the long weeks of their stay in the Cook County Jail.

In Custody

Morning papers of May Thirty-first carried the announcement that "Babe" Leopold and "Dick" Loeb had confessed to kidnapping and murder of Bobby Franks. The exact wording of the confession, at that time was not made public. The town, generally, did not believe it. Even people who had worked upon the case, since Bobby Franks' body had been discovered, ten days before, doubted the truth of the confession.

State's Attorney Crowe and the detectives, who had been in the Criminal Court Building that night, knew that the confession was true, but to the outside world, it seemed like a fantastic story told by two tired, sleepless boys to escape from ceaseless questioning. "Dick" Loeb's mother didn't believe it. A mild and gentle tempered woman, she flew into a passion, when relatives suggested the story might be true. Third degree methods, said many others. Schoolmates of the boys said they were showing off, attracting attention to themselves by this fantastic assuming of the crime. Let them sleep and get rested and they would laugh and deny the whole story.

A group of reporters hurried out to the Leopold home on Greenwood Avenue. Neither Nathan's brothers nor his father, then gave the story the slightest credence. It was not until late in the day that Nathan Leopold, Sr., talking to a group of reporters on his own front porch hesitated in his declaration of his faith in his son's innocence. All day, he had refused to believe that his son had done this thing the papers said he had.

All that first Saturday, when the boys still remained in the custody of the State's Attorney, but not in jail, Leopold's relatives willingly talked to callers and newspaper reporters. The first pathetic break in the brave exterior of that self-respecting man, his father, came at about five o'clock, while he was interviewed by several reporters. "I do not know what to think," he said, and then the tears came to his eyes, he smiled, or tried to smile, at these inquisitive strangers who had brought him the bad news, which in later days so lined his face with marks of grief. In the meantime, the State's Attorney lost no time in collecting the evidence of the crime.

The boys seemed seized with the very mania of confession. You may remember that, at this stage, each was still accusing the other of plotting the crime and of striking the blows which killed the Franks boy. Their friendship of four years, during these days, was shattered. Neither spoke to the other, and each blamed the other for his own predicament. No longer were they the master criminals, but two bad little boys, scared half to death, trying to crawl out of the terrible mess the best way they could, but how they did talk! Once they had made a clean breast of the affair, they seemed to take a delight in tightening the strands of the net that gathered about them.

When they had had some sleep, some food, and a change of linen, instead of repudiating their confessions, as the world expected them to do, they deliberately set about to substantiate every claim of their self-accusations.

With Mr. Crowe, and members of his staff, detectives and newspaper men, the boys started out, Saturday afternoon, to travel over the course of their May day adventure. They went to the drug store where they had bought the hydrochloric acid. They showed Mr. Crowe the place they had bought the chisel. They explained in detail just how they had dismantled the portable Underwood typewriter, with which they had written the ransom letter. They told how they had stolen the machine from a fraternity house in Ann Arbor early in the fall.

They directed detectives to a lagoon near the big bronze statue in Jackson Park. With hundreds of curiosity seekers looking on, the two boys, still ignoring each other's presence, leaned over the rail of the bridge and indicated the spot where they had flung the typewriter into the water. They smiled and talked and were quite cheerful.

They seemed almost proud of what they had done, and fairly basked in the close attention their every word received. They gazed about, quite unabashed, at the curiosity seekers who pressed them close, as they stood on the bridge in Jackson Park.

They led detectives to the drug store from which they had telephoned to Mrs. Franks. They followed the exact trail they had taken as they drove about the evening of May twenty-first, waiting for darkness to come, so that they could dispose of the body of their victim.

They went with the State's Attorney out to the prairie where they thought they had so cleverly hidden the dead body of the Franks boy.

They talked continually with their companions about the details of their crime. They talked about other things, too—Leopold especially. He was the brilliant conversationalist that afternoon. Between telling the different steps they had followed in their adventure, he discussed science and literature, his ideas of God, and his knowledge of languages. He seemed to take a pleasure in amazing these stupid yokels who had entrapped him.

Out on the Hegewisch marsh, the boys showed just how they pushed Bobby Franks' body, face downward, into the mud and water of the culvert, where they supposed he would never be discovered.

They traveled back over the road and stopped at the places where they had hidden the different articles of clothing they had taken from the dead boy's body.

Here were his shoes. At another place they found his belt buckle.

They pointed out in turn every article of clothing, every shred of evidence, which the State was later to weave into a rope intended for their necks.

At Loeb's home they helped recover the remnants of a blood-drenched robe in which they had wrapped the boy's dead body.

Detectives, hardened in the study of crime, shivered at the grewsomeness of some of the evidence which these boys uncovered, but not the boys. They basked in the undivided attention they received.

They paused in the driveway of the Loeb home to show just where they had tried to wash the blood from the car they had driven that night.

They went to the place on Michigan Avenue where they had rented the car. Later in the jail yard, Leopold went to great pains to point out dim spots on the high polish of the car they had driven to show where Bobby Franks' blood had dripped.

Their parents vainly tried, during the two days after their confession, to get in touch with the boys—to stem this ceaseless flow of words which the boys were uttering, but the State's Attorney and the detectives kept the boys on the move. Here, there, all over town, out into the country, from one hotel to another, while the boys talked and talked and talked. So they were kept out of reach of habeas corpus proceedings.

It was not until Monday that attorneys, hired for their defense, succeeded in catching up with Mr. Crowe and the two boys, but by that time the boys had told everything they knew, and all the proof of the crime was in the hands of the State.

It seemed as though the boys had been afraid that no one would believe their story. It seemed as though they delighted in their achievement and were afraid of leaving even one tiny detail of their confession unsubstantiated.

Saturday morning, Mr. Leopold and Jacob Loeb, "Dick's" uncle, had retained one of the ablest criminal defenders in the country, Clarence Darrow, of Chicago, and with him, Benjamin C. Bachrach, a lawyer of long and successful experience. If anybody in the world could save these two boys, who had talked so much, Darrow and Bachrach could.

Monday, the two boys had a conference with their relatives and the attorneys. Then, for the first time, the ceaseless flow of their chatter was stopped. That afternoon, newspaper reporters, who had followed every step the two boys had taken, heard the two boys each make two brand new statements. It was the first time, in those hectic three days, that such a remark had been made.

"We cannot talk without advice of counsel," said Nathan Leopold, Jr., and "Dick" Loeb, with a self-conscious grin, repeated the statement. That was the end of the story tellers' holiday.

The boys had not yet seen the inside of the jail. They had lived in hotels, and eaten the best of food. Every word they had said had received the greatest attention. They had not been close enough to the jail to hear the doors clang. Until Monday afternoon they had been as prominent as the band in a circus parade.

Their smiles were not quenched until after their conversation with their attorneys.

Leading from the Criminal Court Building into the jail is a narrow little passageway, only a few feet long, floored in iron and poorly lighted, with heavy steel doors, at each end. It bears the name of the Bridge of Sighs. There were no smiles when, at last, "Dick" Loeb and "Babe" Leopold faced its gloomy entrance, but, even then, they had their one last little flourish in the limelight. As they stepped up three steps to the first iron door, someone from the crowd, which pushed into the corridor to watch their progress, called out their names. Both boys turned and looked over the shoulders of the deputy sheriffs who gripped

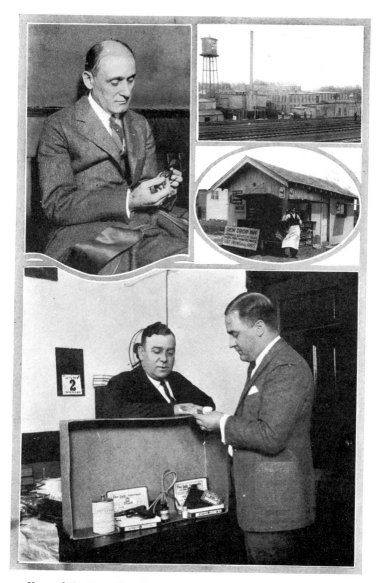

Upper left, Leopold's glasses. Upper right, where the ransom money was to be thrown. Below, lunchroom where slayers ate on day of crime. Lower picture shows the chisel, acids, guns and drugs connected with the murder

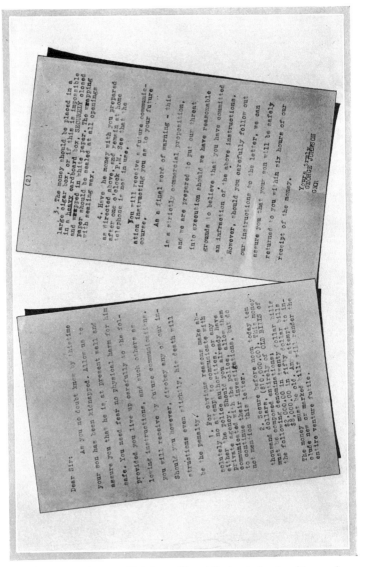

The ransom letter, which Leopold and Loeb admitted writing and mailing to the father of little Robert Franks

their arms, and obligingly each gave a last little smile in the glare of popping flashlights, in the hands of photographers.

The boys were not put in the same cells. They lost no time in getting acquainted with their cell mates. Within a few days "Dick" had taken his part in jail yard athletics. A fear was felt that they might attempt suicide. Something Leopold had said made the jailers very watchful.

The best of meals from an outside restaurant were provided for them by their parents, but all silverware was kept from them. All the time they were in jail, a close watch was kept upon the boys for fear they might end their lives.

Anyone, however, who had expected to see the boys broken and distressed by jail life was disappointed. "Dick," especially, soon adapted himself to prison routine. He made friends rapidly. Before many days passed, one might have thought the boys had lived there forever. At home each had a valet and closets full of the finest clothes. Neither had ever before been without his private bath, yet they fitted into jail life as easily as did the petty thieves, bootleggers and gunmen, who were their companions. They had been in the jail but a few days when, encountering each other in the jail yard, Leopold extended his hand and said, "Dick, we've quarreled before, and made up, let's forget and start again." Thus was mended the friendship which had been temporarily broken when they snarled at each other across the District Attorney's table on May thirty-first, each seeking to heap the crime upon the other.

During the Trial

Long before July twenty-first, the opening date of the trial, Judge Caverly was flooded with requests for passes to the trial. The courtroom, with a capacity crowd, could seat three hundred. More than twice that number of requests for seats were received before the trial. The courtroom was cleaned and newly varnished, everything was ready on the morning of July twenty-first.

The ordinary arrangements of the courtroom were changed, and counsel, defendants, bailiffs, newspaper men, telegraph operators, visiting lawyers, relatives of the Franks, Leopold and Loeb families, and, last of all, the general public, each was assigned their own little preserve. Before the bench there was a table for the counsel. Near them the defendants, guarded by bailiffs and deputy sheriffs, who watched their every move. There was the jury box, minus its twelve good men and true, but plus a dozen telegraph operators. Special correspondents from all the big newspapers of the country were wedged into the jury box and in any little space close to the bench that they could find.

There was row on row of benches to the right to accommodate the local press representatives. To the left, the seats for the families of the two indicted boys and the one dead boy. Back of the rail were more zones for correspondents, not a few of them from New York papers, and here and there, wherever he could insinuate himself, was a representative of the general public.

Judge Caverly ruled that everybody had to be seated. He issued two hundred cards of admission to official representatives and news writers and reporters. So the other hundred which the courtroom could accommodate had to follow the rule of "first come first served."

Up until the very last day of the trial, mid-afternoon would find sidewalks in front of the main door of the Criminal Court Building seething with humanity, hoping in some way or other to slip into the Criminal Court Building and then to find a way into the courtroom itself. So large were the crowds who flocked to attend the trial that a cordon of police was stationed, during the whole trial, at the front door. Those seeking admission to the Criminal Court Building had to show their passes or, having business to transact, had to explain it in detail to the guards at the door. Elevators ran only to the fifth floor for the general public. Guards had to be stationed at the foot of the stairs on the first floor, and they checked everyone who came in the elevators to the floor where the trial was held. Past those three lines of police, one still had to brave some half dozen bailiffs and policemen at the door of the courtroom.

All this because every day three thousand people tried to get into the space that would accommodate three hundred. The excuses made by courtroom fans to gain admission to Judge Caverly's courtroom would fill a book. All the relatives of any man who then held or ever had held a city or county position must have tried to get into the courtroom, for that was one of the favorite excuses used in trying to wheedle passes from the doormen. One woman, day after day, fought and quarreled with every guard in sight, declaring that she was a special representative of some publication, the name of which she could not divulge. Occasionally she slipped by, but when she did not, the corridors rang with her declarations that it was politics and fear of her caustic, truthful pen which kept her from the courtroom.

Pretty girls by the dozen pouted and rolled their eyes at the doormen. They were either sweethearts of "Dick" or "Babe," or they "just once wanted to see those dear boys," they said. The grewsomeness of the crime seemed to have no effect upon the feeling of the giddy little flappers, who begged to get into the courtroom.

A survey of that crowd who daily stormed the courtroom gave much material for speculation about the mind of the average citizen. This was no crowd of close friends and relatives, who fought to hear the trial of "Dick" and "Babe." It was not the jobless or the idle who came to while away the hours, but a well dressed, prosperous crowd, and curiosity was the most common motive. A few friends of the boys attended all the sessions of the trial. Only their closest relatives were there. Comparatively few lawyers and doctors, whose professions made the trial of great interest, were to be found in that seething multitude that daily fought for admission. Most of them were total strangers drawn there by some curious urge to look at these two boys whose lives were in the balance, to gaze upon the grief ravaged countenances of their relatives. There were more women than men, sleek, well dressed dowagers, and girls in their teens. All day long, in the stifling courtroom, scarcely able to hear a word, they would sit on the edges of their seats, loose lipped, eyes shining, intent, straining every nerve to catch some word of the story of blood and grief which was unfolded. In the trial little of the erotic or obscene came out in testimony. Day after day the story unfolded with only now and then some shred of evidence revealed that was not already known to the world. Yet, these nice women and kindly faced men daily fought for seats and daily sat sweltering in the hot courtroom, hoping to hear some forbidden testimony. Not a pretty story, this tale of Loeb and Leopold, and not a pretty sight, the mob that came to listen to it.

The attitude of the boys throughout the trial amazed everyone who watched them. Every day newspapers carried pictures of them smiling in the courtroom. When the crowd laughed, they laughed. Sometimes they laughed alone. Everyone commented on their cheerfulness and even levity, through the whole proceeding, but those who watched them closely came to see that often it was the nervous giggling of two frightened, foolish boys who found themselves in a terrific mess with the eyes of the world upon them.

Tyrrel Krum, a reporter on the Chicago Tribune, only a few years older than the boys, came to know them during their days in the County Jail, perhaps better than anyone else. A story which he wrote for his newspaper gives the most comprehensive and the fairest record of the spirit in which Nathan Leopold, Jr., and Richard Loeb went through their trial:

"Nathan Leopold, Jr., does not feel any remorse or regret for what he has done. Furthermore, he doesn't crave expressions of sorrow for him. This was the answer Leopold sent to the world from his cell last evening (July twenty-fifth, the fifth day of the trial), to the question that has burned the lips of millions of people throughout the country:

" 'The boys are so cool, do you suppose they feel any sorrow for what they have done?'

"Barbers ask it between swipes of the razor. Stenographers in loop offices toss it across to girls who sit at the next desk. Bootblacks look up from their work and wonder aloud. The farmers in the field discuss it across the fence.

"So newspaper reporters attempt to answer this question with their pen observation of the boys as they sit in the courtroom and smile and jest at the proceedings in which their lives are the pawns. And this answer seemingly is reached after all such speculation:

" 'I guess from their manner they don't feel sorry, and if they do, they certainly conceal their feelings wonderfully.'

"A reporter stopped at cell 604 shortly after the boys returned from Judge Caverly's courtroom last evening.

" 'Babe,' he said, 'I feel sorry for you. Do you know that?'

" 'Now listen, I certainly do not like that,' Leopold shot back. 'I don't want you to feel sorry for me, and if you do, I wish you would change your mind. I do not feel sorry for myself for what I did. I did it, and that's all. I got myself in this jam, and it is up to me to get out.'

" 'Everyone,' said the reporter, 'feels that the murder of Bobby Franks was cold blooded and vicious, but the thing that causes wonder is that two boys, with the prospects you and "Dickie" Loeb had before you, should find yourselves in a place like this.'

" 'I feel sorry for you and "Dick" for that reason. It is not a feeling for you as murderers, but as a man to man proposition. That's all.'

"The youth waited a moment or two before he spoke.

" 'Well, if that's the way you feel, it's all right, but don't get the idea that I agree with you. I have great feeling for my father and my brothers, but not for myself. No!

" 'As far as being remorseful, I can't see it. Life is what we make it, and I appear to have made mine what it is today. That's my lookout and nobody's else.'

"The reporter slid down a tier of cells to number 600, where Loeb was reading newspapers.

" 'People on the outside are saying you are the coldest blooded mortal in the world, because of the way you are acting in court. You laugh and josh and appear to be having a good time,' the reporter said.

" 'Well, what do they want me to do? the boy smiled up.'

" 'I don't know. I suppose they want you to act natural.'

" 'That's just exactly what I am doing,' Loeb replied. 'I sit in the courtroom and watch the play as it progresses. When the crowd laughs, I laugh. When it is time to be serious, I am that way. I am a spectator, you know, and like to feel myself as one.'

" 'You can tell the people on the outside there is no faking or pretending. I have watched you in the courtroom across the table, and you laugh, smile, yawn, look bored and all the other things. Why should I be different?'

"The reporter couldn't answer."

There you have Loeb and Leopold during this trial, which they knew might end with their heads in a noose. Only once did their smiling exterior break and that was during the plea of their own attorney, Clarence Darrow, when he asked that these two boys, sick of mind, be sentenced to life imprisonment instead of hanging. Temporarily, the smiles were erased from their faces, and fear and a certain hang-dog sheepishness took its place. Along toward the end of the trial, Leopold's nerves gave way one day, and after a scathing denunciation by one of the attorneys for the State, he became hysterical. Otherwise they remained throughout the whole trial the most interested of a courtroom full of interested listeners.

The Trial Begins

Leopold and Loeb were promptly, on the sixth of June, 1924, indicted by the grand jury of Cook County for the murder of Robert Franks, and also for the kidnaping for ransom. They were arraigned on the eleventh of June and pleaded not guilty. They were represented by Clarence Darrow and Benjamin C. Bachrach, two of the best known criminal lawyers in Chicago. At this time, the case was set down for hearing on such preliminary matters as counsel in the case might see fit to present on July twenty-first.

On July twenty-first, the defendants again appeared before Chief Justice John R. Caverly, of the Criminal Court of Cook County, and to the great surprise of everyone, pleaded guilty. The plea of guilty involved, as to each offense, a maximum punishment of death or a minimum punishment of fourteen years' imprisonment in the penitentiary. Under the law of Illinois, notwithstanding the plea of guilty, the State must prove the crime, before sentence is imposed. At this time the case was set for trial on July twenty-third, before the court, without a jury. The only question to be determined by the court on the trial was the degree of punishment, death or imprisonment in the penitentiary for not less than fourteen years.

On July twenty-third the trial began. Walter Bachrach entered the case at this time as additional counsel for the defendants. The state was represented by Judge Robert E. Crowe, State's Attorney, Thomas Marshall, Joseph P. Savage, Milton Smith and John Sbarbaro, assistants.

The trial proceeded day by day until the thirtieth of July, during which time the State produced some eighty witnesses to prove every detail of the crime, about which there was no controversy and very little cross-examination, by the attorneys for the defendants. On July thirtieth, the state rested its case and the defense began the introduction of its testimony.

The only defense sought to be interposed was "mitigating circumstances," to avoid the extreme penalty of the law, death. The mitigating circumstances claimed by counsel for the defendants did not consist of the facts surrounding the commission of the crime, but of the alleged abnormal diseased mental condition of the defendants.

The first witness placed on the stand for the purpose of testifying as an expert to the mental conditions of the defendants, "Dick" Loeb and "Babe" Leopold, was the distinguished alienist, Dr. William A. White, Superintendent of St. Elizabeth's Hospital, Washington, D. C.

Dr. White was asked his name, his profession, age and professional connections, whereupon all further testimony was objected to by the State's Attorney on the ground that it was apparent that the purpose of the testimony was to prove the mental condition of the defendants, at the time of the commission of the crime, and that all such testimony was precluded by the plea of guilty.

Whereupon, a memorable legal battle began between the State and the defense, over the question "Is there such a thing as degrees of mental responsibility short of insanity in the legal sense?"

All day the thirtieth and thirty-first of July, and nearly all of the succeeding day, August first, the argument lasted. For the negative, "That there is no such thing as degrees of responsibility," Robert E. Crowe, the State's Attorney and his assistant, Thomas Marshall, presented the case for the prosecution.

For the affirmative, "That there is such a thing as degrees of mental responsibility," the argument for the defense was made by Clarence Darrow, Benjamin C. Bachrach and Walter Bachrach.

The question had been discussed before in other cases with reference to degrees of crime but rarely, if ever before, certainly not elaborately, upon a plea of guilty, with reference to the question of degree of punishment. Here there was no dispute as to the degree of the crime. It was murder in the first degree. The punishment fixed by the statute covered a wide range. At one end was death. At the other was imprisonment in the penitentiary for fourteen years.

Between these two the court and not the jury must fix the penalty. And in fixing the penalty, it is the duty of the court "to examine witnesses, as to the aggravation or mitigation of the offense." Is mental abnormality or disease short of insanity in the legal sense "mitigation" within the meaning of this rule of law?

The state said "No"! The defense said, just as loudly, "Yes"! Mental abnormality or disease amounting to insanity in the legal sense is, of course, a defense. But insanity in the legal sense was eliminated from the case by the plea of guilty. An insane man cannot be legally guilty of anything, because an insane man is not legally responsible for his acts.

But may proof of mental abnormality or disease, short of insanity, be considered by the court in "mitigation"? That was the question.

And this in turn depended upon the answer to: "Is there such a thing known in law as degrees of mental responsibility?"

If the question of fact as the mental condition of Nathan F. Leopold, Jr., and Richard Loeb, about to be discussed by Dr. White and the other alienists, amounted to a discussion of the sanity or the insanity in the legal sense of the defendants, then the court had no power to hear the testimony, because this was a question of fact for the jury, upon a plea of not guilty.

On the other hand, if the question about to be discussed by the alienists was a question of degrees of mental responsibility short of legal insanity and if the law recognizes any such thing as degrees of mental responsibility short of legal insanity, then the question was one for the court to consider, in "aggravation or mitigation of the offense." The position of the state on this very interesting question was thus stated by Mr. Crowe, the State's Attorney.

"Our interpretation of this is, your Honor, that they are attempting to show degrees of responsibility. There is nothing in law known as degrees of responsibility. You are either entirely responsible for all the consequences of your act, or you are not responsible at all.

"Whether they term that legal insanity or whether they term that moral insanity, or whether they call it by some other name and leave insanity out, it still presents to the court, in our judgment, a defense of insanity; and I insist that in a murder case where counsel cannot waive any of the rights guaranteed to the defendant by the constitution; where even the defendants themselves cannot waive them, the defendants could not sign a jury waiver in this case. They cannot agree to this or that. The law places these safeguards around them. While counsel may say that this peculiar mental disease does not amount in our judgment to a legal defense of insanity, your Honor may think, or I may think that it does. There may be a wide difference of opinion, as to the exact legal effects of that. We might all be in accord. Your Honor might think, I might think and counsel for the defendants might think that this evidence of mental disease did not amount to legal insanity, but the Supreme Court, reading the records later, may come to a different conclusion, and say that is the defense of insanity, and ought to be submitted to the jury."

On the other hand the position of the defense of this question was thus stated by Mr. Walter Bachrach, "Our plea of guilty in this case admits that on that day (the day of the murder) they were legally sane; therefore we do not propose to offer any evidence to show that on that day they were legally insane.

"We do propose to offer evidence, however, to show a mental condition, a mental disease, functional in character, not an organic brain disorder like paresis or something of that kind, that would affect the capacity of the defendants to choose between right and wrong, but that there was a functional mental disease which would have been insufficient for the defense to have asserted here on an issue before the jury on the question of guilty, that these defendants were insane. But we still say that that evidence falling short of a competent legal defense is a circumstance which this court may take into consideration and should, in determining the punishment to be meted out to these defendants in the exercise of the discretion conferred upon the court by the statute."

After three days' argument along these lines, the court reached the conclusion that "under that section of the statute which gives the court the right and says that it is his duty to hear evidence in mitigation as well as evidence in aggravation the court is of the opinon that it is his duty to hear any evidence that the defense may present, and it is not for the court to determine in advance what it may be."

Whereupon a week's time was devoted to the discussion by the alienists for the defense of the mental condition of the defendants, claimed to support the plea for "mitigation" of punishment.

The alienists for the defense were Dr. William A. White, Superintendent of St. Elizabeth's Hospital, Washington, D. C.; Dr. William Healy, director of Judge Baker Foundation, Boston, Massachusetts, formerly director of the Juvenile Psychopathic Institute, Chicago; Dr. Bernard Glueck, formerly director of the Psychopathic Clinic, Sing Sing prison, and Bureau of Children's Guidance, New York City; and Dr. H. S. Hulbert, formerly connected with the Rockefeller Foundation and now in general practice in Chicago.

Prior to testifying, Drs. White, Healy and Glueck, together with Dr. Ralph C. Hamill, a neuropsychiatrist of Chicago (who did not testify in the case) prepared and submitted to the attorneys for the defendants, a joint report on the mental condition of the defendants.

This report was never introduced in evidence but furnished the basis of all of the expert testimony for the defendants and so accurately and concisely states the position and conclusions of the alienists for the defense, that is here given in full, in lieu of quoting any of the testimony given from the witness stand.

Prior to entering upon the preparation of this report the alienists for the defense and the counsel for the defense made a proposition to the State's Attorney and to the alienists for the State, that the alienists for both the defense and the State make joint examination of the defendants with the view of making, if possible, a joint report to the court.

Mr. Crowe could not see his way clear to accept this suggestion, therefore, the idea of the joint report was necessarily abandoned. One cannot help regretting that the suggestion for a joint report was not carried out. The result might have been a contribution to the science of psychology of crime of unique and lasting value. As it is, the report of Drs. White, Healy, Glueck and Hamill, though not receiving the sanction of the alienists of the State, will no doubt be studied by neuropsychiatrists the world over, as being an interesting and valuable contribution to the psychology of crime.

Probably never in the history of criminal trials has there ever been before such a painstaking, elaborate and detailed examination of any person charged with a crime, by such a distinguished corps of scientists as was made of Nathan F. Leopold, Jr., and Richard Loeb, in this case.

Prior to the preparation of the joint report, by Drs. White, Healy, Glueck and Hamill, an elaborate examination of the boys was made by Dr. H. S. Hulbert of Oak Park, Ill., and Dr. Karl M. Bowman of Boston. There was apparently no secret of the soul of either boy that they did not drag out into the light.

These distinguished scientists made separate reports on each of the boy slayers, showing the result of their examinations. These original reports were not only too long for publication but also contained unprintable matter concerning the sex life of the defendants.

These reports, here quoted, are of great interest, especially to students of psychology of crime. They are quoted in full, except for the unprintable matter:

Medical Report

By Doctors Hulbert and Bowman

The examination covered a period of eighteen days, namely, from June 13th, 1924, to June 30th, 1924, inclusive.

The examination included a careful and painstaking history of the patients' life, obtained by interviews with their relatives and friends, as well as from the patients themselves, an extensive psychiatric study and a physical examination, which included, as well, a thorough neurological, endocrine and X-ray examination, as well as the usual laboratory studies.

The actual examination of the patients took place at the Cook County jail in Chicago. The conditions for the exaimnation were exceptionally good. A large, well-lighted room about fifteen feet square was assigned for the examination. The room was completely isolated from all noises and contact with officials and prisoners, and complete privacy was thereby possible. The room was furnished with a large table, chairs, a bed, and a sink wiith running water, both hot and cold. There was a toilet in connection with this room, and the jail authorities were extremely co-operative and gave every facility possible in their power to aid in the examination. Later the examinations were held in the large room formerly used as the jail hospital. This is on the top floor, and is more private and secure.

Richard Loeb

FAMILY HISTORY

The family history was obtained from the mother, the eldest brother, the uncle Jacob, and the patient.

The paternal stock is of German-Jewish descent. In general,

the stock is characterized as being of high intelligence, good ability, and a number of the members have been prominent in social and philanthropic enterprises.

A first cousin of the father developed a definite insanity when about eighteen, and was adjudged insane and committed to the Elgin State Hospital. Aside from this there have been no other mental disorders.

The paternal grandfather was a quick, alert man, who was quite abusive to his children and beat them severely. The patient's father has been exactly the opposite in his treatment of his children, probably as a reaction to the excessive severity of the grandfather.

There are three paternal uncles, living and well. They are all somewhat sensitive and high strung in their makeup, but not abnormally so. One paternal aunt died at birth.

The maternal stock is of German extraction, and the mother is a Catholic. The maternal stock has, likewise, been composed of individuals of high intelligence and good capacities. The maternal grandmother is living and well, at seventy-one years of age. She had an operation for exophthalmic goiter ten years ago. She was somewhat nervous and apprehensive at that time, but before and since she has shown no peculiar traits of personality.

There were ten maternal uncles and aunts. Four died in infancy. One maternal uncle died at the age of twenty-two of "flumonia." One maternal aunt died at the age of thirty of childbirth and influenza. She developed a goiter while she was pregnant. Three maternal uncles and one maternal aunt are living and well. All are married, and all have children. They are considered of normal make-up, and show no peculiarities.

There is no history of any insanity or mental disorder in the maternal stock.

The patient has three brothers, all of whom are living and

"Dickie" Loeb, one of the confessed slayers, helps recover the buried belt of the victim. Below, boots worn by Leopold while concealing the body, and ashes of blood soaked robe

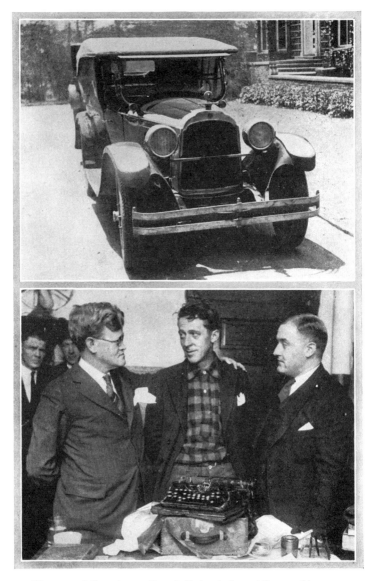

The rented "murder car" and (below) Leopold's portable typewriter on which the ransom letter was written, with the diver,
Frank Blair, who recovered the machine from lagoon

well. Allan is now twenty-seven, Ernest is twenty-four, and Thomas is ten.

PHYSICAL HISTORY

The patient is the third of four children. The other pregnancies have been normal in every way, except that the youngest boy, Thomas, was a premature baby. Prior to the patient's birth the mother was not in very good health, although not severely sick. She had much morning sickness. She had an antrum infection with some fever and had "grippe" with some complications. As far as can be ascertained the father's health prior to conception was good. The delivery was natural. There was a subsequent hemorrhage, but no ill effects were noted.

At birth the patient was regarded as a perfect baby. He was breast fed for three months. He was not very strong during his first few years of life. Before he was five years old he had whooping cough, measles, mumps and influenza. He was regarded as rather weak during all this time. At about four and a half years of age his tonsils were removed, and he increased slightly in strength until the age of nine, after which there was a marked increase in strength and growth. When nine years of age, he had some eye trouble and his lids would tend to stick together for a period of several weeks. At thirteen the first pubic hair appeared. The auxiliary hair first showed at sixteen. At eighteen his voice is still changing. He shaves now every two or three days. During the past five years he has had numerous attacks of frontal sinusitis. He had gonorrhea when fifteen years of age, was treated for nine months and considered cured. He had an operation for hemorrhoids two years ago. For the past year he has worn glasses for reading purposes only. He has had rare headaches. About a month ago he had an acute conjunctivitis or inflammation of the eyes.

There is no history of fainting attacks, except that once during an initiation ceremony at school he fainted.

When a small child he once had a severe fall from his veloci-pede, cutting his chin so that the scar still shows. He was un-conscious at the time, and no bones were broken. When fifteen he had an automobile accident and suffered a concussion of the brain. At the age of twelve he stammered some, especially when associating with stammerers. For the last two or three years he has had tremors of the face which have been increasing, and which are now easily noticeable when he is at all emotional. He has had considerable dental work done, in straightening of the teeth. He still has three baby teeth, and an X-ray shows that there are no unerupted adult teeth imbedded.

In his early life the patient was rather weak and lacked en-durance. At four and a half, following the tonsillotomy, there was some improvement, and since the age of nine he has been in excellent general physical condition.

GOVERNESS

When the patient was four and a half years old a governess by the name of Miss Struthers was employed. She is a Canadian, who had had a high-school education, and was twenty-eight years of age when she first entered the Loeb household. Her influence upon the patient has been of importance in shaping his later de-velopment. She had definite ideas of strictness and obedience. She was prompt with her punishments, but never excessively severe, and she never used corporal punishment.

The patient's earliest recollection of her is that shortly after she came he locked her in a room. She promptly punished him by making him sit upon a chair. This was a new form of pun-ishment to him, and he was somewhat taken back by it. The patient himself feels that she was over-severe, and tended to repress him. He states, "I always obeyed her to the minute—second. Her word was law. To myself I would think certain things were not as they should be. I would brood some.

"To 'get by' her I formed the habit of lying."

He further states, "As a boy I was kept under and did not do the things other boys did. When she left I sort of broke loose."

Although she was strict and enforced obedience, she was apparently very much attached to the patient and endeavored to and acted for what she considered his best interests. As the patient expresses it, "With all her faults I am convinced she loved me intensely and felt she was doing it for my betterment."

The patient soon discovered that he could escape detection and punishment by lying, and he started at this time the habit of lying, which has increased and persisted up to the present time.

The Governess read to the patient a great deal and read him suitable works for a boy of his age, a number of the books being books dealing with history or historical characters. She also encouraged him in his school work, and coached him outside. Her influence probably had a great deal to do with the rapid progress he made in school. She accompanied him to and from school until the fourth or fifth grade.

During his early childhood he was not allowed to indulge in athletics to the extent other children did.

He early became very much attached to his governess, and she to him. When he went to camp for his first summer he was very homesick, so that she came to visit him.

In their early relationships there was a profound attachment. The patient felt much attached to her, as he had toward his mother. Apparently her whole life was largely wrapped up in the patient.

In sex matters she was very repressed, never discussing such matters with the patient, always skillfully turning aside questions he might ask on such topics, and always being very careful that she did not expose herself in any way before him. As a result, the patient was eleven years old before he appreciated that there was any real difference between the two sexes.

His governess took his part against his two older brothers,

and was most fond of him. As he grew older, and she was assigned to take care of the patient's younger brother, she didn't like this, and the result was more or less friction in the family, and she was finally dismissed. Before she left she encouraged the patient to take her side in this disharmony between herself and Mrs. Loeb, and apparently at this time she was becoming very paranoid and suspicious, and he uncritically accepted her unusual methods of thinking as normal.

She left the household when the patient was fifteen years old and went to Boston, and later married. Her marriage has been unhappy, and seems to have increased her abnormal and peculiar ideas. Sometime recently she returned to Chicago and made a scene in front of the patient, expressing some sexual delusions of persecution and ideas of reference. The patient at this time apparently did not return her intense attachment, and she was still further upset by this. An opportunity was obtained to talk with her, and at this time she was very much on her guard, very suspicious and irritable. She refused to discuss a number of topics. She showed no insight whatever into the mental attitudes of small children. She made extreme claims as to how well she had brought up the patient and what a perfect boy he was until she left.

Her claims are obviously untrue, although she doubtless believes them, and simply demonstrates her complete lack of understanding of human nature. She is unquestionably a paranoid person, with various misinterpretations and a suspicious and seclusive attitude toward others.

Her influence upon the patient has been very great, and it has had a most unfortunate effect, although she herself desired only his best interests, and endeavored to secure them. She was too anxious to have him become an ideal boy. She effeminized him and would not allow him to mix enough with other boys. She would not overlook some of his faults, and was too quick in her punishment.   He, therefore, built up the habit of lying, without compunction and with increasing skill.

ACADEMIC HISTORY

He received tutoring by his governess from the age of four and a half to seven, when he entered the third grade.   According to his account, he finished the seventh grade at twelve, there were only seven grades, and he graduated.   He then entered the University School at Hyde Park, Chicago, which was in the neighborhood of his house.   He graduated from High School at the age of fourteen, after two years' study.   He secured extra credits in German and French, and he took a summer correspondence course in history, and also special Latin lessons.   After graduating from High School he entered the University of Chicago in 1919, when fourteen years of age.   The first two years at the University of Chicago he took the regular course, and lived at home.   His governess was still with him, his first year in College, and still tutored him.   He entered the Junior Class of the University of Michigan in 1921, when sixteen years old. His credits from the University of Chicago were out, so that it was necessary for him to take extra courses at Michigan.   He graduated from the University of Michigan at eighteen, and received considerable notoriety as the youngest graduate that they ever had.   He received no scholastic honors.   During his summer vacations he played most of the time.

After his first year at the University of Chicago he started a course in history during the summer, but discontinued it because of lack of interest.   Again, the next summer, he took correspondence courses, but soon dropped them.

In the fall of 1923 he entered the graduates' department of the University of Chicago and studied American and European history.

The patient himself states that after high school his education was along the lines of least resistance, that he was intellectually lazy, and only exerted himself as much as was necessary, and that he never received any honors. He intended to study law next year at the University of Chicago. His arrest prevented his graduate degree this scholastic year.

The patient specialized in history while at college. He states that history was always very easy for him, and that he had received a good start in it because of some correspondence course which he took, under a Miss Frances Knox. The history of the South was most interesting to him. He thinks that this may be due to the fact that he had it under Professor Phillips, whom he admired immensely, and who was a Southerner. The most interesting characters in history to him are Calhoun and Clay. He admired Calhoun because of his arguments in favor of nullificaton. He was interested in Clay at first, because he was very fond of Church's Life of Henry Clay, and also because Clay was unable to secure his ambition in life.

His governess read him from histories, particularly stories of the Scottish Chiefs and the Rise of the Dutch Republic. He feels this may have had something to do with his interest in history. He does not feel that he has any one favorite or ideal character in history. When asked what historical movements were of most interest to him he said that the American Revolution had been interesting, and he had always particularly admired the frontiersmen.

The patient had expected to go on with the study of law next year at the University of Chicago.

SEX LIFE

The patient had no sex knowledge of his parents, of his brothers, or of his governess. He had no realization of the difference between the sexes until he was eleven years old. At this time the chauffeur told him something about such matters. He states that it was not until after he had entered college, at fourteen, that he knew that people had sex intercourse. His first experience was at fifteen. He sought advice from his older brother and from one of his uncles, being particularly desirous of keeping a knowledge of all this from his father, whose respect he wanted to maintain.

. . . .

EARLY DEVELOPMENT AND PHANTASIES

In his early life he had good books read to him by his governess. While none of the family, except his brother, knew of it, he was reading a great many detective stories. He was also developing into an easy and glib liar. He was boastful and selfish. Once he talked to his mother about his running away because nobody at home liked him very much, especially his older brothers. He frequently expressed self-pity.

In the family's estimation he developed very much as any average boy would, except he was intellectually quite precocious.

At about the age of ten or eleven he commenced to develop phantasies, usually at the time of retiring. These phantasies gradually assumed more and more importance in the patient's life, and were worked out in more and more detail. Usually before going to sleep and while lying in bed he would imagine himself living out some scene. He speaks of this as "picturization." There were several phantasies which recurred with great frequency. Perhaps the earliest of these was that he would picture himself in jail. He would imagine that he was being stripped of his clothing, being shoved around and being whipped. There was a great feeling of self-pity in this, but no feeling of fear. "I was abused, but it was a very pleasant thought. The punishment inflicted on me in jail was pleasant. I enjoyed being looked at through the bars, because I was a famous criminal."

Linked up with this idea of being in jail was the idea of being a famous criminal. This seemed to evolve from the first phantasy of being in jail, and came on slightly later. He would particularly imagine himself as the "Master Mind" directing others.

In his phantasies about crime the patient gradually commenced to imagine himself doing all sorts of crimes. He derived intense pleasure from such phantasy, and particularly had a feeling of being superior to others, in that they didn't know who was connected with the crime and he knew the truth about it while they did not.

It is important to note, that a number of his actual crimes were the direct result of a great deal of pleasurable phantasy in regard to a particular type or form.

One particular point connected with all this phantasy was the idea that he was the "Master Mind" and was so clever at planning crimes that he could escape detection from the greatest detectives of the world. Thus he would be, in truth, the "Master Criminal Mind of the Century" and would work out a wonderful plan for a crime which would stir the country, and which woud never be solved.

In this connection it is interesting to note that he paid a great deal of attention to the mysterious disappearance of Charlie Ross, and was greatly interested in the fact that this mystery had never been solved.

In all his criminal phantasies the thing that gave him pleasure would be the prestige to himself as the "Master Mind" directing the criminal operations which no detective could solve. There was never any particular emphasis on financial profits to himself, and when that did appear it was merely to make the "picturization" consistent and logical.

In all his phantasies of crime he always had one or a few more associates with him, and he was always the leader.

In all of his phantasies there is no instance of his performing a crime alone, where there was no one to appreciate his skill.

He did phantasy somewhat of becoming a professional criminal and a gentleman of leisure ostensibly engaged in business, but this phantasy was not vivid or extensive.

Another type of phantasy which occurred early, and tended to be dropped, was to think of himself as a frontiersman shooting at others. In this phantasy he would get under the bedclothes, which, in his imagination, were impregnable to bullets. He would then live out, in his phantasy, various scenes of frontier life.

Another type of phantasy, which has persisted up to the present time, was to think of himself as an ideal fellow. In this phantasy he would imagine that he was extremely good-looking, very athletic, rich, owning several automobiles, a member of a College Fraternity and a great football hero. His audience was always very vague. They were usually good-looking girls and a college group, but there was never any one particular person whom he felt anxious to impress with his great qualities.

The patient's phantasy of crime and of himself as the "Master Criminal" was doubtless stimulated by the large number of detective books which he read, and he describes in detail some of these books and tells of the clever way in which the criminal succeeded in evading the detectives.

DELINQUENCIES

At an early age he discovered he could evade punishment from his governess by lying, and he quickly and skillfully adopted this reaction to escape unpleasant consequences. At no time did he ever experience the slightest feeling of guilt or remorse for his lies. His lies were practically always successful since his governess and family and friends all considered him a very frank and truthful lad, and his appearance was straightforward and honest. Sometimes his brothers were aware of the fact that he was lying to his governess, but he often managed to conceal the truth from them. He has continued to lie, to evade any unpleasant situation, up to the present time. In fact he has carried this to such an extreme that at times he would lie to his parents without sufficient cause. This led some of his friends to tell him, in a quiet way, that he was "crazy," and his cousin specifically told him that he thought he was crazy to lie to his folks when it was not necessary, nor advantageous.

The patient would also lie, in a boastful way, to his friends and acquaintances. For instance, he would tell them what exceptional grades he had made at college, although this was not the case. He boasted of his sexual prowess and his numerous affairs with girls, whereas he now states that he has always been relatively less potent, sexually, than his companions. Recently he has derived a great deal of satisfaction from telling a girl acquaintance that he was a bootlegger, which was not the case. He would also tell her of fictitious dates with other girls. Once he tore his shirt, shot a hole in it, and then put it on and wore it to visit the same girl. He took a revolver with him. He showed her his shirt and told her he had had a fight in a saloon and that was how it happened. He enjoyed very much shocking her and hearing her beg him not to do this. He also told another girl, about this same time, that he was a bootlegger.

He states that he knows that it is wrong to lie, and yet his own lies do not bring him any sense of guilt.

When about ten or eleven years of age he commenced to put his "detective phantasies" in actual use. He would follow people about, imagining that he was a detective shadowing them. He invented a game of "Detective" with his younger brother, which he has played as recently as two years ago.

About two years ago he "shadowed" one of his uncles home. At that time he wore a mask, and just as his uncle came to his own front door step, the patient said to him, "Hold up your hands," but his uncle said, "Run along home, don't be foolish."

When about eleven or twelve years of age he used to walk from his house to that of his French teacher, after supper, as he was taking French lessons. He would walk alone. While walking along he would phantasy himself the "Master Criminal" directing other criminals what house to rob. He would actually give signals with his hands, which were to be interpreted, by his imaginary confederates, as directions for them to follow. This phantasy has continued as recently as two months ago. When walking along by himself he made these signals with his hands, phantasying that he was directing his confederates.

The patient was deceitful in other ways. He would cheat at cards, and perfected an elaborate system of signals with his companion for doing this. He cheated his closest companion with regard to the price of bootleg gin, so that he would secure his own share for nothing.

When eight or nine years of age he stole a sum of money, probably about a dollar, from a boy living next door. He hid the money, and does not think he ever made any use of it. He had absolutely no compunction or feeling of guilt or fear connected with this theft. He got quite a "kick" out of the feeling that he had stolen this money and knew where it was, and that the rightful owner did not.

Shortly after this he again stole money, from a toy cash register, when he and another boy were keeping a lemonade stand.

He soon developed the habit of picking up things in stores, whenever opportunity offered. He would take anything that he could get. It made no difference whether he needed it or whether he would be able to use it in any way. He feels that the thrill and excitement of doing it was the principal cause, and the actual value of the thing taken played a very minor role.

On two occasions when caught he had no feeling of guilt

or remorse, but felt "ashamed" at being caught, that is, at no being clever enough to get away with it.

As he grew older he saw to it that someone was associate with him in the carrying out of the thefts which he himsel planned.

When fifteen years of age he discovered that the keys o his mother's Melbourne electric car would fit any other Mel bourne electric. At the patient's suggestion, he and his com panion twice stole Melbourne electrics. The first time the were followed and had to jump from the moving car to escape The second time they parked the stolen car near a restauran and were in the restaurant when a policeman inquired if anyon there owned the electric near the entrance. The patient got a intense thrill from these two episodes.

About this same time he developed the idea of having hi associate drive him around town while he, the patient, woul throw bricks through the windshields of unoccupied cars. Thi has been varied with throwing bricks through the plate-glas windows of stores. Once they were shot at by a man in a ca and once by two policemen near a store. All this gave the patient a great deal of satisfaction and thrill.

When the patient was fourteen years old he stole a one hundre dollar liberty bond from his eldest brother's desk and put it ir his own desk. This was found by his brother at one time while casually going through the patient's desk.

When sixteen years old the patient stole two bottles of liquo from a second cousin at Charlevoix.

When eighteen years old he planned with his associate the robbing of a wine cellar of some friends who lived in Hubbard Woods. The plan was worked out in great detail. The patient bought a chisel to break into the house. He bound the chisel with adhesive tape. They took ropes with them to tie up the maid, if discovered. They carried two loaded revolvers to shoot anyone, if necessary. They made two unsuccessful attempts to carry out this plan, and then gave it up.

In November of 1923 the patient planned to return to Ann Arbor to rob his own fraternity house, with the assistance of his companion. The plans were elaborately worked out and every precaution taken, including excuses for the patient and his companion for being away from home. The patient and his companion motored to Ann Arbor, arrived at about the appointed time, three o'clock Sunday morning. They wore masks, carried flashlights, two loaded revolvers, rope to tie anyone who might interfere with them, and the patient carried a chisel wrapped with tape, to knock anyone over the head. The robbery went through as planned. They secured about seventy-four dollars, several watches, knives, fountain pens, a typewriter, etc. They became somewhat nervous hearing noises about the house, and the patient did not desire to rob a second fraternity house, as had been agreed upon. His companion, however, insisted. So they went to the second fraternity house, but things there were such that they agreed it was too dangerous to go on, and they left after having picked up a camera in the front hall.

At various times the patient has sent in false telephone messages, false fire alarms, and has committed arson. He has sent in several false riot calls to the police. As far as is known the patient has never set any large fires, but has confined himself to small shacks or out-buildings.

In the matter of arson the pleasure was not in the destruction of property, nor in revenge; but in both the planning to set fire and escape without identification, and to know more about the affair than the bystanders who collected.

The patient would always try to arrange and return at such times and discuss the matter with spectators, asking their theories and offering various speculations as to the cause of the fire and how it happened to be set.

THE FRANKS CASE

In November, 1923, while the patient and his companion we
on their way home from robbing the fraternity house at An
Arbor they got into a heated argument. Each one was di
gusted with the other's work in the robberies. They raised othe
personal questions, about which they were disharmonious, an
their friendship threatened to collapse. This argument was ver
bitter and lasted for some time. It was suggested that thei
friendship should dissolve. However, both gained by this frien
ship in several ways, and therefore they came to an agreemen
to perpetuate the friendship under certain restrictions. It wa
agreed that the patient should have complete domination ove
his companion so that he might call upon him whenever he wishe
for implicit obedience. In order, however, that his companio
should not accede to the patient in every minor request an
under all conditions, it was understood that the patient's com
panion should use his own discretion about accepting the patient'
suggestions or commands, except when the patient should sa
"for Robert's sake." Whenever the patient used this phrase i
a request it meant that it was a part of this contract, and tha
his companion should do as the patient suggested.

Other cryptic uses of language were developed. For instance
if one of the boys telephoned the other that he saw a bargai
at 12th and 50th streets, the listener would know that he was t
meet the speaker at 12:50 o'clock that night.

The patient was the one who planned and enjoyed planning
these subterfuges. Each felt that the other was his superio
mentally. Each felt that the continuation of this friendshi
would be extremely profitable to himself, and each felt tha
abandonment of this friendship would be very hurtful, and pos
sibly dangerous.

On the way back from Ann Arbor the patient first broached
the plan of kidnapping a boy, coupled with the idea of ransom.

The patient had a definite boy in mind at that time. The patient did not like this boy. The patient's idea was to get hold of this boy when he was coming home from a party and to lure him into an automobile. He could not, however, figure any safe way of securing the money. The patient and his companion discussed this idea quite frequently, the patient enjoying these discussions intensely. They would probably spend two or three evenings a week drinking and discussing further plans for this crime.

In March, 1924, the patient conceived the idea of securing the money by having it thrown off a moving train. This idea was discussed in great detail, and gradually developed into a carefully systematized plan. As time wore on the plan became greatly modified from the original one. They discussed at considerable length the choice of a suitable subject for kidnapping. The patient's companion suggested that they kidnap a young girl instead of a boy, but the patient objected to this. His companion also suggested that they kidnap the patient's younger brother, but the patient apparently did not seriously consider doing this. They then considered half a dozen boys, any one of whom would do, for the following reasons: that they were physically small enough to be easily handled and their parents were extremely wealthy and would have no difficulty or disinclination to pay ransom money.

Since they planned to kidnap a boy who was known to them, because it would be easy to lure them into their automobile, they felt it was necessary to kill him at once to avoid any possible identification of themselves by the victim, should he escape or their plans go awry.

The patient did not anticipate the actual killing with any pleasure. He merely looked upon it as an inevitable part of a perfect crime, since it would aid in covering up one possible trace of identification.

The patient states that they anticipated a few unpleasant minutes in strangling him. (The patient's face registered the expression of disgust), and they planned for each of them, namely, the patient and his associate, to have a hold of one end of the strangling rope and they would pull at the same time, so that both would be equally guilty of the murder. They did not seem to feel that this would give them a closer tie in their friendship. It was the sharing of culpability. It was anticipated that the victim would be knocked senseless by a blow on the back of his head from the taped chisel.

The plan then was worked out as follows: they decided to get any young boy whom they knew to be of wealthy family, to knock him unconscious, then to take him to certain culvert, there to strangle him, then pour hydrochloric acid over his face, penis and any identifying scars to retard identification, and to strip off all his clothes for the same purpose and dispose of them, to push the body deep into this funnel-shaped culvert, through which the water flowed, expecting the body to entirely decompose and never be found.

They had also perfected the plan for securing the money. The victim's father was to be told to put the money in a cigar box and seal it with sealing wax. He would receive a telephone call telling him there was a Yellow cab outside. He would then be told to go to a certain place, a "Keep-the-City-Clean" box, where he would find a note which would tell him that he was to get a phone call at a particular telephone booth in a certain drug store. He would then receive a telephone message to board the 3:18 train, to look in the telegram receptacle in the rear car where he would find a note directing him to throw the money off the train at the proper place, namely, when he passed a red factory on his left-hand side, almost immediately after the train passed a certain station. The boys arranged to have a rented car, with a black cloth over the license plate, backed up to the track at the place where the box would be thrown. They had timed the train. They had arranged that if the train was late it probably meant that there had been some flaw in their plans and that the father had sought outside aid, whereupon they would drive away in the car and not wait for the train.

They then planned to return home, and to enjoy the sensation which would be created, as they themselves, of all the world, would be the only ones knowing the actual facts. They had worked out an elaborate plan to rent a car by means of false identifications. They felt assured that their plans were so perfected that they themselves would never be suspected, and of course never be apprehended. They planned to divide the ten thousand dollars ransom money equally. They had no definite plan as to the expenditure of this money.

PSYCHIATRIC STUDY

While under observation in the jail the patient has been quite well behaved. He eats and sleeps well. He has even been noticed going to sleep while his associate was being examined in the same room. He takes a lively interest in the jail routine and in the affairs of other prisoners. He enjoys using the language of the "under-world" which he has picked up while in jail. He is in excellent contact with his surroundings in every way. His intellectual functions are intact, and he is obviously of high intelligence. He denies any hallucinatory experiences, and there is no evidence of their presence. He has no feeling that people are against him or that he is being treated unfairly at the present time, although he often felt as a child that he was treated unfairly and discriminated against, and still believes this to be so.

While in jail the patient appears to be quite unconcerned and indifferent, he does not show the normal amount of emotional reaction to the situation in which he finds himself.

It is interesting that, although he seems absolutely without emotion while at the County Jail, he states that all his life he has been subject to spells of depression and has frequently contemplated suicide.

Since being in jail he has considered the question of suicide, in a very careful way, and has rejected it because he felt that if he were to die there was no added discomfort in letting the law take its course. He also felt that it would be much better for the family if he were to be hanged, rather than to commit suicide as a way of escaping hanging.

He says, however, that if there were some "simple and graceful" way of committing suicide, which would not allow people to know that he had committed suicide, he would do it.

He discusses his own views of religion and morals. His companion has often insisted to him that the only wrong that he, the patient, can do, is to make a mistake, and that anything that gives him pleasure, is right for him to do. The patient states that he has never been able to accept this view of morals, that his viewpoint is the conventional one, although he has not lived up to it. He believes that there is a definite and universal right and wrong, depending on convention in part. He does not believe in a life hereafter, but is not absolutely sure. "When you die, that's all." He does not believe there is an immortal soul to live after. "Speculation won't solve it, so I gave up thinking about it."

He sees the incongruity of his own standards, compared to his own conduct, but explains it by saying that he is somewhat superior to others, and that conventions, therefore, should not bind him.

He says that he is sorry about his present predicament for his family's sake, and that he should be sorrier. He knows that he has done wrong. He doesn't know what should be done to him. He has felt the law should take its course, unless he could avoid it in some way. He would repeat his crime, however, if he knew he wouldn't be discovered.

THE PATIENT'S ESTIMATE OF HIMSELF

He says that he has always been very curious, but had no abnormal type of curiosity. While lazy at times, he has a tremendous amount of energy, and, physically, he doesn't tire easily. He feels that he is very skillful at making friends, can do so quite easily, and can also drop them in a very skillful manner. He has always felt it necessary to have one or two close friends in his life. He has always liked to be in the limelight and to receive favorable attention and comment from others. He likes to have knowledge which others do not possess, and gets a marked feeling of superiority under such conditions. He is inclined to be a leader and likes to dominate his environments, but can fit himself easily into any sort of a situation, so that he does not become bothered or upset if he is compelled to assume a minor role. He often does things quite impulsively and regrets them afterward. On the other hand, he does plan a great many things beforehand, with elaborate detail. He is open and frank with others as long as he feels it is to his interest to be so, but he doesn't hesitate to conceal or to lie to any one, if he will gain by doing so. He often has swings of moods in which he becomes depressed and contemplates suicide. These pessimistic moods have increased during the past two years. They are, however, fairly superficial and pass off as quickly as he becomes engaged in some form of activity. In actual physical combat he is a coward, but in some ways he is rather reckless in regard to personal safety. For example, he will go out in a storm, in a small boat, when he knows that it is a dangerous thing to do. At such times he has no feeling of fear. He has always been much inclined to self-pity, and to feel that he is always right. He has never done anything because he thought it was the right thing to do. He has simply done what he considered to be expedient. He was fond of outdoor sports and is interested in camping and outdoor life in general. This, however, has not been linked up with any intellectual pursuit, such as botany, zoology or the like. He is very fond of bridge and is a very excellent player. He is fond of dancing and mixed society. He has used alcohol considerably since he was fifteen, and has gotten drunk a number of times. He has always been careful of his personal appearance and neat and clean about his person and has liked to appear well dressed. He has always had a pleasant consciousness of his own body.

The patient denies ever having had any hallucinations.

PHYSICAL EXAMINATION

The physical examination is essentially negative. In general he is a well-developed and well-nourished individual without deformities and without evidence of physical disease. His blood pressure is rather low, being 100 systolic and 60 diastolic. The neurological examination is largely negative. The only point of interest is that on the inner posterior and frontal aspects of the middle third of each leg there is a well defined area of poor thermal discrimination. Pinpoint and light touch are normally discriminated everywhere, including this area. The basal metabolism is minus 17 percent. This is, possibly, of some significance. It may be an indication of a lack of secretion from the sexual glands, since we know the patient has very little sex urge, and that lack of secretion from these glands does produce a low rate of the basal metabolism.

The examination of the blood, including hæmoglobin, cell count, Wassermann, blood chemistry and blood sugar tolerance curve, are all within normal limits.

The urine examination is negative.

The X-ray examinations of the head, thorax and wrists are

quite negative, except that they show that some of the permanent teeth are missing.

PSYCHIATRIC INTERPRETATION

To understand this case the following facts must be kept in mind:

The patient has always had a marked feeling of inferiority. This appears to start at the time when he felt he was being too severely punished and not understood by his family or governess, and when he felt he was not receiving sufficient affection from his parents and brothers.

Up to the age of nine he was inferior physically, being rather frail. He was not allowed to play freely with other boys in strenuous outdoor games. As a result he tended to spend a good deal of time by himself thinking over his unsatisfactory life of reality and constructing a world of phantasy, in which he occupied a dominant role and in which his emotional life was satisfied. It was at this time he first encountered some detective stories, which he read surreptitiously and with great avidity. These made a profound impression upon him. It should be noted that he was able to read earlier than the average boy, with a consequent discrepancy between his reading and his judgment.

He actually put some of his phantasies of crime into operation at an early age, and derived intense pleasure from them. He invented the childish game of "Shadow" and of "Detective and Robber," which he has played up to as late as two years ago.

From earliest age he never seems to have experienced the slightest feeling of remorse or guilt for any misconduct, and his only self reproach has been when he has not been sufficiently clever to escape detection or to lie out of a difficult situation.

As he grew older he grew stronger physically. But another physical defect became noticeable, which prevented his feeling on equal terms with other boys. This was his delayed maturity and his lack of sexual potency. He soon recognized that he was lacking in this respect compared with his associates, and to compensate for this he stressed his intellectual superiority and scholastic maturity and sought opportunities to demonstrate his superiority over others in this way.

To cover up his relative impotence he boasted of his excellent marks at school, although he received only moderate grades. He convinced his friends that he was quite superior to them mentally, and derived an intense feeling of satisfaction from being considered their superior in this respect. His closest associate, who was considered by many as being more brilliant than the patient, frequently told the patient that he, the patient, was the "greatest mind of the century." All this focused the patient's attention upon the emotional satisfaction gained from demonstrating his intellectual superiority over others.

To him the possession of knowledge which others did not possess was a great thrill, and he found that by committing crimes and knowing the true details he could discuss them with others who were unaware of the true facts, and thus receive a secret thrill and satisfaction, which was most pleasurable.

The only thing that he desired of other people was that they should look up to him.

As a matter of fact, many of his boy associates considered him immature in judgment and did not acknowledge any marked superiority on his part. They even criticized his behavior severely at times. Some told him frankly that he was "crazy" to act the way he did, because he would lie to his parents many times when no useful purpose was gained by doing so.

From a very early age the patient has been subject to fits of depression, particularly during the past two years. These spells now come on whenever he is alone, but disappear whenever he is occupied, therefore he has tended to have a close companion and to discuss and plan something that is interesting to him in order to avoid these spells of depression. During these depressed spells he has frequently contemplated suicide, but never has attempted it.

The patient has some insight into his peculiarities and says that the idea has often come to him as to whether he was "all there." He states that during the past year he has felt different. He feels that he cannot concentrate so well, that his memory is not so good and that he cannot carry on conversation and small talk with others as well as formerly.

The total lack of appropriate emotional response to situations is one of the most striking features of his present condition. This is not carried out in a consistent manner, but is full of contradictions. Thus we see the patient refusing to escape from jail because it might hurt the family in some way, and yet contemplating kidnapping and murdering some member of his own family, without the slightest emotional reaction to it. Although he is quite anxious for his mother to have the minimum amount of suffering, and not wishing to do anything to bother her, he tells how his sense of humor is aroused by his mother's indignation against the kidnappers and murderers of Robert Franks.

Another example of this split between his emotions and his ideas is the robbery of his own fraternity house. There are many such instances. He has also tended to carry out his crimes in a rather stereotyped way.

From this evidence it must be concluded that the patient is markedly different from the average individual; that he has gradually fallen off in his efficiency, contacts and interests with the world of reality; that he has gradually projected a world of phantasy, which was satisfactory to him, over into the world of reality, and at times even confused the two. There is a definite splitting between the emotional and the intellectual faculties. There has been a great deal of abnormal mood reaction, and a total lack of appropriate mood to certain situations.

During the past year the patient himself has felt that there was something the matter with him, and has vaguely appreciated that he was not "all there."

His crime is to be explained by his peculiar phantasies, which have grown to such an extent that they now dominate him and control his actual behavior. Although he is, in one way, in excellent contact with his surroundings, his world of phantasy is much more important and interesting to him.

In our opinion this tendency will continue and increase so that he will become more and more wrapped up in his world of phantasy and less and less in contact with his world of reality.

There is no reason to feel that the patient's condition is of a hereditary nature or that it will be transmitted to future generations by any of his siblings or relatives.

Neither is there any reason to feel that the family are responsible in any way for this boy's condition.

Nathan Leopold, Jr.
FAMILY HISTORY

The family history was obtained from the father, aunt Birdie and the two brothers, Foreman (Mike) and Sam, and from the patient.

The paternal stock is German-Jewish. The father is a successful business man. The maternal stock is also German-Jewish, and one of the ancestors, namely, Grandpa Foreman, was especially bright mentally.

On the father's side there are three cases of diabetes, and two cases of insanity, of the paranoid type.

On the maternal side there are several instances of nephritis and the patient's own mother died of nephritis.

The known causes of death are of the usual variation: Carcinoma, gastro-intestinal, gall stones, anæmia, childbirth, and acute infections.

The mother was sick throughout her pregnancy with this boy. She had constant albumen. Eclampsia was prevented. She never fully recovered from this nephritis, but lived for seventeen years.

PHYSICAL HISTORY

He is the third of three children, all boys, and the last of six pregnancies, the other three being terminated by disease. Delivery was normal. Breast fed baby, wakeful, and he showed early mental and nervous-system precocity. His first step was at three months, his first word at four months, first tooth at eight months, and he had six teeth in one year. He walked when fourteen months old. Abundant hair developed early. He had measles when five years of age. Until he was nine he had gastro-intestinal disorders, which were complicated by fever, headaches and vomiting. At the age of nine his tonsils were removed, which resulted in a marked improvement in his physical condition. Previously he had been rather effeminate. Following his tonsillotomy he played much more with the boys. He had whooping cough at seven. Earaches were frequent during childhood. At ten he had several minor injuries and infections. Mumps occurred at nineteen. Head colds have been frequent all his life. Adolescence started at thirteen, and was very rapid. He started to shave at fourteen. When fifteen he became overweight and had to reduce.

There has always been a marked instability in the control of his blood vessels. He usually developed a rash when he had eaten the wrong foods. His appetite has been enormous. There has been considerable dental work done. His sleep has been quiet and refreshing, but he could go without sleep for a night and the next morning would be exhilarated. His physical endurance has not been unusual.

About 1920 he had three unusual sicknesses, which resembled in many ways chicken pox, measles and scarlet fever. In all of these the skin symptoms were delayed, and were unusually severe. Within this period he also developed a case of giant hives, showing the extreme sensibility of his skin circulation. During one of these sicknesses he had an unusually high fever and some signs of involvement of the central nervous system, such as twitchings, stiffness of the neck, and over-irritability, which are found in all cases, even very mild cases, of meningitis.

He would grow faint easily, without much provocation. For instance, when he saw his mother's blood pressure being taken, or when his aunt's throat was examined, or when he was vaccinated, or when any sharp physical pain was impending; and this parallels his blood-vessel instability. He has shown in his nose an abnormal degree of sudden engorgements.

There have been no serious injuries.

His urine has never shown albumen.

GOVERNESSES

His first governess was Marie Giessler, or "Mimie." She came when he was about six months old, and stayed about five years. Her main effect on him was that she taught him German, which gave him some advanced credit in school at a later time.

The next governess was a little Catholic girl, named Paula, who stayed six months. Her main effect on him was interesting him in the lives of the minor saints. She carried on his previous desire to become acquainted with the various churches of all denominations in his neighborhood.

The next governess was Mathilda Wantz, or "Sweetie," as she taught the boys to call her. She was a woman ignorant of the English language. She was homely, suspicious, irritable, not tactful, jealous, over-sexual in unusual ways, scheming, and very immature in her judgment. She trained the patient to love and respect her more than he loved and respected his mother. She exposed herself indecently to the patient. She had encouraged the boy to steal some stamps from another boy's stamp collection, and then intended to blackmail him, threatening to tell on him.

The psychiatric importance is that this woman, of very peculiar mentality, was so close to the boys that the boys, especially the younger one, took her abnormal ideas as normal. She gave him a wrong original conception about sex, about theft, about right and wrong, about selfishness and about secrecy. He was so constituted that he never was able to emancipate himself from her erroneous teachings and mistakes.

ACADEMIC HISTORY

The patient entered school when five years and eleven months of age, attending first a school for girls, which had, until very recently, been a school for boys and girls. After two years he entered the public high school, but did not like it, and returned to the school for girls. He was one of the three boys at this school for girls. When eight years old he entered the Douglas Public School in the third grade, but rapidly advanced. In the fifth grade his teacher, Mrs. March, became especially interested in him because of his intellectual advancement and because of his interest in birds. She helped him arrange to skip a grade. When he was eleven years old, in the middle of the school year, he entered the Harvard Preparatory School by taking examinations and thus advanced himself half a year. When he was fifteen years of age, by taking extra studies and by taking examinations, he found he would be eligible for college.

At sixteen he attended the University of Chicago for one year. The next year he went to the University of Michigan at Ann Arbor. The following year he went to the University of Chicago, living at home. Altogether he attended college for three and a half years and received a Bachelor of Philosophy degree and Phi Beta Kappa at 19. He then took one quarter, that is, one term, of post graduate work, and this last school year he has been studying law at the University of Chicago.

During his school days he realized his superiority over the other boys in wealthy parents, in the location of the home, in the fact that a nurse accompanied him to and from school, and that he couldn't attend the toilet in school. This nursing supervision was not quite strict enough because, at least in one instance, some of the tough boys at school came home with him, part way at least, and implanted in his mind some obscene sexual ideas.

He learned to play piano in a surprisingly short period of time.

He enjoyed languages. He spoke German as well as he did English. He took Greek instead of further French courses, and at the University he majored in languages.

As early as his days in the Harvard school, before he was sixteen, he was recognized by the other boys as being distinctly unusual. They called him the "Great Nathan," they called him the "Crazy Bird," they called him the "Flea," and they recognized his superiority in languages, birding and psychology. They recognized, further, his scholastic superiority and rather envied him his ease of attaining high grades. He said that he never had worked because he never had to.

His college course was complicated by absence, due to sicknesses which have been mentioned, but at that he graduated in three and a half years. He took several supplemental courses, some in residence and some by correspondence. He even took correspondence courses during his vacations. These courses were mostly in various languages. They include English, German, French, Greek, Latin, Sanskrit, Umbrian, Russian, Spanish, Modern Greek, Oscan, and he had an idea that he might find *the* universal language.

The other courses which he followed up to quite an extent were in history, psychology, zoölogy, and business.

His college course was complicated, in part, by the fact that some professors and administrative officers did not like to see a student so young advance so rapidly, and it was complicated, on the other hand, by some of his teachers encouraging him to advance much more rapidly than the average boy could.

His interest in language appeared early. He was surprised to find that the idioms of one language were not verbatim translated into another.

He then became interested in comparative language study, and he enjoyed it because languages could be so definitely and accurately classified. He said that he had a "mania for exact classifications." Furthermore, he liked languages because they were intellectual and cold-blooded, not emotional studies.

He writes in his memoranda with Sanskrit characters forming French words.

In his law course he did not exert himself, but had plenty of time for extra mural interests, and yet he was able to take examinations to enter Harvard Law School in its second-year course.

He read extensively in non-academic books, along a great many different subjects, but rather especially along unusual lines. For example, Russian novels of vivid morbid psychology, ancient books, many of them bizarre.

NOTE-BOOK DRAWINGS

It will be recalled that this man spent on an average an hour and a half a day in preparing for his class. He graduated with very high honors, at a very youthful age.

While tending his classes it was impossible for him to maintain his attention. His note-books are full of sketches, drawings and notes, showing his non-attentive thinking in class, and these indicate, directly or symbolically, his remote and recent thoughts.

A list of these drawings, etc., taken from just two of his note-books, takes twenty typewritten pages.

In brief they show religious ideas, the Crucifixion, the Pharaohs of Egypt, crosses, hooded figures marked "K. K. K.," kings, priests, sheiks, gallows. There are almost countless pictures of birds, some drawn carefully, some carelessly, some only in part and in various positions, occasionally two birds together, caricatures of birds. There are pictures of people, and of people's hearts and bodies. Some of these pictures are, obviously, sexual, others are not. There are pictures of animals of many different kinds, dogs, muskrats, seals, pigs, horses, snakes. There are many pictures of stars, 5 and 6-pointed, and clocks and watches pointing at various times of day, pictures of things such as violins, telephones, bones, hearts and body, whisky bottles, pistols and vases. There are notations in various languages, some of which can be identified as French, German, Sanskrit, Russian, English. There are calendars with some dates crossed off and illegible notes there. On the whole these pictures show that the man's subconscious mind had a much greater range than the average person's and turned to subjects quite foreign to the thinking of normal people.

FRIENDSHIPS

With few exceptions he has never formed close friendships. As a boy he was secluded from the company of other boys by having a governess. Two school boys, however, did have an effect on his life by telling him that his governess and his teacher had "pussies," and that he was their "pet." He realized that this was obscene in some incomprehensible way. He was much younger than his nearest brother. He never developed any great appetite for outdoor games and sports, and seldom participated. He used to be bored at watching a baseball game, although he enjoys now watching football and basketball games. While he was at Harvard school he was manager of the basketball team, but not a player.

When he was about sixteen he was rather sickly, and when he was eighteen he was away from school quite a bit because of his mother's sickness and death.

He was especially sensitive to the opinion of others and to their criticism, but he did not let this attitude become known. He assumed the attitude of indifference or superiority, and, on the whole, found it difficult to make friends. The advantages that he took of other boys also interfered with deep friendships. For example, the robbing of another boy's stamp collection. Another thing which prevented enduring friendships was the fact that he was promoted at school much more rapidly than the other boys, and therefore, from year to year almost, his group of school playmates changed. He got along with fair adaptability, and only once in his life did he get into a fight. He much preferred making friends with boys than girls.

When he went to Ann Arbor he was not invited to join the same fraternity that his closest acquaintance from Chicago had previously joined, because the older boys in that fraternity thought he was not a help to his companion.

Dick Rubel was, to some extent, a third member of the close friendship of himself and Dick Loeb, but he was rather patronizing of Dick Rubel, saying that he was only of fair intelligence. His nickname for Dick Rubel was the "Bastard Jew."

While at Ann Arbor he would occasionally go on dissipation parties with other boys from school, going to Detroit. He preferred an intellectual, cold-blooded life, to an emotional one.

Doctor Bernheimer of Chicago, familiarly known as "Murph," is slightly older than the patient and they have been social friends for years. He has looked up to "Murph" for his superior knowledge and has often questioned him about medical and quasi-medical things, such as the pain suffered in operations, the perversions, and the conflict between science and religion. Recently, since "Murph" has become a physician specializing in nose and throat, the patient has consulted him medically, and he often discussed his growing philosophy with him. To this older man the patient's philosophy was not very impressive. He told how he felt, that selfishness was the ideal life, and said he would not raise his hand, nor cross the room, to save the doctor's life. He also told the doctor that each man was a law unto himself, and that conventions were not binding on those of superior intellect. He was very sincere about this. He discussed atheism and the denial of immortality, with Doctor Bernheimer. The doctor's attitude seems to be quite a normal one, and the patient did not learn to correct his own mistakes by conversation with the doctor.

He made no close friendships with his teachers, but was very supercilious and sarcastic towards some of them.

He did find, in Richard Loeb, an intelligence which he regarded superior to his own. Whereupon he offered Richard Loeb his closest friendship. It soon became impossible for him to live without this friendship. His affection grew out of bonds, and he felt willing to be the slave of his friend and co-operate with him in any delinquency which his friend might suggest as the price he would pay for the maintenance of this friendship. The friendship was much too close, but it served for each of them a purpose which they regarded as essential. Because of its abnormality there were certain drawbacks and the boys debated, sometimes acrimoniously, about the perpetuation of this friendship, and finally they reached a very definite, formal compact. If the patient would do as Loeb wanted done in carrying out Loeb's phantasies, Loeb would do what the patient wanted done in the carrying out of the patient's phantasies. Their phantasies were quite dissimilar, but each required one other confederate.

In the jail the patient has not established any friendships, although he has been pleasant mannered, and he has taken an attitude of superiority and slight annoyance towards those whom his family have engaged in his behalf.

PHANTASIES

His phantasies have always been unusually vivid, and, in more than the ordinary way, he has tended to react to them actually.

His anticipations were very vivid and his reactions pronounced. For example, he almost fainted when he saw his mother's blood pressure being taken, he having heard of this and thinking it was a "bloody" process. He gave the signs of real physical upset with a lowered blood pressure, sweating, and generalized weakness, when he was to be vaccinated or when he knew that any hurt was impending.

. . . .

His religious phantasies have always occupied a very prominent part in his life. They began somewhat by his desire to catalogue various churches in his neighborhood. He studied them all in their architecture, and he attended the services when he could. Even during his summer vacation he liked to attend church services in all kinds of churches. He remembers most distinctly Madonna pictures or stained glass windows. He was too young to be confirmed when he had learned the necessary lessons for confirmation. Due in part to his self-guided study of comparative religions he decided not to be confirmed when he had reached a sufficient age.

The most interesting part of the Crucifixion for him was somebody being nailed to something, and this reappears twice later, with pathological significance.

He regarded his mother as *the* most superior woman. After she died he regarded his aunt practically as her equal. He confused their two identities, and he confused the two of them with the Madonna.

His contemplations on God led him to believe that God made mistakes, therefore there was no infallible God, therefore there was no God. One mistake God made was taking away his sainted mother, and leaving a lot of worthless women in the world.

He gave up the idea that there was a God, saying that if a God exists some pre-God must have created him.

In this line of thinking he reasons by analogy, saying that time is the fourth dimension, and insists that if there is no beginning and end of space, there is no begining or end of time, but he cannot conceive of there being a God without beginning or end.

．．．．．．．．．．．．．．．

After the episode when the two older boys brought him home from school one day he indulged in sexual phantasies about his governess. These phantasies were somewhat inaccurate and based upon his present forgotten memories of actual incidents connected with her in his earlier youth.

His earliest phantasies that he can recall began at five, when he phantasied being in command of a large number of men, similar to the officers of the company to which his brother belonged at the time his brother went to military school.

This phantasy changed then to the phantasy of king and slave. This king and slave phantasy lasted for years, was ruminated upon frequently, for various lengths of time, and the phantasy underwent some change as he mulled it over in his mind.

He identified himself at times with the king, and at times with the slave, but he usually preferred to play the role of slave, about 90 percent of the time, he estimates.

His first account of the phantasy was that there was a king who had a slave, and the slave was intensely devoted to the king. This slave was the strongest man in the world. In some way or other, and the way frequently varied, he saved the life of the king. The king was very grateful and wanted to give him his liberty, but the slave refused. The slave was usually comfortable as regards his living conditions, but occasionally, in some of the phantasies, the slave would be in a cell.

There were often "kings' banquets" where each king brought his body slave along to serve him. The slaves were all chained, but the patient was only chained with a tiny gold chain, which he could easily have broken.

When he was in the role of a slave he was always very good looking and very strong. Often there were combats when a champion would be picked from each side to settle a question. The patient would be selected to represent his side and would always win.

The patient had some insight to his phantasies at the time, and was much disturbed because he couldn't work out his phantasies logically. For instance, he states that in one phantasy there would be thousands of men armed with guns trying to overpower him, but he would kill them all off. Then his critical reasoning would assert itself and he would inquire how it would be possible that none of these thousands of armed men should have managed to shoot and kill him. He was so troubled by the impossible and illogical aspects of this, that he gave up that phantasy.

In another phantasy the king would be holding court, and the patient, as his slave, would be lying at his feet. Someone would endeavor to murder the king, but the patient would prevent this.

.   .   .   .

When he was not quite twelve years old he first attempted to fit any of his companions or his associates into his phantasies. This was in the summer of 1916 when he was at a summer camp for boys. The Counsellor in his tent was a well-developed and good looking boy of eighteen. The patient proceeded to fit himself into the position of slave. At this time his phantasy was a nightly occurrence. At night he would lie on his side or stomach, with his arms under the pillow, hugging the pillow. He would notice a certain odor which would be partly from the pillow and partly from his own body, and he regarded this odor as extremely pleasant.

At about this time he developed a great love of symmetry for the human form. He continued to develop his phantasies. A later development was that the king would get this slave when he was a boy, even when he was a baby, at least before he was ten or twelve years of age, and before he had been completely developed physically, then the king would find the boy being beaten by cruel slave drivers, and he had been neglected until he was dirty and sick. Thereupon the king would take the boy for his slave. After the slave had saved the king's life, the king would try to give the slave his liberty, but the slave would refuse saying that the king had saved his life. The king would then say that this had caused no effort on his part and, therefore, he was entitled to no particular gratitude. The slave, however, would persist that this made no difference and would refuse to accept his liberty.

These phantasies continued up until about a year ago, and during that time the patient would add other good-looking boys to his list of slaves.

His ideal for the slave has been a man who was large, muscular, beautiful, and with practically the conventional type of face, such as the advertising models used by Hart, Schaffner & Marx.

The phantasies developed certain variations, in that there was a chief slave named "Bill," who would own two or three slaves himself. These slaves in turn would own two or three more, and so on down. The king, however, would own all of them.

.   .   .   .

During the past two or three years he has fitted his closest companion into this king-slave phantasy. At first his companion had not seemed very good looking to him, but after a while became the patient's ideal of good looks. He then idealized his companion in other ways, thinging him more athletic than he actually was, and regarded him as an ideal athlete.

He regarded his companion as a superior student, and although he actually knew that his companion was not getting the best of grades at school, he preferred to believe his companion's boasts of his high grades. He felt, and still believes, that his companion was much more brilliant and much more intellectual than he himself was.

About a year ago he made a table or a chart for the "perfect man." He gave his companion a score of ninety, he gave himself a score of sixty-two, other friends receiving a score of about thirty or forty. "It was blind hero-worship. I almost completely identified myself with him."

The phantasies, however, continued along other lines, and the patient continued to consider every boy who appealed to him as eligible for the part of slave.

The slave or slaves eventually were always branded with a crown or seal on the inner calf of the right leg, and this branding usually took place in a locker room of the gymnasium of the Harvard School.

One of his extensive phantasies was that he and his companion, with others, were taking a sea voyage and were wrecked on an unknown island. The patient was the only one of those saved who could speak the language of the natives. A piano was saved in the wreck and the patient was the only person able to play upon it. No one on this island knew anything of music. The natives of this island were divided into two groups, nobles and slaves. His companions were all made slaves, but because of his own ability to make music he was made a noble.

He then bought, to be his slave, a certain one of his companions. He would sometimes phantasy that this companion had been the property of someone else and had been very sick, and he would then nurse this companion through his illness. He would then generally give this companion his choice of three things:

First: Liberty, in which case the brand-mark on the inner calf of his right leg would be obliterated and he would be set free, only, however, to be at the mercy of the first noble or lord that saw him, who could take him for his slave.

Second: To remain as his personal slave, in every sense of the word.

Third: To sell him to some other noble. He would develop this phantasy so that his companion should receive worse treatment elsewhere than with him, and that, therefore, his companion would not be desirous of leaving him.

On this island there were two words which were especially used as terms of endearment. These words were "pussy" and "kitten."

Parenthetically, the patient remarks that he has always been very fond of cats, and that as a small child he used to play that he was a kitten, often indulging in this phantasy, over a considerable period of time and on many occasions and in all directions.

. . . .

If the patient is now indulging in phantasies while in jail, he has not disclosed them spontaneously.

His phantasies have been so delightful to him that he would prefer to actually play the role of slave to some one whom he regarded as his superior, than he would to be independent, or take the role of superiority. On the other hand, towards persons to whom he is indifferent he has an attitude of superiority, and very deliberately he affects a still greater attitude of superiority.

His phantasies mean so much to him that they have become compulsions and have permitted whoever he selected to be king while he was slave, to do with him as the king thought, without the patient using his critical judgment as to what is right or wrong.

The phantasies when confused with realities are definite, ir-resistible impulses.

SEX LIFE

His earliest sexual experiences were with his governess. Most of the memories of these have been dropped from his con-scious mind. None of these experiences with her were alto-gether normal.

At seven or eight he learned that sex conversation was taboo. He had no real conception of sex. He did not believe the story that the storks brought babies, because when his nurse said it to him she said it with a sneer. But he did believe his father, who told him that babies were bought at a store.

When he was ten years old he found out that girls were dif-ferent from boys. At about this same time, with two other boys, Henry and Joseph, a club was formed for initiation purposes, and Joe, who was younger than the others, was always the in-itiate. They locked Joe in a closet one day, and when Joe ob-jected to this his cousin, a girl the same age, told the other two boys that if they would let Joe out of the closet they would be told a great secret. So they let Joe out, and she told them, as a secret, that girls were different from boys.

. . . .

When he was fifteen and a half years old he had, for the first time, sexual relations with a woman. It was the custom among the boys of his group, who had automobiles, to take a friend and drive out and pick up two girls and then endeavor to have sexual relations with them. He had been out on a number of such parties, but the girls they had secured would never permit anything more than fondling or caressing. That night he and his friend picked up two girls who at once, in a business-like way, offered sexual relations in the car.

However, he has had since then numerous sexual relations, but he has noticed that his desire toward women has always been essentially an intellectual one and that he has merely gone with them because it is the "thing to do."

His sex urge has been very strong. He realized this, but he has felt that his mental superiority gave him the right to do as he wished sexually without the ordinary conventions of right and wrong applying to himself.

While the patient does not believe there is any such thing as intrinsic right and wrong, he feels that the general ideas of right and wrong are good enough for the average person, but that the person who is superior intellectually is also superior to convention.

During the physical examination at the jail he spoke of his testes as being small, but powerful.

He denies any versions of bestiality.

LOVE LIFE

He has never been greatly attracted towards the opposite sex, nor has he ever had any true love affair, leading to an engagement. He is not now engaged, nor has be ever been married. With the exception of his mother, his aunt and the Madonna, he has always looked down on women and despised them, because he felt they were intellectually inferior.

As a growing boy he had no "puppy-love" affair. He thought he ought to have a girl, because his friends had girls. He never looked forward with much emotion towards marrying. He did decide that he probably would marry. He thought he would marry some one and have first a boy and a girl, then another boy.

He had some definite ideas about how he would raise these children. For example, he thought that they would be superior to the average children. He would never allow taboos to spring up, nor would he impose such fictions as "Santa Claus" upon them, unless their mother was very insistent upon telling the children there was a Santa Claus.

He would send his children to Sunday School until they were eleven or twelve years of age, and then allow them to decide for themselves.

He wondered, if he did marry, if he would be able to satisfy his wife, and he wondered if his wife would be able to satisfy him. The reason he doubted this was that no woman had ever satisfied him. He has had three girls whom he has considered as prospective candidates for a wife. When he was eleven years old he met a girl, "R." This affair did not develop to any length. When he was 17 he met another girl, "D." She was very good looking and attractive and very tender-hearted, but he said she was "dumb and came from a low strata." She was very pretty, but after they became intimate he dropped her.

He has at the present time a very good friend in Miss "M. D.", who was his good pal, but love and sex did not figure in that friendship. Apparently the family appreciated her more than the patient did. His last candidate has been "S," whom he describes as "beautiful, a good dancer, and intelligent." She is a very nice girl, chic and petite, but she is not quite as intellectual as the patient thought she was, and she is too young for him. However, he arranged with his aunt to entertain the young lady at luncheon. He enjoyed very much her intellect, her stimulation and her interest in himself.

DELINQUENCIES

He indulged in petty thefts as a little child, but these were not of any great importance in his life.

He sold his brother's necktie for some cigar bands at the time when the collection of cigar bands was a fad among the boys and others. He did not conceal this theft, nor was he embarrassed when accused, but admitted it quite frankly, saying "It's my business."

He stole some fruit from a Greek restaurant.

When he was about fifteen he began using alcohol, and began to go about with women. About the same time he commenced to cheat at cards, at the suggestion of another. He needed a confederate. He got no thrill or satisfaction from this, nor did he get any sense of guilt or remorse. He felt that if his friend requested him to develop a scheme for cheating at cards and put it into practice, that that was reason enough. In much the same way, on account of friendship he would indulge in other delinquencies, which his companion thought up and planned out.

He stole some pipes from a department store in Chicago.

With the keys of their own electric car they stole another electric. This theft was not very successful because a truck from the garage where the stolen electric had storage space followed them down the street, and the two boys jumped from the moving electric and ran down an alley. This was not thrilling to the patient, nor did it leave him with any desire to repeat. But they did steal another car, at his companion's instance, and the police almost apprehended them, whereupon the patient concluded this was too dangerous.

About this same time the boys indulged in the practice of driving around town and throwing bricks through automobile windshields, and finally through store windows. Twice they were shot at before they gave up this practice, because the patient said it was too dangerous. The only reason the patient indulged in these practices was at the instance of his companion.

They also indulged in false telephone messages, false fire alarms, and later they set fire to buildings in three instances. The companion got a great thrill out of this, but the patient himself thought it was too dangerous. He did not disapprove of the harm done to others. He did not like to think about the risk of being apprehended.

He was apprehended for violating certain game laws in several instances, but his parents got him out, and replaced the tackle, which had been taken away from him as part of the penalty. He had also been arrested for speeding, but the folks paid the fine. None of his experiences contrary to law, when he was apprehended, left him with the idea that the law was superior to him and that he should have to abide by it.

His companion suggested the novel crime of robbing his own fraternity house, and planned it out. The patient concurred, without any emotion. They went to Ann Arbor and robbed this house at two o'clock in the Sunday morning the day after a football game, and then went to another fraternity house and robbed it a bit before they got scared away.

They took with them at that time ropes to tie up anyone who might interfere, guns to shoot, and a chisel whose end had been wrapped in tape so that it would not cut the hand of the one who wielded it, if he had occasion to crash in the skull of someone who might apprehend them. It was at this time the patient acquired the typewriter on which was written the "Ransom letter" to Mr. Franks at a later date, although when the typewriter was taken he had no specific use for it in mind.

On the way home from Ann Arbor the two boys discussed whether or not they should keep up their friendship and whether or not they should keep up their career in crime, and it was decided for friendship's sake, the patient volunteering to play the role of "slave," that they should keep up their career in crime. Their slogan for friendship acts was, "For Robert's Sake."

They next planned the robbery of a house in Hubbard Woods, where some friends lived whom they knew would be out of the city for a few days. They twice went to this house to rob it. On the first trip their automobile was too noisy and slow, being out of good mechanical condition, and in the second instance they were unable to break through the window.

Here again they were prepared to murder, if necessary, to complete the crime, and took with them again rope, pistols, flashlights and taped chisel.

If they indulged in any other crimes, they are loath to talk about them.

Following these crimes there was no remorse, no normal adequate emotion, but he rationalizes that the only wrong he can do is to make a mistake, and the things which might be right or wrong for ordinary persons have no right or wrong significance for him, he being what he was.

THE FRANKS CASE

In November, 1923, on their return from the fraternity house robberies at Ann Arbor, the patient and his companion first quarreled, and then came to a distinct understanding as to their future conduct together, to endure until June, 1924, when the patient was going to Europe.

Dictated by his "king-slave" phantasies the patient's contribution towards this compact was that he would absolutely comply with the requests, criminal requests, of his companion, in exchange for his companion's friendship.

His companion at this time was angry at a certain youth called William, and his companion suggested that they kidnap William for ransom, and incidentally kill him and destroy any marks of identification, in order that William could not escape to incriminate them later.

They began to devise elaborate plans for this kidnapping, and soon the planning became the all-important thing. They gave up the idea of kidnapping this particular person, and settled on the idea of kidnapping anyone who would fit in with their kidnapping plans.

The patient did not enter into this planning with the enthusiasm that the other man did. He felt that the plan probably would never be executed. He made some impossible suggestions in order to delay the carrying out of the plan, knowing that the compact had only a few more months to run. On the other hand, he made several practicable suggestions which were of value in perfecting the plan. The boys would meet several times a week and engage in animated conversation over their plans. Occasionally at these times they did some drinking. But sober or not, neither the patient nor his companion had any moral scruples against carrying out the plan. The patient felt it was dangerous and that he would derive no pleasure from it, but he was anxious to be "the perfect slave to this perfect planner."

The first person they contemplated kidnapping they decided was too large and strong, and they also knew that he would be out of town, away at school. So they decided to secure any small boy who had wealthy parents and who would probably ransom him, to lure him into an automobile, immediately knock him senseless by hitting him over the back of the head with a taped chisel, to take him to a secluded spot, to strangle him, each holding one end of the strangling rope so that they would share in the culpability, to destroy any marks of identification, to leave the body where it would not be found, namely, in a culvert with which the patient was acquainted from his birding trips through the swamps, to burn the clothing, to secure ransom according to a complicated plan, and to be the only ones in the community who would have full knowledge of this most extraordinary crime.

They next concentrated on the plan of securing the ransom, and this in turn became a most important part of the plan, in their minds, as the whole thing went through its evolution. They finally decided to have the father of the kidnapped boy notified by telephone to go to a certain street corner and look in one of the rubbish boxes marked "Help-Keep-the-City Clean," against the cover of which would be stuck an envelope. In this envelope would be directions for him to go to a certain drug store and wait for a telephone call in the public booth there. The telephone would tell him to take a Yellow Cab, which would be sent to the drug store, awaiting him, and go to a certain railroad station, and take a certain train. On the train, in the holder for telegraph blanks, would be a letter of directions. This letter would tell him to throw the money off the train on a certain side immediately after passing a large red brick factory on the southern outskirts of a certain town. In the first letter, which told him to go to the "Help-Keep-the-City-Clean" box, would be sent directions about wrapping up the money, ten thousand dollars in old bills, in a cigar box, and wrapping that in paper and sealing it with sealing wax, to make him think that it was to deliver it in person.

After they had planned how to secure the ransom their thoughts next turned mostly toward the money they would get. They devised a way whereby they could establish credit in town and eventually rent a car which would enable them to do the kidnapping, and in this same rented car go to the railroad tracks beyond the factory, and there wait for the money to be thrown to them. They planned to divide the ten thousand dollars ransom money equally.

They felt absolutely competent in their ability to carry out the plan and to avoid detection.

THE KIDNAPPING AND MURDER

The patient described in detail the carrying out of the kidnapping and the murder. Everything went as planned, except that the first blow over the head of the boy with the taped chisel did not knock him completely unconscious and when he was dragged from the front seat into the back seat he was struggling and crying and a hand had to be placed over his mouth to suppress the noise. While the boy was struck again several times over the head with the chisel, the boy bled some, which was very upsetting to the patient. He said, "My God, this is awful." And at the same time the patient experienced a sinking feeling in the pit of his stomach, his hands trembled, and he lost some of his poise and self-control. The other one, however, seemed to be quite cool and self-possessed, laughing and joking, and helping the patient get back his self-control.

When they got to the culvert where they planned to strangle him and dispose of the body they found that he was quite dead, and there was no need to strangle him. They stripped the body as planned, poured hydrochloric acid over the face, penis, and an identifying scar on the abdomen. Some of the hydrochloric acid ran into the mouth. There was no sexual significance in pouring the acid on the body, and there was no mistreatment of the body. The body was stripped, and later on the clothing was burned as planned. The body was put in a funnel-shaped culvert, but, unfortunately, not pushed in far enough, so that a foot protruded, and it was visible in daylight the next day and was seen. It was at this time the patient dropped his glasses, but he didn't notice it. They returned home, washed the car, and continued their every-day life, that night.

The ransom plans did not work out exactly as they anticipated. The envelope would not stick to the "Help-Keep-the-City-Clean" box. So they telephoned Mr. Franks to go directly to a drug store and wait for orders, and to take the money with him. They drove to the neighborhood of the brick factory to get the money, but on the way read in the newspapers that the body had been found, and so they decided that Mr. Franks would not bring the ransom money, they did not wait for the train, and they turned the car back to the agency that afternoon.

SUBSEQUENT BEHAVIOR AND REACTION

He had no feeling of remorse, fear or guilt. He was not apprehensive. He did get some "kick" from reading the newspaper accounts of the murder, but not as much as his companion did.

On the other hand, he was somewhat disturbed by his companion's behavior, who seemed to seek to discuss publicly, at every opportunity, theories about the crime. He was annoyed that his companion would be so friendly with the detectives in tracing down clues. He remonstrated that this was a dangerous way to act. He became distinctly alarmed when he read in the newspapers that his own glasses had been discovered near the body, for he knew that he had lost his glasses during the trip, but he did not feel that the glasses could be identified as his own.

His companion then suggested that they work out an elaborate alibi as to their whereabouts on the night of the murder, claiming that they were out on a drinking and "jazz" party with some girls, and could not remember exactly where they had been or what they had done.

His companion also said that this alibi should only be used if they were apprehended within one week after the murder. The boys were apprehended eight days after the murder. The patient gave the alibi agreed upon, although the Statute of Limitations had run against it, according to their agreement.

He denies any feeling of remorse at the crime or his mistakes since then. He states that he has no feeling of having done any-

Upper left, Sven Englund, Leopold family chauffeur, who shattered the slayers' framed alibi. To the right, Leopold's brother, Foreman, on witness stand. Below, one of Loeb's college sweethearts

The two strategists, State's Attorney Crowe and Clarence Darrow, conferring during the trial. Below, the defense alienists (from left to right), Drs. Healy, Hammel, White and Glueck

thing morally wrong, because he doesn't feel that there is such a thing as morals, in the ordinary sense of the word. He maintains that anything which gives him pleasure is right, and the only way in which he can do wrong is to do something which would be unpleasant to himself. He does not think he is insane. He knew what he was doing at the time, and he knows what the law says in regard to this. However, he wouldn't commit such a crime again, because one can never be sure of escaping detection, he realizes.

He got no pleasure from the crime. He got no sexual reaction from the crime. With him it was purely an intellectual affair, devoid of any emotion.

He does not like to see people suffer, it is unpleasant for him, but he has no sympathy for them in their suffering. He states that he is rather fond of small children. When he sees a crying child he wants to take it into his arms and comfort it, and on such occasions he almost notices "a function of my lachrymal glands."

He makes no effort to shift the blame for the crime on to his companion, although he insists he did not really desire to commit the crime and he derived no special pleasure from doing it. Apparently he does not try to excuse himself, nor to make himself appear less guilty in the eyes of others. Rather, he seems to be perfectly honest in his statements, and is trying to give an accurate account of the whole affair.

His reason for going into the crime was his pact of friendship with his companion, and his companion's desire to do it. Once they started into the plan he had no feeling of guilt or remorse.

He says that he proposed to his companion that they kidnap his companion's younger brother, and that he would have been quite willing to go through with this plan if his companion had agreed to it. They also contemplated kidnapping their respective fathers, but this idea never got very far, because it immediately occurred to them that they couldn't secure money from a man who had been kidnapped himself. And furthermore, if either of their fathers had disappeared the boys would remain under a good deal of supervision, and would, necessarily, have to stay with their families, and of course couldn't collect the ransom money, even if it were available.

It is difficult to estimate how serious they were in discussing the kidnapping of members of their own families. In their discussions with each other apparently they were very cold-blooded and matter of fact, but one doubts whether they ever very seriously entertained the idea.

They also contemplated kidnapping their next most close companion, Dick Rubel, but they gave up this idea because they felt that Dick Rubel's father was very "tight," and that he would not give up the money. Also if Dick Rubel disappeared they probably would be questioned because they were such close associates of his and they would be less free to come and go, such as claiming the ransom money, because they would be under some observation.

During the examination the patient apparently enjoyed being the center of attention and he was very anxious to discuss his personality and his past history. At first he said that he looked forward, with a great deal of pleasure, to these examinations. However, when the examinations became physical, and he had various tests, such as blood taken from his arm or his ear, he became much more irritable and rather less friendly in his attitude. He was quiet, but not absolutely frank in his statements. He omitted certain data, lied rather plausibly when questioned about the parts he omitted, and was quite unconcerned when he was told that knowledge on these things was already in the possession of the examiners. He was more interested, however, in trying to be sure that his account of everything agreed with his companion's.

OF LEOPOLD AND LOEB

PSYCHIATRIC STUDY

While under observation in the County jail the patient has
been quite quiet and well behaved.

He eats and sleeps well. He has had several transitory attacks of minor sicknesses which seem to be accompanied with
very severe prostration, especially in his heart and blood-vessel
system. He is correctly oriented. He takes a lively interest in
jail life and in the examinations. He shows a very lessened degree of emotion over the loss of his liberty. He seems to have
made no plans as to his life, if he is not executed, whether he is
given his liberty or whether he is permanently confined. He has
not seriously contemplated suicide, nor jail escape, but adapts
himself, with good grace, to his incarceration.

In the past he has had a few vague hallucinatory experiences.
Several times he has seen a white hearse in the sky. Several
times he has imagined he saw the tail light of an automobile in
front of him while driving, but there was no car there.

．　．　．　．　．　．　．　．　．　．　．　．　．　．　．

He has had always very strong and very vivid phantasies,
which at times approach actual hallucinations. His phantasies
have actually affected his behavior to a profound degree. His
phantasies or reveries about his dead mother have been insipid
and colorless. His sexual phantasies, on the other hand, have
been very intense and very vivid.

The most striking of his phantasies was the "king and slave"
phantasy, in which his feelings of inferiority made him usually
take the role of a slave; but his knowledge of his own actual
superiority made him occasionally take the role of king. For
years he searched for a companion who was his own actual superior, and when he did find one whom he regarded as his
superior he desired to become his abject slave. More recently
he has identified his companion as king and himself as slave,
both in the world of phantasy and in the world of reality, and

he finds it difficult to differentiate the two. The result was that he became pathologically suggestible to the ideas of his "king."

He has been subject to compulsions and impulses. For example he would get up always after he had retired to see that he had set his alarm clock although he had set it before retiring. He would get up several times at night to turn off the gas, or to be sure the gas were turned off, if the room had gas-piping in it for lighting. He actually reacted to his superstitions, crossing his fingers while passing an undertaker's shop, avoiding a black cat, and spitting over his shoulder, refusing to light his cigarette from a match if two others had already lit theirs from that flame.

He has always been extremely self-centered, egotistical and selfish. He regarded himself inferior physically, and would try to overcompensate in such a way that he could boast that he was superior physically. This was followed in his sexual life especially. His sexual life, which was especially pronounced in a boy with his physical constitution and endocrine make-up, had an abnormal start due to the abnormal introduction to sex life that he had acquired from his insane governess when he was a boy of tender years.

In most matters he has been quite unemotional all his life and lacking in the normal ethical sense. He has no proper amount nor proper character of emotion or feeling for the crime. He did not even get a thrill from it. His fear of being apprehended was only slight. He has no grief for the harm and suffering he may have inflicted upon others. Emotionally he lacks the reactions of either the normal individual or the hardened criminal. This split between the intellectual process and the emotional process is very striking, and is considered by the international authority, Professor Kraepelin, to be an essential feature of Dementia Praecox (Schizophrenia).

Abnormal, or sub-normal, emotionalism is frequently found in persons with disorders of the endocrine glands. This patient is of the dyspituitariasm type, with associated disorder in the other endocrine glands, and the vagatonic or autonomic segments part of the sympathetic nervous system.

He has a marked disorder of the attention. He is easily distracted; his attention fatigues. The stimuli which distract him are not other stimuli of his environment, to which he would not he expected to pay attention, but are stimuli arising in his subconscious mind from his totally or partly forgotten memories.

In judgment he is quite immature. He has never developed to the healthy adult level, where the individual's emotions are harnessed and directed by his intellectual processes for his own well-being and without sacrifice to an individual in his environment. He has used his intelligence rather to rationalize and explain his behavior, and his explanations have been satisfactory to himself. He lacks a proper sense of proportion, and has assigned very high emotional values to certain topics and very low emotional values to other topics.

In his early life the patient had an intense interest in religion. He has confused his Mother, and the aunt somewhat took her place, and the Madonna, as one person. He denies the existence of God, and yet he is following the insane trend of thought so frequently observed in persons who undergo a change of personality and consider themselves to be Christ.

ENDOCRINE

In summarizing his physical examination one is struck with the very definite disorder of the control of his heart and blood-vessels, as shown by his low pulse rate, low respiration rate, low temperature, and very low blood pressure. His blood pressure has been found to vary from 80 to 100 millimeters in its systolic pressure and from 30 to 60 mm. diastolic pressure. The basal metabolism was minus 5. He has an abnormal blood sugar tolerance curve, and sugar in the urine during the glucose test.

His fasting blood shows 100 mgs. of dextrose. A half hour after the ingestion of sugar it is 173 mgs., and a half hour later it rose to 210 mgs. and two hours should be back to the fasting level. He has a slight tendency towards acidosis, as shown by the carbon-dioxide combining power of the blood, which is 52.2 volumes per cent, the normal value being 65 volumes percent. The non-protein nitrogen in his blood is 44 mgs. per 100 cc. of blood, which is higher than the normal, which varies from 20-40. He probably has incipient Bright's Disease. He certainly has cardio-renal disease.

The X-ray examination of the skull reveals a small sella turcica, which is the part of the skull in which the pituitary gland of the brain lies. There is marked calcification of the pineal gland, which should not occur in a man of his youth. The union of the bones of the skull show osteo-sclerosis. There is usually found intellectual and sexual precocity linked up with involvent of the pituitary and pineal glands, as is frequently found in cases of tumor on the pineal gland.

Associated with these disorders scientific research has recently shown there usually is a disorder of the increased function of the sex glands, and these in turn, with the thyroid, usually have an effect on the heart blood pressure and on the kidneys. The whole endocrine chain of glands via their chemistry and via the sympathetic nervous system profoundly affect the intellect and the emotion; in his case the endocrine disease contributes greatly to his mental disease.

PSYCHIATRIC INTERPRETATION

To understand this case the following facts must be kept in mind:

When extremely young he acquired ideas which he thought were normal from a person (his governess) who was distinctly abnormal, and some of her ideas, such as on sex, attitude towards others, and responsibility for conduct, were of themselves distinctly abnormal ideas.

Before conception his mother was not healthy, and during his childhood he was not healthy. His sicknesses seemed to fall into several groups, namely, abnormal skin diseases, diseases of the heart and kidney, and dieases of the endocrine glands. The mental effect on him was that he tended to regard himself as inferior to others. He found that by phantasies he could escape from a realization of this inferiority, or he could compromise this feeling of inferiority in such a way that he found great satisfaction in it. His phantasies, therefore, became more important to him than the actualities of life.

In childhood he was precocious mentally. He first tried to classify the universe, and became interested in nonemotional academic subjects, like comparative languages.

His mental growth was so rapid that he never established close friendships and maintained them, and he has always been a solitary creature. His judgment did not mature as rapidly as his knowledge. His sexual life did not bring him the satisfaction it does to average persons, as judged by the way the other boys boasted of their prowess with women.

He went through school very rapidly and graduated at 19, receiving Phi Beta Kappa. At the same time he took many extra curricular studies and really became very proficient in ornithology.

His religious ideas became so unusual that at first he criticized God, then denied the existence of God, and he has the symptoms that are so frequently found in persons who eventually come to believe themselves to be God.

There has been a marked discrepancy between the development of his emotional life and the development of his intellectual life, and he is not able to have the ordinary emotional reactions for his ideas that most persons have. He has been extremely suggestible. His phantasies have played so important a role in his life that they have dominated his behavior and made him willing to accept ideas from other sources than his own mind without criticism, and he has reacted, in behavior, to these unusual ideas.

He has substituted for the conception of morals which the ordinary man has and which is regarded as normal a bizarre philosophy which he has evolved, based on selfishness, superiority, atheism, denial of the existence of right and wrong, intellectuality, and scraps of metaphysics which he has picked up here and there. At the same time his conduct, insofar as others knew him, has been quite orderly, well-mannered, and he has been regarded as an extremely brilliant, likable person.

There is nothing in the family training, either of omission or commission, which is responsible for his present condition. Nor is this condition to be regarded as hereditary.

His abnormal or individualistic type of thinking will become more pronounced with the passing of time. The world of phantasy will bring him so much greater satisfaction than the world of reality that he will continue to deny, more and more, the unpleasant facts of reality, to engage himself, in solace, in the realm of unreality or phantasy. The rapidity of this dementia will be enhanced because of his constitution, especially his endocrine make-up, and under ordinary circumstances one can expect that his years will be shortened because of the diseases of his heart and kidneys.

Joint Medical Report

By Doctors White, Healy, Glueck and Hamill

The study and opinion recorded below represents an attempt to combine into a single report the findings and conclusions of the examination of the defendants by Doctors William A. White, Superintendent of St. Elizabeth's Hospital, Washington, D. C.; William Healy, Director, Judge Baker Foundation, Boston, formerly Director of the Juvenile Psychopathic Institute, Chicago; Bernard Glueck, formerly Director Psychiatric Clinic, Sing Sing Prison and Bureau of Children's Guidance, New York; and Ralph C. Hamill, Neuropsychiatrist, of Chicago.

The examinations were carried out at intervals between July 1st and 27th, 1924, at the Cook County Jail, in Chicago, in the presence of Walter Bachrach, Esq., one of the attorneys for the defense. The facilities furnished by the jail authorities, the complete co-operation of the defendants, and the ample time allowed for the examination made it possible to approximate the conditions of the examination ordinarily obtaining in the consultation-room of the physician, and our conclusions are believed to be as reliable as are those ordinarily reached by us after a thorough-going examination of a patient applying to us for treatment. The data obtained as a result of the direct examination of the defendants was supplemented by data taken from the reports of the original examination by Doctors Bowman and Hulbert, and by conversations with relatives and acquaintances of the defendants.

The two defendants, neither of whom has reached the age of twenty, have maintained a very intimate and peculiar relationship since 1921. The Franks crime, as is well known, was carried out by them together, and, it might be added, that in our opinion the mental condition and conduct of the two defendants, certainly in so far as this crime is concerned, can best be understood when adequate consideration is given to the nature of this relationship between them and to the factors which led to its establishment and maintenance.

An unbiased estimate of the facts pertaining to this association between the two defendants leads us to the conviction that their criminal activities were the outgrowth of an unique coming-together of two peculiarly maladjusted adolescents, each of whom brought into the relationship a long-standing background of abnormal mental life. This has made a situation so unique that it probably will never repeat itself. There is justification for stressing the uniqueness of this case if, for no other reason, than that it has created wide-spread panic among parents of young people.

How is one to account for this most peculiar relationship of the defendants and their criminal action? Our studies have revealed the following evolution of the situation:

NATHAN F. LEOPOLD, JUNIOR

The characteristics that Leopold presents today and which make his criminal conduct comprehensible, have their roots in his mental life, his thinking and his feelings, during the years of early childhood.

Early Peculiar Tendencies

We find that already from five to seven years of age peculiar tendencies were shown quite at variance with the trends of normal childhood. He was not only precocious in his mental interests, but these interests assumed a degree of intensity and showed themselves in special directions which were in themselves indications of abnormality. As examples we may cite that when about five he showed an intense pre-occupation with questions of religion, cataloguing churches, insisting upon visiting the different ones in his neighborhood, learning the names and something of the lives of the minor Saints of the Catholic Church, dwelling upon the idea of the crucifixion, which he now states had a very peculiar fascination for him, and wondering greatly why there should be so many different ideas about God. And at this time he exhibited other curious interests, such as in the specific meanings of words, especially the meaning of "Yes" in different languages, he wanted to complete series

of numbers, to be roused up at odd hours of the night, to visit
a street that had a certain attraction because of its number, to
visit the church where there was a Madonna picture.

His Delusionally Disordered Personality

There are many well substantiated facts concerning Leopold's
gradual development of a pathologcial, disordered conception of
himself. Beginning very early in life with conceptions of his
own superiority, which in intellectual ways were founded on
fact, there has been a steady growth of delusional tendencies
concerning himself, and to the extent that he definitely conceives of himself as a superior being, quite, set apart and not
called on to be amenable to the social regulations or legal restrictions which govern the ordinary human being. His ego
is all-important, right or wrong, his desires and will being the
only determinants of his conduct. There is conclusive evidence
of this conception and attitude developing years ago and being
steadily cumulative in his world of ideas as well as his world
of behavior. He says without the slightest exhibition of doubt
or uncertainty that anything which gives him satisfaction is
justified by this fact itself. Even the commission of murder is
perfectly tolerable to him on this basis of his conception of himself.

This abnormal tendency had its beginnings early. Early
recognition of his superior attainments by his teacher and by
his mother made him feel unlike and apart from others and
superior to them.

As a young child he placed his mother and favorite aunt on
the same level with the Madonna, about whom he came to know
through having a Catholic nurse at four years of age, as being
the most wonderful persons of whom he had any conception.
And later in life, as he looked down with contempt on women
on account of their intellectual inferiority to him, he steadily
maintained the above exceptions. He thus transferred his own
abnormal egotistical standpoint to his own immediate family
life and, what is most significant psychologically, to his own
origin.

He early showed a well-defined tendency to whip himself into
superior accomplishment, and to do those things which would

set him apart from others on the basis of his superiority. He believed, for example, that his mental ability was stepped-up about twenty per cent. following a night without sleep, and that when he showed increased ability as a result of the lack of sleep it demonstrated to the world his uniqueness. He prides himself on the fact that he has done something important at every hour during the twenty-four hours of the day, something that others have not done. Many of his college studies, such as Sanskrit, Oscan and Umbrian dialects, Russian and modern Greek, were chosen to emphasize his being different. He says he strove for perfection, he trained himself to think in the fourth dimension, he hoped to find the universal language.

While yet a child he began to strive to be the cold-blooded egocentric intellectualist, turning gradually from the unusual and intense early childhood interest in religion to a deliberate over-throwing and eliminating of God, conscience, sympathy, social responsibility and loyalty as being thoroughly unnecessary to him and unworthy of him as a completely intelligent individual.

(And, as his career shows, he developed these ideas to the extent that they have led him into conduct which, if it had not been for his delusions and his defective judgment, he might have seen would certainly cause his own destruction.)

As it stands now, he looks upon his present predicament for the most part as offering him occasion for the utmost satisfaction. He says that in the eyes of the world, although despised and hated, he is considered as a Napoleon on St. Helena.

Through the pathological development of his ego he has gradually come to develop a personal philosophy which admits of only one motive, his own advantage. He estimates murder as a very small thing to weigh in the balance as against his pleasure. In a class on Torts this year he challenged the professor in open class with the argument that legal regulations should not apply to one who is a superman.

It is of interest to note that for years he has been excessively hypercritical of others and has studiously avoided the making of friendships which might even through ordinary demands interfere with his delusionally cherished ego.

As it is now he ridicules the idea that he may be considered as mentally diseased, unbalanced or insane; saying that while he knows he is different from others, the difference is one of superiority only.

If he is going to have to die at the hands of the law, he has two main plans: First, he will write down ten of the world's riddles as he conceives them, put them into a safety deposit vault, select a committee of scientists who will try to get into communication with him after his death and get his aid in solving these riddles. Then he wants to write a book or books, particularly his autobiography, because he thinks he is different from others and has led a most unusual and interesting life and one that is worth recording. He would include an apologia or interpretation which would, among other things, show that he played his part and went to his end consistently, that he did not change as many expect him to. (At another time, speaking of his childhood ideas of self-perfection, he stated that consistency has always been a sort of God to him.)

Furthermore he wishes to be allowed to go to his death in his own way, and to address the public freely. It is vastly more important for him to preserve his dignity than to have his life preserved.

Another feature of Leopold's personality characteristics, which students of abnormal psychology all recognize as belonging to the same picture, namely, that of the paranoic personality is concerned with the abnormal and intense energy which he has for many years displayed. His relatives and friends speak of his restlessness and excessive mental energy, and we have various records of his great mental output. He has not been subject to the normal limitations of ordinary fatigue. There is much that bears upon this point. When interested in the study of birds he would remain up all night in preparation for his early morning observations. He was continually reaching out for new subjects to study, and a list of what he has undertaken is really formidable. In the same way he continually sought new life experience, new ideas, new sensations. He is a tremendous talker and arguer. His tense physical and mental attitude has been continued over many years and was noted by us throughout our examinations. In all this he presents what is known as the manic drive of the paranoic personality.

Emotional Life

Another outstanding abnormality in Leopold's life is related to his emotions. From childhood on there has been a definite and often very conscious effort on his part to suppress sentiment and sympathy, as being entirely out of accord with his well defined idea of himself as a being primarily intellectual and superior, one who could and should rule his actions by coldly logical notions of what he was pleased to do.

His pursuance of this idea of inhibiting emotions stimulated and made further possible an intensely energetic activity. We note that he not only liked to make collections in a normal boyish way, but he pursued a search for information about his numerous collections and about groups of ideas in his mind, which were themselves of the nature of collections, with an avidity that was altogether far beyond what is normal in child life. He wasted but little energy even then in emotional ways, and as time went on his conscious repressions in this sphere, made possible excessive and feverish exhibitions of mental activities in many directions, some of which have been thoroughly unhealthy from a mental and moral standpoint.

These peculiarities pertaining to his emotional life started in a direction determined by his early feeling of inferiority. His repression of feelings and emotions began with conscious realization of his own sensitiveness to the opinions of others, by discovering that he readily suffered from what others said or thought of him, notably in his school life. His feelings he found interfered with his self-satisfaction and soon he consciously determined that he could get most out of life by destroying emotions in favor of intellect, or, putting it in another way, by freeing his thought life as much as possible from admixture with normal emotions. But his continuously planned antagonism to emotional expression has led to a most abnormal dependence upon his own phantasy life and its expressions for the satisfaction which make life tolerable.

Comparing his emotional life with his intellectual precocity we can definitely say that his emotional nature in its development (and in this he strangely enough, closely resembles his comrade), is on an immature childish level. He now demonstrates a well defined incapacity for appreciating through emotional life his place in the social order; there is abnormal lack of ordinary ethical motivations. The normal "sense of right and wrong" is no longer a part of his makeup, having been effectually forced into the background by the manifestation of his delusional ego.

All through the various examinations by each of us, Leopold spoke with the utmost indifference and lack of emotional display concerning the details of the Franks crime, freely acknowledging that he had not the slightest remorse of what might be considered anything like an appropriate emotional reaction. The same absence of feeling characterizes his adjustment to his confinement in jail, under conditions so utterly different to what he has been accustomed to, and particularly as a prisoner awaiting sentence.

He expatiates on his own coldness and speaks of it as a desirable phenomenon in that it makes it possible for him to enjoy the dramatics of the situation, stating that he looks forward to his trial as the moment of the keenest intellectual enjoyment of his life. In this his attitude resembles that which he evidently displayed before the murder itself—he had considerable interest in the thought of observing himself as a murderer. Indeed, he goes further and sets up the picture of the possible and probable enjoyment of his own execution, if that takes place; his nature showing such an abnormal hiatus between normally constituted and correlated emotion and intellect that he can look on such an ending of his life as a keen-minded observer of human behavior.

The essence of his abnormality in this clearly perceivable lack in his emotional life is found then, in the fact of the constant subordination of normal feelings of loyalty and obligation and sympathy to his intellectual life, and to the demands of his diseased ego. Herein lies the explanation of the absence of natural feeling on his part about the commission of criminal acts.

This separation of intellect and emotions with certainty indicates mental abnormality. It is a symptom belonging to the same group of mental abnormalities as the manifestations of the pathologically developed ego or self.

ABNORMAL PHANTASY LIFE

Related to many important phases of his subsequent career has been Leopold's early and intense turning of his interests to phantasy life (conscious dreaming), spending a considerable part of the time each day in the weaving of phantasies. These daydreams which have persisted continuously and with great vividness up to the present, have been indulged in to a tremendous extent and variety, forming for years a sort of serial story with many variations. The psychological significance of the persistent intrusion of this kind of abnormal imaginative life into the daily existence of a child, and particularly into the life of an adolescent, is very great, since it has the power of eventually leading to the confusion of reality with unreality—as was the case here.

In contrast to the imaginative life of normal childhood which is always in touch more or less with the realities surrounding child life, Leopold's phantasies were from the beginning out of accord with the usual demands of social life, and never seem to have undergone the natural fate of phantasy life in being increasingly matched or assimilated into the facts of reality. Thus the normal child identifies himself with the persons in his immediate invironment, he day-dreams of being a motorman, an engineer, a policeman, showing thereby in his desires a normal response to the influences which surround him. These responses lead to the evolution of ideals and interests of a social quality which accords with the social status of the individual. Of peculiar significance in this case is the extent to which the ideals of the boy Leopold deviated from what might have been expected of him in his social setting—his ideals and behavior have evolved in line with the thoroughly abnormal phantasy life which since childhood has dominated him.

One of the earliest of Leopold's waking dreams was related to his peculiar religious interests; he persistently visualized the crucifixion—the idea of somebody suffering, or, as he states it now, the idea of some one being nailed down to something, had an abnormal appeal for him. And it is most important to note that in his later phantasies he very frequently indeed played the role of the one who suffered.

Earliest and throughout his life the most predominating has

Assistant State's Attorneys Savage and Marshall and (below)
State's Attorney Crowe demanding the extreme penalty—death

Clarence Darrow, chief counsel for the defense, delivering his notable plea before Judge Caverly. Below, Attorneys Walter and Benjamin C. Bachrach

been a series of what may be called his King-Slave phantasies. He began these, as he remembers, before he was ten years old, and even recently these imaginations have played an immense part in his thought and in the directing of his impulses. They began with imaginings about a slave who was intensely devoted to a king or master. This slave was extremely good looking, the strongest man in the world, and in some way or another, the way varying greatly in different pictures, this slave saved the life of a king. The latter was very grateful and wanted to give the slave his liberty, but he refused. As a rule, the lot of the slave was good. He belonged to a class or caste of slaves, each of whom was bound to his special king by a chain—our day dreamer himself, who was in the vast majority of his phantasies the slave, was bound to his king in later phantasies by a golden chain which he easily could have broken. There would be combats and slaves chosen to represent a side; the dreamer would always be chosen and would always win.

Other variations of this theme were that the dreamer thought of himself as a boy captured and beaten and then the king would come along and save his life; or that he was stolen away by gypsies and brought up subject to much punishment, or that he was taken during war times and made to serve a nice young girl, being frequently beaten by others but always saved by her.

When his phantasies grew too impossible or illogical for him even in his dream life to entertain, as when he found himself combatting and overcoming a thousand men in trying to save his king, he would consciously dismiss the idea as too absurd and improbable, and readjust his phantasy to accord more with the possibilities of real life.

The above is but a slight sketch of this realm of Leopold's mental life where abnormal thoughts and phantasies held sway. Very many details and variations of the above topics have been given to us.

We are impressed with the validity of his recital of this phase of his mental life because it is so explicitly similar in type to the phantasy life of which we are accustomed to learn during our studies of patients who have various sorts of psychoses (mental disorders). All of it came to the surface spontaneously in the original examination and then has been told to the different physicians with a free elaboration, which is so characteristic in some forms of abnormal mental life.

Carrying His Phantasies Over to Reality

Even as early as at twelve years there was outcropping of phantasy life in the world of reality—he began to identify actual persons with the characters in his imaginings. There began then a confusion of the real with the unreal, which has come to play an increasing and most important part in his daily intercourse with others. A specially good looking counsellor at camp was nightly fitted into the role of slave. Other boys gradually were identified with characters in his life of phantasy. Every boy who appealed to him became eligible for some part in his inner dramas; an elaborate system of capturing them and even of branding them, with a very specially designed brand, on the inner surface of the calf of the leg, was evolved.

But of most significance is the fact that for three or more years his companion Loeb has been very definitely woven into his phantasy life. For the most part it has been a King-Slave affair, with Loeb as king, but there have been many variations to it. Latterly, Loeb has been transfigured into an individual who has played the part of an ideal man, wonderfully good looking, an athletic star, a brilliant scholar, who gets the highest marks in college. Although in life none of these things have been true, Leopold has forcibly transformed his companion and, even apart from his definite day-dreamings, tried to make himself believe that he was this perfect individual. Thus he actually made a chart of the "perfect man," in which Loeb received a score of 90, Leopold himself grading as only 62, and other acquaintances ranging from 30 to 40. But as he says when looking back on these phases of his inner mental life, "There was at this time an almost complete identification of myself with Dick. It was a blind hero worship."

The abnormal and puerile unreality of Leopold's mental life is exhibited in the fact that he frequently told others that his companion was the superman, and often tried to convince Loeb himself that his mental powers were far above his own—knowing all the time that Loeb was thoroughly untruthful in boasting and that he was much inferior intellectually to Leopold himself.

We can see how the ready acceptance of Loeb's suggestions with respect to their joint criminal activity fitted in perfectly with Leopold's phantasying for years himself in the role of a slave, first to a phantasy king and then transferring his allegiance to his idealized king-like companion.

The pathological admixture of inferiority and superiority concepts and strivings not only in his abnormal imaginations, but also in his behavior reactions to real life, is a matter of great practical as well as professional interest in this case. It reflects, on the one hand, the profound disorder of judgment which permits such contradictory ideas and impulses to live side by side, and it indicates, on the other hand, a tremendous and altogether abnormal rift between Leopold's intellectual precocity and the emotional immaturity which made possible the ready acceptance by him of either role. The strange admixture demonstrates that no normally integrated or consistent personality was ever evolved in Leopold's mental life.

Concerning Possible Causes of Leopold's Mental Abnormality

If one attempts to discover underlying causes of Leopold's above described abnormal mental life, one comes upon possibly significant factors in the following background:

Leopold, who is not quite twenty years of age, a first-year law student in the University of Chicago, comes from a well-to-do and socially well placed German-Jewish household. His father is a successful business man, who impresses one distinctly with his earnestness and solidity of character. The mother, who died about three years ago, was a socially minded, gentle and highly esteemed member of her community. Nathan Junior is the youngest of three boys, and with the exception of the fact that his mother was considered dangerously ill with nephritis during the pregnancy with him, there is nothing of special interest in his early physical development. He was unusually precocious in talking; it is recorded in his baby-book that he spoke his first words at four months. Up to the age of nine he was considered poorly developed. His inferior physical status, together with the fact that he attended for the first two years of his school life a girls' school, on account of which he was taunted by other boys,

and also because he was regularly taken by a nurse to and from
public schools until he was eleven years old, tended very clearly
to give him the feeling, which he himself now remembers well,
that he was a person apart from the ordinary and physically inferior. It was all through this early school period that he was
particularly sensitive to the opinions and criticisms of others.
Among the people with whom he came into contact at this time
most influential, probably, was a nurse, a woman who was dishonest, suspicious, irritable, jealous, and who showed marked
indiscretions in her physical contacts with this boy. For a considerable time he was very fond of her. She succeeded in winning his affections to the extent of his being fonder of her than
he was of his own mother.

At school, where his intellectual precocity was at once recognized by his scholastic performance, he was pushed ahead one
grade. Later, in preparatory school, we find that he was characterized in the school publication as "The Great Nathan," "The
Crazy Bird," "Flea" (because the boy was smaller than average
in stature), and "This Crazed Genius."

He progressed very rapidly, and at the age of fifteen years and
ten months he entered the University of Chicago, from which he
graduated, although his studies were interfered with by illness
of himself and in the family, with Phi Beta Kappa honors at
eighteen years and four months. Throughout his academic
career he has engaged in considerable extra-curricular studies,
during the school term or in vacation time. His studies and
field researches in ornithology represent decidedly good work,
and he has contributed articles of note in that field and has also
taught classes in this subject. This and his work in languages,
including philology, represent his best efforts. In much of this
there is evidence of expression of his own desire for superiority
through being different from others—once he was the only
student in a course of advanced Greek.

Of significance in the case of Leopold (although probably of
not so much import as in the case of his comrade) is the fact
that this boy, who had during his early years lived such a guarded
life in respect to his contacts with other boys, at the age of fifteen
was thrown with college students much older than himself and
exposed to the temptations and obvious desirability of living up

to what, in his particular set, were considered standards of manly behavior. He began to drink at the age of fifteen, and has been a more or less frequent consumer of alcohol ever since. It was when he was fifteen that he became intimate with Loeb, who is a little younger, he having barely known this boy before then. It is significant that up to this time no tendencies were shown to criminal behavior.

FINDINGS AND DATA OBTAINED THROUGH DIRECT EXAMINATIONS

PHYSICAL STATUS

There are definite signs of instability of the nervous system, a neurotic makeup. Even in ordinary conversation is noted exaggerated use of facial muscles, nervous gestures, flushings and pallor of the face. The examination of Doctors Bowman and Hulbert brings out the point that beyond these neurotic conditions, there is some evidence of pathology of the endocrine system (the glands of internal secretion) and the sympathetic nervous system.

MENTAL STATUS

Given a number of mental tests, Leopold is found to have very considerably super-normal general intelligence, as indicated by all tests where the use of language, the comprehension of language and vocabulary are mainly involved. Up to a certain point he is good in abstract reasoning. His mental activity is extraordinary, his mental reactions are tremendously quick, his associations are abnormally rich—so much so that they are rather difficult for him to control. He is voluble, self-assertive and indeed aggressive in the use of his mind, thoroughly enjoying mental tasks and doing special memory stunts by the use of associational memory devices—and altogether being very much interested in his own mental processes. In his reasoning power, and especially in his common sense judgments, as might, indeed, be known by his life career, he is extraordinarily lacking in comparison. Shrewdness is shown in only a very limited field and rarely takes into account the validity of premises which he assumes.

PERSONALITY TRAITS

Leopold's personality traits have been mainly indicated above. In review we may restate that he is pathologically egocentric; extremely energetic, showing a great pressure toward mental activity; hypercritical of others but not at all of himself; very appreciative of the dramatic when he plays a main part; astonishingly and quite abnormally devoid of any show of feelings of sympathy or obligation or conceptions of gratitude; persistent and obstinate in mental attitudes and behavior trends; enthusiastic and forceful about anything that he himself undertakes. Beyond this we note that he is not changeable in mood or subject to depressions, even under most unfavorable conditions. Whatever his native endowment of normal emotions may have been, they have been schooled by his intellect to remain in the background. Only occasionally, as noted during some mental testing periods, he may momentarily show evidences, however, of feelings which ordinarily do not come at all to the surface. He is a play-actor in a play-world of his own constructing and proposes to play out his part.

There have been alterations in his personality that show the progressive deterioration that is going on in his mental life. But all the evidences are minor as compared to our knowledge of his having gone down hill steadily along the paths of defective judgment in relation to the part which he should and might play in the world and of his development of various pernicious interests —all in utter contradiction to his notions of himself as a superior being and to his self-formulated desires of wishing to play the part of a superman.

THE PROBLEM OF MENTAL DISORDER IN LEOPOLD'S CASE

We could draw no other conclusions from Leopold's abnormal phantasy life, his delusional development of notions about himself, his defective or deteriorated judgment which has not permitted him to see the pathological absurdity of mixing up phantasy and real life; his repression and misplacement of emotional life; his abnormal urge towards activity and search for the experience of new mental and physical sensations; his disintegrated personality to the extent that he has shown an essential and abnormal lack of foresight and care even for his much beloved ego

—we can draw no other conclusions from the above than that Leopold is and was on the twenty-first day of May, 1924, a thoroughly unbalanced individual in his mental life.

He represents a picture of a special abnormal type, the paranoid psychopathic personality. His ability as a conversationalist and as a student had led to his being unrecognized for what he really is, and his delusional conceptions about himself have therefore not been taken seriously. His very manic (over-excitable and over-energetic) tendencies have been misinterpreted as evidence of cleverness. The fact that he has been able to carry himself along in the world without being recognized as being abnormal is in itself typical of individuals who belong to this special group of mental disorders.

RICHARD LOEB

The facts and circumstances which have, as leading forces, combined to make this adolescent what he is and which serve to explain his criminal conduct reach back, as in the case of Leopold, to his early boyhood days.

The challenging fact in the personality of this boy as we see him today, lies in his most remarkable unscrupulousness, untruthfulness, unfairness, ingratitude, disloyalty, and in his total lack of human feelings and sympathy with respect to the deed, to which he has, with his companion, pleaded guilty. His characteristics assume a particularly abnormal nature when one views them in the light of the kind of home and social setting that he came from. The Loeb home has been noted for its high standards of virtue and culture and a place where the task of bringing up children was viewed with unusual seriousness.

It is therefore clearly indicative of some abnormal tendencies in this boy himself that he should have developed the above characteristics and that he should have felt from early childhood estranged and not wanted in his home, so that at one time he told his mother that he was thinking of running away, and that he should have missed during his developmental period the feeling that he could find some one who could understand him and to whom he could reveal his inner mental life.

It is astounding to contemplate how this boy's mind, from the time before he was nine years of age, was filled with a curiously abnormal and criminalistic set of ideas and visions. For example, at this early age he very strangely pictured himself frequently as being a prisoner in a jail yard. He would imagine himself stripped of clothing, shoved around and being whipped. This "picturization," as he calls it, was worked out with great detail. There were other people in the yard; he was ashamed of seeing the others, and particularly the women naked or partly clothed; he made a burrow in the earth, where he felt warm and comfortable; people looked at him through a fence that separated the yard from the street; at first it was only people in general, and then it was young girls who looked at him with wonder because he was a criminal and they sympathized with him. There was a great feeling of self-pity in this, but no feeling of fear. "I was abused, but it was a very pleasant thought; the punishment inflicted on me in jail was pleasant. I enjoyed being looked at through the bars, because I was a famous criminal."

(As bearing upon the validity of Loeb's testimony concerning these phantasies, we may note that the detailed picture which he gave us of the jail yard and fence was suggestive to us of the fence around the Chicago House of Correction as it was years ago. Although he does not remember it, the family state that the boy occasionally was driven with his father to the latter's place of business, going over the boulevard that passes the House of Correction.)

Linked up with this phantasy of being in jail and evidently directly evolved from it and coming some time later was the notion of being some sort of a celebrated criminal. Still later grew up the phantasy of being a "master-mind" directing criminal activities.

There seems to have been an endless variety to his imaginings about his own sufferings as a prisoner and about his being a criminal, working up to his being "the master criminal mind of the century." In his phantasies about crime he gradually imagined himself committing all sorts of crimes. He derived intense pleasure, he says, from this, particularly in having a feeling of being superior to others, inasmuch as they would not know how the crime was committed and who was connected with it, whereas he did.

He as the "master mind" was so clever at planning that he

could escape detection from the greatest detectives of the world. He phantasied working out a wonderful plan of a great crime which would stir all the country and which would never be solved. None of this was undertaken for financial profit and if the question of money did appear in his imaginings it was only to make the "picturization" consistent and logical. In all of his phantasies he had one or more associates, but he was always the leader. One reason for this was that others might appreciate his skill.

He states that these imaginings have recurred with very great vividness, so that he remembers them now as well as he does the actual occurrences of his earlier every-day life.

Among other types of phantasies which occurred early, but which was stopped, was that of thinking of himself as a frontiersman shooting at others. In this he would get under the bedclothes, which in his imagination were impregnable to bullets. We speak of this particularly because we note a photograph of Loeb as a child in cowboy outfit holding a toy pistol, and in this photograph he exhibits an extraordinary set, intense, facial expression; he is doing a bit of acting out of his phantasy life with a zest that remarkably changes his ordinary appearance, and indicating a deep leaning toward adventure.

(Here it may be noted that throughout his life, Loeb has shown a very great and, indeed, abnormal love of excitement and adventure. Unfortunately, the repressive and sheltered life in which he was brought up by his governess and family, afforded him no normal outlets in healthy, natural ways for his adventuresome spirit. The main satisfactions which he derived in this connection were through his curious and abnormal phantasies which he indulged in with such regularity.)

How completely his phantasies have controlled him and have been a habit with him is illustrated by the fact that, as he tells us, at night in the jail he has caught himself saying, "As you know, Teddy," this being the formula with which he introduced for many years his phantasy life to himself in his evening reveries. He began with his talking to his teddy bear, who would understand all things and so obviate the necessity for the narrator or day-dreamer squaring himself with the necessities and logic and consistencies of ordinary life. And, of course, this, too, illustrates Loeb's dual nature, his being even now essentially a child in some respects, while otherwise he is so strikingly capable of hardened and vicious behavior.

ABNORMAL MIXING OF PHANTASY WITH REAL LIFE

As early as at eleven years of age Loeb actually began to live out his phantasy in his daily behavior—he would walk down the street as if he were directing people under his command in the carrying out of burglaries; in fact he has kept up this play acting until very recently. It was a trick that his comrade Leopold told us he himself thought extremely foolish and childish as he observed it.

Loeb invented various games in which he played the role of detective, and at about ten years of age he actually shadowed people persistently for hours. Somewhat later he was caught at this game by members of his family, who, however, knew nothing of the real significance of his behavior.

And the pleasure which Loeb first experienced in his phantasies from doing something that others did not know about, thus feeling in a sense superior to them, was likewise gradually carried over into real life. In fact it has come to be one of the chief elements in the so-called thrill that he has derived from the planning of crime and from the mystification of others who did not know the real facts or his part in it.

He appears to have actually stolen first at about the age of nine, and his experiences in connection with that event are still so vivid to him that he relates them in great detail—he had a curious set of physical sensations of the nature of exhilaration and power. He remembers in many such affairs how he has enjoyed the rapid beating of the heart.

As time has gone on, Loeb has endeavored to bring in line more and more his actual behavior and experiences with his phantasy life, with even his earlier phantasies. This is not only shown in the development of his crime ideas as such, but also in the fact and method of the enjoyment of his experiences connected with the crime. Under his present predicament, for example, he is much pleased over the fact that he knows more about the details of the events connected with the Franks case than anyone has been able to find out.

Very remarkable in the light of his early imaginings is the fact that in jail he is endeavoring to obtain sympathy for himself through inviting friends, especially girls, to come and gaze at him behind the bars, to look up at the jail windows where he is, being stationed at places which he designates on the street. Also, his ready adaptation to jail conditions, for a boy of his social status shows the continuous influence on his mind of these early phantasies. Spontaneously, he says on July 27, "It's sort of all right, it seems, to be in jail. It seems to be a sort of confirmation of my early picturization. I had a very pleasant sort of feeling in the jail outfit when I first came in; this self-pity entered into it, but I was a little glad of the jail clothes, of being in jail. I was glad to have a ragged coat. When they offered me a better one, I refused it. The one they gave me was torn up the sleeve. I was living out being subjected to worse conditions than the other prisoners. I feel comfortable here. I am living it out— what I used to picture as a child." In these days the thoroughly abnormal ideas of some of his first phantasies of criminality are shown even today.

(Of considerable interest to students of abnormal psychology and mental disease must be the unquestioned fact that this boy, selfishly seeking in an extraordinary fashion his own peculiar pleasure at anybody's expense, even to the point of entering into situations which were most dangerous to him, is quite in line with his abnormal early phantasy of self-suffering, and almost leads to the conclusion that he has been unconsciously bent, as it were, on self-destruction.)

Emotional Nature

Another outstanding fact in explanation of Loeb's abnormal career is the extraordinary moral callousness which has been growing upon him. He has become incapable of viewing his criminal acts with any natural feeling. Nothing, perhaps, emphasizes this point any more than the fact that it was possible for him to contemplate the kidnaping of members of his own family, particularly his younger brother, of whom he professes to have been fondest.

This pathological moral obtuseness, which all recognize who have been in contact with Loeb, especially when placed side by side with his intelligence and school achievement, points to a disordered condition of his personality and mental life, a type of condition not uncommonly encountered among the obviously insane.

A careful estimate of the way in which this boy has developed his tendencies shows that the divergence between his thinking and his feeling or emotional life had its origin even before he was ten years old. Already that early he hit upon persistent lying as a means of avoiding the difficulties of his environment.

And while he continued to develop intellectually and to be capable of entering college extremely early and to obtain passing marks all through his college life, he has remained pathologically backward in his emotional make-up, and perhaps also retrograded to the point of being now absolutely defective or abnormal in this phase of his personality.

His notoriously unfeeling behavior in connection with his immediate situation, as a person about to be tried for murder, is ample illustration of the depths of his emotional displacement or defect. The absence, all along, of normal remorse, revulsion, disgust, depression, fear, or even apprehension, in any way concerning the planning, discussing and carrying out of the gruesome details of the kidnaping and murder, or in considering the outcome, also sharply emphasizes the thoroughly disordered character of his mental life. His own astonishment at his lack of feeling is worthy of much note. He has repeatedly stated that certainly for years he had hardly any of the slightest evidences of being moved by ordinary sympathy. He says, "I would have supposed I would have cried at the testimony of Mrs. Frank, but I did not feel anything much. I was not sorry about any of the things I did that were wrong. I did not have any feeling about it. I did not have much of any feeling from the first. That is why I could do those things. I think I am getting worse in my mind in the last few years. I used to be quicker in my mind." "There was nothing inside me to stop me." "Of course I feel sorry about my folks, but not so much as I ought to feel."

And to the same point, we have the manifestation in him of the outward characteristics of affability, good manners, desire for friendship, pushed to the point of deliberate planning to achieve better social relationships, desire for sympathy, all in the strangest contrast to his satisfaction in conduct and in the thought of conduct that could easily be seen to include every chance of negating all these desires. This makes a contradictory picture, both in the realms of judgment and emotional life, that is incomprehensible except as it is seen so surely to involve mental abnormality.

CONDITIONING FACTORS OF LOEB'S PATHOLOGICAL MENTAL DEVELOPMENT

The above mentioned pathological features of Loeb's inner mental and emotional life were somewhat conditioned and probably strengthened by the following most important facts:

(a) Between the ages of four and a half and fourteen he was very largely in the company and under the domination and guidance of a peculiarly repressive and jealous governess. Through this he was very considerably deprived of the self-development that comes from free and healthy contacts with other children.

(b) Through this woman's scholastic ambitions for the boy and through her tutoring he was most rapidly pushed through his school classes, the boy having, however, exhibited no special abilities and particularly having developed no normal ambitions and interests. It is all during the period when he was supposed to be doing so well in meeting the requirements of formal education that he was forced to fall back for his real satisfactions upon the abnormal features of his phantasy life.

(c) The culmination of these efforts to push this boy rapidly through school was in his entrance to the University at the age of fourteen years and three months. This proved to be an unfortunate circumstance in relation to his development, one that Loeb himself emphasizes as having been pernicious. Soon after his matriculation he was thrown among young fellows four to six or seven years older than himself, and the ways of some of the wildest and most immoral of them he soon imitated. Like his comrade Leopold, he began to drink at fifteen. His very release at this age from the restraining influence of his repressive governess he reacted to by going rapidly in other and immoral directions.

(d) Beginning at ten years of age, the boy found opportunity to secretly feed his cravings by reading exciting detective stories, which made a great impress upon him and which afforded material for his criminalistic phantasies. A number of books of this kind he read over and over and the characters entered into his imaginative life. This reading interest also signifies that extreme attention was paid to the formal education of this boy without developing normal and healthy interest in his inner mental life, and this left him with no vestige of ambition or ideal to counteract his eccentric and pathological interests.

PRESENT FINDINGS THROUGH DIRECT EXAMINATION OF LOEB

PHYSICAL STATUS

Although this active and well-built young fellow usually preserves a calm and pleasant demeanor, he shows marked signs of some nervous instabilities in certain involuntary twitchings of the muscles of his face and in the asymmetrical use of the muscles controlling the lips.

MENTAL STATUS

Given a number of mental tests of different sorts, we find him grading as having only average general ability for a person of his educational advantages; and we find him evidencing no particularly good abilities of any sort. This is interesting, because it seems out of consonance with his precocious academic record.

Concerning his personality traits we note that he takes very little pleasure in ordinary mental activity and that he appears to be very limited in his interests, to the extent of being almost ambitionless along any ordinary lines. His energies appear to be directed almost exclusively into the channels of his abnormal tendencies. He can easily take command of a situation and is strong in emergency. He has a pathological love of excitement and adventure. There is a very striking pathological contradiction between his desires for sympathy and friendships, and the fact that he is unscrupulous, unfair and ungrateful. His unfortunate qualities he freely confesses and claims to wonder at them in his own makeup. He is rather even tempered and shows no superficial evidence of repressed emotions, no special irritabilities. He can be decidedly courageous on occasions. He does, however, have times of mild and probably pathologically significant depressions, which, however, are easily changed by making pleasant social contacts. During these depressions, he tells us, he has repeatedly contemplated suicide.

Thus a central indication of his abnormality is to be found in the great emotional peculiarities, which are indicated by the extreme lack of feeling and of sympathy in certain spheres of life, by a lack of appropriate emotional response in connection with many situations which normally call forth certain emotional reactions, and in certain curious twists or misplacements, so that the few loyalties that he does express are quite incongruous and relate to issues of relatively minor social consequence. Thus when compared with the normal person, his entire scale of emotional values is seen to be defective and in certain aspects decidedly abnormal.

The Problem of Mental Disorder in Loeb's Case

It is evident from the foregoing that in this case we are dealing with an adolescent who in his development has manifested a markedly pathological divergence or split between his intellectual and emotional life, so that while he may be considered mature intellectually, he is decidedly infantile in his capacity for reacting to the ordinary situations of life with normal, appropriate emotions. His whole behavior in connection with the Franks case before and after its occurrence and up to the present moment, indicates a degree of callousness which is wholly incomprehensible except on the basis of a disordered mentality.

The opinion is inescapable that in Loeb we have an individual with a pathological mental life, who is driven in his actions by the compulsive force of his abnormally twisted life of phantasy or imagination, and at this time expresses himself in his thinking and feeling and acting as a split personality, a type of condition not uncommonly met with among the insane.

We therefore conclude that Richard Loeb is now mentally abnormal and was so abnormal on May 21st, 1924, and, in so far as anyone can predict at this time, will continue, perhaps with increasing gravity as time goes on.

The Alienists for the Defense

Dr. Harold S. Hulbert, one of the alienists for the defense, in collaboration with Dr. Karl M. Bowman, of Boston, prepared the Bowman-Hulbert report, from which Dr. Hulbert later gave his testimony on the witness stand for the defense.

Dr. Hulbert is a graduate of the University of Michigan, class of 1914, from the department of medicine and surgery. He was sent by the Rockefeller Foundation to Tennessee to make a survey of the neuropsychiatric cases in the Tennessee institutions, including penitentiaries, county jails and poor farms. When war was declared he became neuropsychiatrist at the Great Lakes Naval Training Station. He was sent by the navy department to sea as psychiatrist on the Leviathan. Since the war he has been in private practice in Chicago.

Dr. Karl M. Bowman, with whom Dr. Hulbert collaborated in the examinations of Loeb and Leopold, is a graduate of the University of Kansas and of the University of California, school of medicine. He was made first assistant at the Bloomingsdale Hills Hospital, Bloomingsdale, N. Y., soon after his graduation. The institution conducts research in mental diseases and is of very high standing.

During the war he was sent by the medical department of the army, with other neurologists of the American medical units, through the British hospitals for a few months before being asisgned to studying shell shock cases. He spent his time at the military hospital for mental cases at Maghull, England, under the direction of Col. R. G. Rows. Of all the American doctors who went through this hospital Dr. Bowman was the only one retained by the English army as a member of its own staff.

There he remained throughout almost all the war as a sort of liaison officer-doctor between the British government hospitals and the medical units of the American army.

He returned to Bloomingdale Hills Hospital after the war but was soon invited to become chief of staff of the Psychopathic Hospital in Boston, which is a part of the Harvard Medical school. He is a lecturer on mental diseases at Harvard.

Four alienists, called in to study the boys as to their sanity and their responsibility, joined together in a report which was never introduced in trial but which stated most concisely their opinion of the state of the boys' mind. Dr. William Healy, one of these alienists, an Englishman, is a graduate of Harvard and of Rush Medical college. Shortly after his graduation he was given charge of the women's department of the Wisconsin State Hospital for mental diseases. He was in general practice in Chicago for five years after resigning his position at the Wisconsin hospital.

Then he went abroad and studied in Vienna, Berlin and London. Returning to Chicago he was made head of the psychopathic institute of the juvenile court in 1909. He held this position until 1917 when he was invited to come to Boston and plan the Judge Baker Foundation, an endowed psychopathic hospital and research laboratory which is one of the finest in the world. He was then made director of the foundation. The purpose of the institute is to study conduct and behavior problems for court, particularly the juvenile court of Boston. Dr. Healy is a lecturer at Harvard and Columbia University and the author of a number of books, monographs and articles on medical-psychological subjects.

Dr. Bernard Glueck, specialist on mental disorders, was graduated from Georgetown University in 1909. He was at one time president of the Society for Medical Jurisprudence. For a time he was in the service of the government of the United

States, examining immigrants for mental and nervous diseases at the port of New York. In 1916 Dr. Glueck took charge of the psychopathic clinic at Sing Sing prison, established by the Rockefeller foundation and held this position for two years. He resigned to enter the army at the outbreak of the war. In 1919 he was appointed director of the mental hygiene department of the New York School of Social Work. He was also associate neurologist at the College of Physicians and Surgeons at Columbia University.

Later he was appointed professor of psychiatry at the New York Postgraduate School and Hospital. In 1921 he was appointed to take charge of one of the divisions of the Bureau of Children's Guidance. At the present time he is engaged in private practice and lectures at the College of Physicians and Surgeons in New York City, and occasionally lectures at other universities and colleges throughout the country.

Dr. William A. White is superintendent of St. Elizabeth's Hospital, Washington, D. C., and professor of nervous and mental diseases at George Washington University. He is a lecturer on insanity in the United States Naval and Army Medical School. Dr. White is a member of the National Research Council, and is author of many works on nervous and mental diseases.

Dr. Ralph Hamill, of Chicago, was the fourth alienist who joined with Drs. Glueck, White and Healy in examining the defendants, and his name also is signed to the joint report on the mental and physical state of the two boys. Dr. Hamill has a private practice in Chicago and is associate professor of neurology and mental diseases at Northwestern University. He is a fellow of the American Medical Association.

The State's Alienists

The testimony given in the trial of Nathan F. Leopold Jr., and Richard Loeb is too voluminous to be presented in a popular volume. It fills six large books of the official record. Some eighty witnesses were called by the State and about twenty by the defense.

With the exception of the State's alienists, the State witnesses were called only to substantiate the details of the boys' confession and to prove the crime. The laymen called by the defense testified to the uncertain dispositions of the boys, as observed by their friends, classmates and associates, and to prove that the boys had no need of money. A desire and a need for money, the State contended, was the motive back of the murder.

The real contest was between the two sets of alienists. For that reason only their testimony is of real and lasting interest. The State's alienists, who had examined the boys a very short time after the crime, contended that the boys were normal and not mentally diseased.

The alienists for the defense, on the other hand, contended that the boys were diseased mentally. The trial became a contest in psychology and for days the air was thick with terms—"split personalities," "phantasies," "subconscious influence," "basal metabolism"—which the alienists and neurologists of the two sides of the case hurled back and forth before the judge. Only the testimony of these two conflicting groups of alienists is therefore being given in this volume.

Dr. Hugh T. Patrick, a Chicago neurologist, was called by Mr. Crowe the afternoon of May 31st, a few hours after Loeb and Leopold had made their confessions, to observe the boys for signs of insanity. Dr. Patrick is neurologist for the Henrotin, Passavant, Peoples and Wesley hospitals of Chicago. He is a graduate of the Bellevue Hospital Medical College, a part of the University of New York.

He studied nervous and mental diseases abroad for a number of years following his graduation and has been professor of nervous and mental diseases in the Chicago Policlinic since 1896. He is emeritus professor of nervous and mental diseases at the Northwestern University, at Evanston, Ill. He was president of the American Neurological Association in 1907 and twice president of the Chicago Neurological Society. He is the author of numerous articles on medical jurisprudence.

Here are the more important extracts of Dr. Patrick's testimony on the stand as a State witness:

"Were you present in the office of the State's Attorney on Sunday, June first, 1924, at the request of the State's Attorney?"

"Yes."

"Will you state if you recall who were present?"

"There were present the State's Attorney, yourself, Mr. Savage, I think Mr. Smith and there were some officers or detectives whose names I do not know were present; there were two stenographers, and I was there, and soon after I went in Mr. Leopold, Jr., was brought in and almost immediately after, his father, but the older Leopold did not stay very long. He left and then later Mr. Loeb was brought in. Then there were present, not from the beginning when I was there but during the time immediately succeeding there were Dr. Church and Dr. Krohn and then Dr. Wesener, chemist,"—

"By Leopold, Jr., you mean Nathan Leopold, Jr., and by Mr. Loeb you mean Richard Loeb, the defendants in this case?"

"Yes."

"Will you state an observation or examination you made at

that time of the defendants, Richard Loeb and Nathan Leopold, Jr.?"

"I observed these gentlemen and listened to their conversation
practically all that afternoon.   I think this began about two
o'clock.

"After the elder Mr. Leopold left, I got into conversation
with Nathan Leopold—is it Nathan Leopold, Jr.?—and we had
quite a conversation largely about psychology of birds and the
relation of the psychology of birds and other animals to human
beings, the relation of instinct to reason.

"Mr. Leopold told me about a paper he had written on the
psychology of birds based on the observation of some gulls and
their change in migration routes, and that sort of thing.   We
talked about, I should think, perhaps fifteen or twenty minutes, twenty minutes probably, and then Dr. Krohn came in
and he took up the conversation with Leopold and I listened.

"Dr. Vasenor came in and had something to say, not very
much, but it was a discussion of things of scientific interest
largely.

"Then after, I presume I had been there thirty or forty minutes, Mr. Loeb came in and he was asked to tell the story of
this crime from the beginning, which he did, with a few interruptions, some interruptions from Mr. Leopold several times,
but the State's Attorney requested him to reserve his objections
or criticisms until after the story was finished, and then he
would have an opportunity, which he was given, and he cor-
rected some of the statements of Mr. Loeb so that there was
quite a discussion of the event and the preparation and commission of this crime.

"Then there were some questions asked of these young men
by the State's Attorney and by the physicians.

"During this time the young men had something to eat, they
had a lunch.   Mr. Loeb had a little table and Mr. Leopold was

not given a table, and one of the police officers handed him a very cumbersome sandwich—I don't know how thick it was, but it was a very unhandy thing to eat while held in the hand, and Mr. Loeb evidenced some little embarrassment how to handle this grub"—

"You mean Leopold?"

"Did I say Loeb, yes, Mr. Leopold, and nobody seemed to notice his little embarrassment with this thing, and I asked him if he would not like to change seats with me, as I was sitting next to a filing case which would serve very well as a table? He thanked me very pleasantly and we made the exchange.

"Then afterwards I wanted a drink of water. The fact of the matter is that all this recital had made me a little dry in the mouth and there was not any glass in sight. The two young gentlemen had all the available drinking vessels, and I asked Mr. Leopold if I might have one of his glasses and he very pleasantly gave it to me.

"He gave me his glass very pleasantly, and I took a drink of water and then I asked him if he would have the drink, and he said he would. I filled the glass at the water cooler and returned it to him and he received it very politely and pleasantly. That was simply an episode that went on.

"Well now, if you want most of the details that I recall, I will go ahead and give them to you.

"After Mr. Leopold had finished his lunch, he had about half a glass of water and he took a small bottle from his pocket and dropped some fluid, drop by drop, into this glass of water. That looked rather interesting to the doctors, and the State's Attorney stated to us that that was aromatic spirits of ammonia and asked Mr. Leopold if that wasn't it, and he said it was. He drank that.

"After this colloquy in the State's Attorney's office we all went down into the jail yard, I think it was, in order to inspect the car which was supposed to be the car the gentlemen used in this affair, and Mr. Leopold identified it. Mr. Loeb said he didn't know if it was the same car, it looked like it, it was that kind of a car, but he couldn't tell if it was the same car. Mr. Leopold walked around it from the left hand side of the car, around the rear to the right hand side and said presently:

" 'Yes, this is the car, I know it by these scratches on the front door.' Then after being down there a little while these two young gentlemen, and some of the rest of us, went back to the State's Attorney's office, and they were requested to strip, which they promptly did, and Dr. Krohn and I made a rather brief physical examination; we looked them over to see that there were no defects. There were no signs of bruises or any injury.

"We took the pulse.

"I think I listened to the heart. I am not perfectly certain about that."

"That is all."

"The reflexes?"

"Yes."

"Have you an opinion, from the observation and examination as detailed, as to whether the defendant, Richard Loeb, was suffering from any mental disease at that time?"

"Yes."

"What is that opinion?"

"My opinion is that he showed no evidence of mental disease."

"Will you state your reasons for that opinion, doctor?"

"The reasons for that opinion are these: That unless we assume that every man who commits a deliberate, cold-blooded, planned murder, must, by that fact, be mentally diseased. There was no evidence of any mental disease, in any of this communication or in any of the statements the boys made regarding it, or their earlier experiences; there was nothing in the examination; there were no mental obliquities or peculiarities shown, except their lack of appreciation of the enormity of the deed which they had committed."

"Now, doctor, have you an opinion, from the observation and examination as detailed, as to whether the defendant, Nathan Leopold, Jr., was suffering from any mental disease at that time?"

"Yes, I have an opinion."

"What is that opinion?"

"My opinion is that there was no evidence of mental disease.

"And your reasons for that opinion?"

"Well, the reasons are just as I have stated."

Dr. Archibald Church, a specialist in nervous and mental diseases, was called by State's Attorney Crowe on June 1st, with several other doctors, to observe the boys while they were still in the custody of the State's Attorney. Dr. Church was graduated from the College of Physicians and Surgeons in Chicago, in 1884. Shortly thereafter he was appointed on the medical staff at the Illinois Hospital for the Insane at Elgin.

He later went to Europe and studied at Paris, Vienna, Leipzig, Prague, Berlin and London. In 1892 Dr. Church was made professor of nervous and mental diseases and medical jurisprudence at Northwestern University (then called the Chicago Medical College), which position he still holds.

For many years he has been neurologist to St. Luke's, Wesley, Mercy and Michael Reese hospitals in Chicago. He is the author of a number of text books on nervous and mental diseases, and a frequent contributor to medical periodicals.

Following are extracts from his testimony, as he gave it in the trial when called as a witness for the State:

"Now, doctor, were you present in the office of the State's

Attorney on Sunday, June 1st, 1924, at the request of the State's Attorney?"

"I was."

"Will you state if you recall who were present, as far as you know?"

"Well, there was Dr. Wesener, Dr. Patrick, Dr. Krohn, Chief of Detectives Hughes, Mr. Crowe, and his assistants, a couple of stenographers, and then during the four or five hours a number came in and out whom I did not know. Of course, also there were present —"

"Were the defendants present?"

"—the defendants, Leopold and Loeb."

"Will you state any observation and examination that you made at that time of the defendant, Richard Loeb, and Nathan Leopold, Jr.? Will you go on in your own way, doctor, and state what those examinations and observations consisted of, and what your conclusions were as a result of that examination?"

"When I entered the room Dr. Krohn and Dr. Patrick were in conversation with Mr. Leopold, discussing the subject of the psychology of birds, and his studies and courses taken in psychology, and the character of the apparatus used in the psychological laboratory which he was familiar with.

"A little later later Loeb was brought in and then upon the suggestion of Mr. Crowe, Loeb detailed all the circumstances of the Franks crime.

"During his detailing those circumstances, he was interrupted at times by Leopold with disclaimers or objections, and finally Leopold was asked to make notes, and they would be then considered after the termination of the statement by Loeb, and this he proceeded to do.

"Very shortly after Loeb's entrance, both young men were supplied with a luncheon which they ate intermittently during the course of the interview during the next half hour or hour.

"Loeb in a very methodical manner began with his statement dating back to November of last year, at which time they said that they, meaning, as I understand it, Leopold and himself, had determined upon the execution of a murder and kidnapping for ransom, and that they had discussed the details of that plan at frequent intervals over a period extending down to the time of its commission.

"That they had formulated a letter which was to be sent to the father of the victim, that was of an open character so that it might be applicable to any parent; and in the formulation of this letter mutual changes and suggestions had been made until it arrived in a finished form, the form which was used at the time.

He stated how, in order to secure an automobile which would not be easily recognizable, they had arranged for the rental of a car from the Rent-a-Car Company on Michigan Avenue, and to that end how Leopold had registered at the Morrison Hotel under an assumed name, to which name they had forwarded pieces of mail in order that it might give an appearance of substantial fact to such registration; how later they transferred from the Morrison to the Hotel Trenier, and established their identity under that name in the same manner, and directed that the authority or license of the Rent-a-Car Company should be forwarded to Leopold, who had registered under the name of— I can't recall that."

"Ballard?"

"Ballard. That they had provided the car obtained in this manner; and also the character of Leopold had been substantiated by Loeb through a telephone communication made at a certain place on Wabash Avenue, Loeb then giving Leopold a good character as to reliability, so that the Rent-a-Car people would accept his assurances; that they had provided in the equipment of the car a bottle of chloroform, a bottle of hydrochloric acid, which they had some difficulty in buying, owing to the fact that the drug stores where they applied for it were not provided with such a quantity; and had purchased a cold chisel, which had been protected on the sharp end by tape; Loeb said it was done by Leopold, and Leopold said it was done by Loeb, but which chisel was presented to them and identified by them at that time.

"That they also had pieces of rope and pieces of cloth or rags to use as a gag, and had supplied the car also with a lap robe which would be useful in wrapping a body, or in carrying a body; that their plan was to pick up a boy by the name of Levinson; that with the car equipped as they described, they went to the school where Levinson wsa a pupil, and saw him playing in the yard; and then to make sure of his father's address, they drove to a drug store, and the telephone book was consulted, in order that the letter which had been prepared for the parents might be sent to the proper address. That they then found that the Levinson boy had gone from the school to a vacant lot on the corner of Grand and 49th Street, where he was playing ball; that they hung around that corner for an hour or so, first on one side of Grand Boulevard and then on the other, but were unable to keep satisfactory watch of the boy, to which end they then went to the house of Leopold, and secured a pair of field glasses with which they would then be able to see the boy in his play and watch his movements; that this boy with other boys went up an alleyway, and they lost track of him, although they had formerly secreted themselves in an adjoining alley, in order to better watch the boys and at the same time be out of view themselves.

"That they then drove down to the Levinson home, expecting to meet the boy on the road, but were unable to see him. Then in driving back, as they came along on Ellis Avenue, they saw the Franks boy, and immediately decided to pick him up as a suitable victim; that they turned the car about, and came up to the curb stone; that Loeb invited the Franks boy to take a seat in the car, and he would give him a ride home; that the Franks boy demurred, and said he only had a little ways to go, and did not need a ride, but Loeb said, 'Get in; I want to talk with you about a tennis racket that I saw you have when you were playing with my brother two or three days ago at my house,' or something to that effect. And thereupon the Franks boy consented to get in.

"They asked him if he would mind driving around the block, and he said no; that they then drove south to 50th street, and then east on 50th street; that along about Kimbark or Kenwood avenue one of them in the rear seat struck the boy on the back of the head with the chisel, which had been prepared for that purpose, several blows, and he was then dragged over the back of the seat on to the floor of the rear portion of the car.

"At this point Loeb insisted that he was doing the driving, and that Leopold was in the back seat, and did the striking. Leopold denied this, and said that he himself was driving, and that Loeb was in the rear seat.

"Some discussion was held between them on this point, each accusing the other of having struck the blow.

"When Loeb made this statement that Leopold was in the rear of the car and did the striking, he looked at him in a furtive, rather frightened way, showing some emotion in making the assertion.

"They said they then drove south somewhere toward the Midway and after driving about in order that the time might pass until darkness ensued, they stopped at one place and sent a telephone mesage to a young lady on the north side, stopped at another place to get something to eat, and if my memory serves me right, they said at that time they found that the boy was dead; that his eyes were glazed, that he was rigid, and as they said, rigor mortis had developed.

"They also said that immediately after he was struck and

pulled into the back of the car, he made some noises, and rags which had been prepared for the purpose of gagging him were stuffed in his mouth.

"Later they drove on to the prairies and disposed of the body, carrying the body in the bdanket a distance of perhaps three hundred yards, one at the head and one at the feet, to a culvert, at which place he was disrobed entirely, part of his clothing having been removed previously.

"That then Leopold, because Loeb hesitated to do it, poured the acid over the face and genitals; that the body was then taken and thrust head first into the culvert, Leopold having prepared himself for the purpose by taking with him a pair of rubber boots to enable him to wade into the stream.

"That they then gathered up the clothing, and Leopold's coat, which had been taken off so that he might pursue his job, and with these garments they returned to the car and then to the residence of Loeb, where everything was burned except the blanket and the belt and the shoes, because they thought these would not be consumed thoroughly in the fire of the furnace.

"That the belt and the shoes were subsequently buried at a certain point on the south side, and that the robe was subsequently burned somewhere near the right-of-way of the Illinois Central tracks by pouring gasoline over it, and that they then returned and posted the letter at the post office on 55th street, directed to Mr. Franks, and went back home, leaving this rented car, I think, at the Leopold house. That the next morning they found that the car had been stained by blood on the floor in the rear portion, and they washed it out, telling the chauffeur, who made some inquiry, that they had been out on a drinking spree and that the stains were wine stains.

"They also washed off the rubber boots and the clothing that they wore, which had been spattered during the night.

"In the afternoon, I believe it was, they said that they returned the rented car to its owners, and either at that time or on a subsequent occasion, threw away the chisel which they had used in beating the boy over the head.

"Then certain questions were asked Loeb by Leopold, tending to confirm his contention that he did the driving, and that Loeb did the striking.

"And Leopold at the request of Mr. Crowe also printed his name or wrote his name and the name of Mr. Franks on a piece of paper several times, knowing that it was for comparison with the address he had used on the envelope of the letter mailed to Mr. Franks on 55th street.

"Mr. Loeb then detailed how he had planted a letter in the rear of the last car on Michigan Central train in the box for messages and directories, and how they had mailed instructions or had telephoned instructions, rather, to Mr. Franks, regarding taking that train, their first plan being to direct him to a 'Keep-the-City-Clean' box, where they expected to plant a letter with such instructions, and that they had sent a Yellow Cab to his house so he would have just time enough to take this train, the purpose being that he should throw from the train a cigar box containing ten thousand dollars in certain denominations of bills which were to be old and so not easily marked, at a given point on the right-of-way of the Illinois Central, opposite the Champion factory, which is to the east of the right-of-way somewhere near 72nd street, where they expected to be on hand with a rented car, provided with something to obscure the number, the license number, so as to be enabled to pick up the box, make their getaway, and if they found that the train was slowing up at that point or if it did not reach that point on scheduled time they would realize that methods or means were being taken to interfere with the progress of their plans, and that they could then get away.

"All of this matter was gone into at much greater length and detail than I have taken or should take. And I then asked Leopold why in Heaven he did such a thing, whereupon, his face trembled, he almost broke into tears, and he said he didn't know why in the world he ever did such a thing.

"Leopold said to me that they were able,—they knew exactly what they were to do, and they were able at any time to have desisted from the pursuit of their plan, but that he was not a quitter; and I said, 'Wasn't one of the purposes of the whole thing to beat the detective forces?' and he said, 'Yes, that was a very large part of it.' He said, 'I suppose it was egotistic.'

"During the latter part of this interview, Leopold said to me, 'You won't be able to find anything in this that would be of any help to us, not a thing.'

"He said this in an undertone. Why he said it I didn't know, but that is what he said.

"During the course of the examination, of course, the young men were under continuous observation and watchful attention on my part. Their physical conditions and attitudes and emotional reactions were observed as carefully as I could, and at the end of the interview it was announced that the automobile was in the jail yard, and we all adjourned to the jail yard.

"Shortly after we reached the jail yard there was quite a crowd of reporters and court officers and physicians, Dr. Kektone and Dr. Ralph Webster joined us at that time, and somebody let off a flashlight and Loeb collapsed against the wall of the jail. Leopold looked at him sneeringly and said, 'Poor weakling,' or that is what I understood him to say.

"At this time they evidently were not in entire harmony and sympathy owing to these mutual accusations or charges.

"I think that covers my observations and experiences and contract with these two young men."

"Doctor, do you recall having heard Dr. Krohn ask any questions, or Dr. Patrick?"

"Yes, after I asked Leopold if he understood just what he was doing, the nature of his act, its criminal character, and the penalty provided, to all of which he said 'Yes, certainly.' Dr. Krohn asked similar questions of Loeb, who replied in the same way."

"Was there anything said about the ransom?"

"Yes, I asked Leopold what the ransom had to do with it, and he said, 'Well, that was a secondary consideration, but of course it was an important one.'"

"They also said about the ransom money that they had agreed between them that it should be divided half and half, or fifty-fifty were the words used, and that it was understood and agreed that none of that money should be spent in the city of Chicago within a period of a year, but that it might be spent at a distance, either abroad or in some distant city."

"Doctor, do you recall having heard the State's Attorney ask about picking a pocket of ten thousand dollars?"

"Yes, he asked Leopold if he would pick his pocket, that is, Mr. Crowe's pocket, of ten thousand dollars, and Leopold took it rather laughingly and said he did not suppose he would have ten thousand dollars in his pocket, or something to that effect."

"Didn't he say that if he could get away with it, he would?"

"Well, he may have said so; I am not clear about that."

"Now, doctor, you stated that you observed certain emotional reactions. What are your conclusions?"

"Conclusions as to what?"

"With reference to those emotional reactions?"

"The emotional manifestations were entirely on the part of Loeb. Leopold showed no emotion of any kind, but he intimated that his philosophy was one which dictated the suppression of emotion and that he had practiced their suppression so that he was on his guard against manifesting any emotion—"

"Loeb, you mean?"

"Loeb, yes; when asked why he did such a crime."

"Have you an opinion, doctor, from your observation and examination, as to whether the defendant, Richard Loeb, was suffering from any mental disease on that day, at that time?"

MR. B. C. BACHRACH: "What day?"

MR. SBARBARO: "June 1st."

"There was no mental disease of any character."

"Will you state your reasons for that opinion?"

"The young men were entirely oriented—"

MR. DARROW: "Just a minute. Are you talking about both of them now?"

DR. CHURCH: "Yes."

MR. DARROW: "Do you want it that way?"

MR. SBARBARO: "I would rather have you address yourself to Richard Loeb, please."

DR. CHURCH: "Your question, I thought, was comprehensive of the two."

"No, as to Loeb."

"As to Loeb. The young man was entirely oriented, he knew who he was and where he was, and the time of day and everything about it. His memory was extraordinarily good; his logal powers as manifested during the interview were normal, and I saw no evidence of any mental disease."

"Now, doctor, have you an opinion from your observation and examination of Nathan Leopold, Jr., as to whether he was suffering from any mental disease at that same time?"

"I have."

"What is that opinion?"

"There was no evidence of any mental disease."

"Will you state your reasons again, please?"

"Because he was perfectly oriented, of good memory, of extreme intellectual reasoning capacity, and apparently of good judgment within the range of the subject matter."

"Now, doctor, assume a hypothetical person who on examination disclosed the facts and circumstances that you gained from your examination of Richard Loeb, and add thereto these other facts that have been testified to here:

"That he is immature in his sexual development;

"That he still has three baby teeth;

"That the growth of hair on the body is scanty; and he only requires to shave twice or three times a week;

"That he has had several fainting spells during his life;

"That he has tremors of the hand and tongue and enlarged inguinal glands;

"That he also has dermagraphia, and that his basal metabolism, when examined on one day, averaged minus 17 per cent.

"Have you an opinion whether such an individual was suffering from any mental disease on May 21, 1924?"

"I have." "What is your opinion?" "My opinion is that there was no mental disease."

"And will you give your reasons, please?"

"The additional facts which I am expected to assume are of insignificant importance and most of them are entirely trivial, have no bearing on mental qualities."

"Now, doctor, add further these further facts: That this same hypothetical person has a high or average intelligence for a college graduate; that he has been observed to be nervous and restless; this being indicated by facial twitching and slight stammering, his speech being rapid and rather jerky; that he smokes cigarettes in a curious, jerky way, drawing deep breaths; that he frequently changes the topic of conversation; that he picks out the pin points in arguments; and that he runs up and down stairs, taking two or three steps at a time.

"Assume further that he has shown a marked criminalistic tendency, which began with lying when he was quite young, and grew to include larceny, burglary, arson, drunkenness, and cheating at cards.

"Assume further that in his inner mental life he is stated to have had phantasies in which he would lie and preface his lie by saying, 'And now, Teddy,' as if talking to a teddy-bear; of seeing himself in jail undergoing tortures and being exhibited to crowds, which caused a feeling of pleasure rather than pain; and that he phantasied himself as a cowboy or frontiersman, as a leader of a gang of criminals, committing a perfect crime; and that in relation to some of these phantasies he has attempted to act them out by shadowing people on the streets, making signs with his hands as he walked along, as if he were signaling to his gang concerning which houses should be robbed and which should be left alone. Assume, further, doctor, that he has been in the habit of reading detective stories, and of acting out some of these stories.

"Assuming these additional facts, have you an opinion as to whether this hypothetical person had a mental disease on May 21, 1924?"

"I have an opinion."

"Will you state that opinion?"

"That there was no mental disease."

"And will you give your reasons, from those additional facts which you have assumed?"

"Those additional facts have very little significance except as relates to the phantasies. Phantasies are day dreams. Everybody has them. Everybody knows they are dreams. They have an interest in relation to character and conduct, but they do not compel conduct nor excuse it. Those additional facts would imply a slowly growing criminal character, but would not furnish the basis for an opinion that there was any mental disease in that individual."

"What would you say, doctor, as to reading detective stories?"

"It is a very common practice."

"You have read some yourself, haven't you, doctor?"

Mr. B. C. Bachrach: "I object."

Mr. Darrow: "Wait. He is not being examined. He is the witness."

Mr. Sbarbaro: "Well, does reading detective stories indicate any mental disease?"

"No."

"Now, doctor, assume further that the following were true of this hypothetical person; that, having confessed to the commission of a homicide and kidnapping for ransom, he showed a lack of emotion in describing the crime; that he had at various times swings of mood, occasionally becoming depressed and thinking of suicide; and assume further that, though he graduated from a university at the age of eighteen, he had shown a lack of ambition and steady purpose during his life; and assume further that at the time of your examination he is eighteen, going on nineteen years of age. Would you have an opinion as to whether this hypothetical person had a mental disease on May 21, 1924?"

"There is nothing in those additional assumptions which would enable me to say there was any mental disease."

"Have you an opinion, first?"

"I have."

"And what is that opinion?"

"That there is nothing in those additional assumptions upon which you could predicate mental disease."

"Now, doctor, you have read the so-called Bowman-Hulbert report as to the various examinations of Richard Loeb, and which is in evidence here?"

"I have."

"Now, doctor, assume further, in addition to what has already been asked of you to assume, that the facts stated in this Bowman-Hulbert report with reference to Richard Loeb are true in connection with this case or with this same hypothetical person, doctor, that I have asked you to assume in previous questions. Have you an opinion as to whether this hypothetical person was suffering from a mental disease on May 21, 1924?"

"I have such an opinion."

"Would you state what that opinion is?"

"That there was no mental disease on that date."

"Give your reasons."

"This report, which is very carefully and thoroughly prepared, and based upon painstaking examinations, fails to present anything which is significant of mental disease."

Dr. Harold D. Singer was called Monday, June 2nd, by the State's Attorney, to observe the two boys, a few hours before they were finally locked in the county jail.

Dr. Singer at present is engaged in private practice in Chicago, making a specialty of mental diseases. He was graduated from the University of London, England, in 1898. After graduation he took six years' post graduate course in St. Thomas Hospital in London. From there he went to the National Hospital for the Paralyzed and Epileptic at Queen's Square, London. In 1904 he came to this country, to become associate professor of neurology in John Creighton University, Omaha, Neb. He then became assistant superintendent of the Norfolk State Hospital for the Insane of Nebraska.

From there he came to Illinois in 1907, to be director of the State Psychopathic Institute in Kankakee. In 1917 he was appointed state alienist for the State of Illinois. Later he became advisory consultant to the surgeon general of the United States Public Health Service in its mental work. Still later he was appointed advisor in neuropsychiatry to the surgeon general of the United States. Still later he was appointed advisor in neuropsychiatry to the director of the Veterans Bureau. Extracts of his testimony given when he was called as a witness for the State follow:

"Doctor, were you in the State's Attorney's office on Monday, June 2nd, at the request of the State's Attorney?"

"I was."

"Will you please describe who was present and what occurred?"

"I went there about three-thirty in the afternoon and at that time there were present in Mr. Crowe's office, yourself and Mr. Sbarbaro and Mr. Savage and one or two other people who came in and out.

"Shortly afterwards the two defendants in this case were brought in by several deputy sheriffs, three of them, I think.

"I believe there was also a stenographer present, and later Mr. Crowe, the State's Attorney, came in.

"Later still Mr. Darrow and another gentleman whom I did not know came into the room for a short time, and then left.

"When the defendants were brought into the room various questions were asked of them, chiefly by the Assistant State's Attorneys, one after the other, to each one of which, regardless of its nature, they made exactly the same reply.

"The one who did the most answering was Leopold, and that reply was to the effect:

" 'I respectfully decline to answer on the advice of counsel.'

"Loeb also made the same answer to the questions put to him. There were a number of such questions asked, many of them very trivial, joking remarks."

"Do you recall any of the questions?"

"I recall some of them. The majority of them, I do not.

"One of the earliest questions, I think by Mr. Savage, was he asked Leopold whether he understood how it was that a certain person whose name I did not know and do not now recall had been interviewed in that morning's newspaper."

"Do you remember if that was with reference to a young lady or not?"

"It was a young lady, yes,—to which he replied with the same answer that I have already given."

"That is, he answered with——?"

" 'I respectfully decline to answer on the advice of counsel.'

"Mr. Savage then gave an explanation that the State's Attorney's office was not responsible for this lady's name appearing in the paper, that she had given it, as he understood it, voluntarily to the newspaper. Mr. Savage made several remarks, to the effect that he wanted him to understand that he had not violated his confidence, and such remarks as that.

"The only answers received were still in exactly the same terms, that he respectfully declined to answer on the advice of counsel. They were asked questions about some of the various trips that had been made about the city in the last day or two, and asked about places where they had lunch.

"I remember some comments were made about some sandwiches, as I recall.

"The answers were always in exactly the same form or substantially the same form.

"After Mr. Crowe came in he asked them some questions, and got the same answer, and I remember that he then asked Leopold whether he thought there was anything that he could tell that he had not already told.

"Leopold laughed, and said he respectfully declined to answer."

MR. DARROW: "Upon the advice of counsel?"

THE WITNESS: "On the advice of counsel every time, Mr. Darrow, I remember just one spontaneous remark on the part of Leopold that I heard at that time, and that was to one of the deputy sheriffs, when he said:

" 'Say, Mr. Sheriff, I am in your control, and I protest against this proceeding,' or words to that effect. When Mr. Darrow came into the room, he and Loeb both talked to him. I didn't hear what was said at all. They appeared to be conversing with him in a natural manner.

"Mr. Darrow made some remark to the State's Attorney to the effect: 'I thought I had taken these boys out of your charge.' Mr. Darrow was only in the room a very short time and then left.

"I recall another series of questions that were asked in connection with the disposition of the suit cases belonging to the defendants. They were asked whether they wished to take those to jail with them, and they replied that they respectfully declined to answer on the advice of counsel.

"One of the Assistant State's Attorneys told the defendants to take the suitcases. They went over and took them and carried them to the door. They were then told to put the suit cases down and they complied with that.

"During the interview the defendant, Leopold, was self-possessed."

MR. DARROW: "Was what?"

"Self-possessed, laughed, and on one occasion he mimicked the laughter of someone who had been speaking to him, and laughed at the time.

"Loeb on the other hand was quiet, but restless, and his face had the appearance of being worried.

"He was smoking cigarettes for a short time, and throwing them away. He repeatedly got up and went to the water cooler, and took some water.

"I think in substance that about covers the nature of and the things that happened at the interview."

"Now, doctor, you have been present in court during the hearing of all the testimony offered by the State and the defense from the very beginning of this case at the request of the State's Attorney, have you not?"

"I have."

"Have you observed the defendants, Richard Loeb and Nathan Leopold, Jr., while here in court at any time?"

"I have."

"Will you tell his Honor, Judge Caverly, what you observed?"

"I have observed that the defendants have been free and easy in their movements, which were natural, easy and smooth; I have observed them especially during the early part of the trial laughing and conversing with one another; I have observed them both consulting on frequent occasions with their attorneys, they taking the initiative in those conversations by calling the attorneys back to speak to them.

"I have noticed that during the last two weeks, since the alienists for the State started to testify, their demeanor has been distinctly different. There has been much less laughing, although occasionally they do laugh now, particularly Leopold.

"I have noticed that they smile and nod to persons in the courtroom, and to witnesses on the witness stand. That they have occasionally, particularly Leopold, shaken their heads as if in dissent from various things that have been said. The laughing on the part of Loeb has changed frequently and quite abruptly to a very serious expression."

"Now, doctor, from your observation as detailed by you on Monday, June 2nd, and from your observations of the defendants in court, have you any opinion as to whether or not these defendants are suffering from any mental disease?"

"I cannot answer that question without qualification."

"Well, will you qualify it, please?"

"The answer I would give is that there is nothing in those observations that would indicate mental disease."

"Have you read the Hulbert-Bowman report which was presented in evidence on behalf of the defendants, Richard Loeb and Nathan Leopold, Jr.?"

"I have."

"Now, doctor, you have listened to the testimony of all the witnesses, both for the State and the defense; is that correct?"

"Yes, sir."

"Now, I will ask you to assume all the testimony as to the facts, exclusive now of all opinion evidence, that was detailed here from the witness stand as applied to Richard Loeb, and assume that with reference to a hypothetical person and assume also the observations that you have detailed both on Monday, June 2nd, 1924, and in court here; assume all these as applied to a hypothetical question——person, rather, and assume also in this hypothetical question the reading of the Hulbert-Bowman report, have you an opinion as to whether such hypothetical person was suffering from a mental disease on May 21st, 1924? You say you have an opinion, doctor?"

"Yes."

"What is that opinion?"

"That he has no mental disease."

Dr. William O. Krohn, a Chicago specialist in mental and nervous diseases, made a study of the boys at the request of Mr. Crowe, and his testimony was given for the State.

He received his Ph.D. at Yale University in 1889 for special study in psychology. Shortly thereafter he was made head of the department of psychology and mental science in the Western Reserve University at Cleveland, Ohio. After two years in that position he went to Europe and pursued his studies in various universities, including Freiberg with Prof. Muensterberg. He was delegated by the United States government to visit all different European universities that were devoted especially to the study of psychology, and published a report on the result of his investigation under the Department of Education. In 1892 he was made senior teacher fellow at Clark University, Worcester, Mass., where he was associated with G.

Stanley Hall. Later he was made head of the department of psychology at the University of Illinois, which position he held for five years. In 1897 he established a laboratory at the Kankakee Hospital for the Insane and was made psychiatrist of that institution, for the study of the life of the insane. He has also been an instructor at the Northwestern University Medical School. During the war he was psychiatrist at Camp Travis, Texas, and had charge of the mental examinations of all the draftees who came to that camp. Later he was made psychiatrist for the 18th Division.

Extracts from his testimony, given for the State, follow:

"Were you in the State's Attorney's office on June 1st, at the request of the State's Attorney?"

"I was."

"Will you please state who was there, if anyone?"

"There were present yourself, Mr. Savage, Dr. Patrick, Mr. Leopold, Dr. Wesener, Dr. Church, Mr. Loeb, Mr. Crowe, one stenographer when I first went in the room, a little later joined by another.

"At one time in the course of the afternoon I saw Chief of Detectives Hughes.

"A little later in the afternoon Captain Shoemaker came in, and Mr. O'Malley, sergeant of detectives.

"There were two other officers whose names I do not recall."

"Will you now state, doctor, what occurred on that date?"

"The first thing that was said, or observed by me first and then the first thing that I said afterwards, I noticed Dr. Hugh T. Patrick talking to Mr. Leopold. Mr. Loeb had not yet come into the room. This was about three o'clock. I had just gotten into the office at about three o'clock or three five. They were talking. The words I heard were 'materialism' and 'centralism.'

"I was introduced to Mr. Leopold by Dr. Patrick; and I

might say, in passing, the reason I called these men, the defendants, Mr. Leopold and Mr. Loeb, is that is what they called each other all during that afternoon, except on two occasions there was reversion to another name; but I learned to call them 'Mr.' at that time and have done so ever since. I simply wish to explain that in passing.

"Dr. Patrick introduced me to Mr. Leopold. Mr. Leopold spoke up at once and said, 'Oh, I have heard of you, Dr. Krohn. You are the doctor that has been sold on the Binet test.'

"I said, 'Not exactly sold on the Binet test, but it has some usage. What do you think of it?'

"He said, 'I do not believe that there is any unit or standard by which you can measure intelligence. There is no unit that will be applicable to the study of the mind in all of its parts.'

"I asked him what he knew about it, had he given it any attention or study, and he said: 'Yes, I studied psychology out at the University of Chicago.' I asked him what he had studied along that line. He said, 'Laboratory psychology.'

"I said, 'To what extent?' 'Well, we measure the time rate, reaction, time; the time rate of mental processes.' I said, 'What unit of time do they use?' I thought maybe he was just giving me a little account without showing any depth of preparation. So I asked him a few questions. I said: 'What is the unit of time that they measure by?' He said: 'Sigma,' using the Greek letter Sigma. I said: 'What does that indicate, in point of time?' He said, 'A thousandth of a second.' I asked him if they had any finer instruments than that, that is, instruments that measured smaller portions of time. He said:

" 'Yes, even the ten-thousandths of a second,' and on my asking him if the name of the instrument was the Hipp Chromoscope, he agreed with me. I asked him in what way his mind differed from another mind.

"He said, 'Only as you can find out from the study of behavior.' That he was a behaviorist. That his mind was the sum total of the behavior of his nervous system, and therefore there was no test, no arbitrary test like the Binet test, that would measure the mind.

"I then referred to the fact and asked him why it was that the mental age as given by the modified Binet-Simons test—that the mental age of all the men in the United States army during the war was less than twelve years.

"He said: 'That is because of the bulk of the army came off the street.' That they were not men of education. I say: 'You take the average of all?' and then Dr. Patrick spoke up and he wanted to know if I thought that was true of the Yale battery to which his son had belonged, and we found on reference it was a little over twelve years that their scale of intelligence was.

"In that same connection we discussed the adequacy of any form of measure and used the term 'adequate.'

"About this time Mr. Loeb came in and a short time afterwards Mr. Crowe, and about a quarter of four Mr. Crowe stated that he thought it would probably be best to give the meeting some purpose, to have one of the defendants start and tell the story.

"And so asked Mr. Loeb to tell his story, first telling the fake alibi story of what he had done on the Wednesday, May 21st.

"Mr. Loeb started by telling how that he had told Mr. Crowe that on the Wednesday they had lunched at Marshall Field's, that they had gone to Lincoln Park; that Leopold had become interested in a specimen of gull or some such bird.

"That later they had gone to the Cocoanut Grove. Later he had become somewhat intoxicated from the use of gin that they had with them in the car.

"They met two girls on 63rd street, he said about twenty-one and twenty-three years of age.

"Did not remember much about those girls except his girl's name was Edna. That they afterwards turned them out in Jackson Park and let the girls walk home.

"That he told Mr. Crowe that he was really too much under the influence of liquor to give much of the details.

"In explanation of that he said a few minutes later, 'I couldn't figure out what in the deuce to tell. I knew that if I told the actual facts of what had transpired on Wednesday it would go probably no worse than if I had told what was not true and was caught at it, but that is the reason I first told this alibi story.'

"He said: 'All the time I was figuring out what in the deuce to tell, and I couldn't get out of my mind how it would affect my folks.'

"He then started to tell what was his true account of the events that had transpired on Wednesday, the twenty-first, on Tuesday, the twentieth, and on Thursday, the twenty-second.

"He began first by telling what occurred on Tuesday, and he stated that he and Mr. Leopold had bought certain articles that they thought they would need; that Leopold bought hydrochloric acid; that he himself thought sulphuric acid would have been better.

"Dr. Church at this point asked him how much acid they had bought. He said it was a pint or quart, but the bottle fitted snugly into the pocket of the seat, the front seat, so that it would not tilt, anyway.

"Dr. Wesener suggested it was a pint bottle. That he, Loeb himself, had purchased the chisel and the rope; that on this Tuesday they had further determined about how to plant a letter on a Michigan Central through train whose first stop was at Gary or Michigan City, that would stop at 63rd Street; that this train would leave the Illinois Central Station at three o'clock; that at precisely two thirty they would call up a Yellow

Cab to proceed to Mr. Franks' house to go to a drug store at
63rd and Blackstone; that they had planned to paste a note or
directions on a Keep-the-City-Clean box, but they found it
would not stick, so they left that step of the program out.

"In this connection he started to tell how they had first begun to plan the crime.

"He was asked before he went on with the details of the acts
to tell the very beginnings.

"He stated that:

"'I think it was about two and a half or three months ago.
Mr. Leopold here says it was last November. In discussing
the commitment or commission of crimes in general, we finally
hit upon the crime of kidnapping in particular. One great difficulty that we met with in our planning was how to get the
money. The second difficulty was how to get a car that would
not be readily identified.'

"The result of the first question was the letter, so Mr. Loeb
told how both he and Mr. Leopold had framed the letter, Leopold doing the actual typing, but he, Loeb, making many suggestions as they proceeded in the writing of the letter.

"At this point Dr. Church asked: 'Did you have in mind the
Franks boy at this particular time when you were writing the
letter?' and Loeb said: 'No, any boy living on the south side
whose father had sufficient funds.' He told how Leopold's car,
red car, was too conspicuous and too showy, that they hit upon
the scheme then of renting a car, and described then their negotiations with the Rent-a-Car people.

"In the first place, he spoke about their registering at the Morrison Hotel on May 7th, and going there with a suitcase full of
books, four books in it. These books were identified at the time
Mr. Loeb was telling the story, as University of Chicago books,
library books, and the suitcase was identified as his suitcase by
himself, or the suitcase that he took there.

"That they mussed the bed up, but on May 9th found it necessary to change from the Morrison Hotel or to skip, as he expressed it, because when he went to the room he found that the suitcase was no longer there, and they simply left the hotel and made arrangements for receiving mail at the Hotel Trenier.

"The reason for this, he stated, was that they were to receive a letter from the Rent-a-Car people that would be addressed to their hotel address, and they arranged for the receipt of this, having left the Morrison Hotel for a new place to receive the letter, at the Hotel Trenier, on Oakwood Boulevard, and Grand.

"He stated also that in pursuance with the securing of the card of identification he was stationed in a little restaurant on Wabash Avenue and had assumed the name of Louis Mason, stationed near the telephone booth to receive any inquiry with reference to a Morton D. Ballard, the same name under which they had registered at the Morrison Hotel and the name they had given at the Trenier Hotel, and the name under which they had made their application for an identification card at the Rent-a-Car people, and that he was to receive an inquiry as to the standing or dependability of this Morton D. Ballard direct from the Rent-a-Car people over the phone. That he did so station himself in this restaurant, did receive the message and did give the guarantee as to dependability over the phone.

"He stated further that they had tried out this car, had gone less than twenty miles, and then did not use it again until Wednesday, the twenty-first.

"He stated that——he started then to tell about Thursday, after telling about Tuesday, because he said that was shorter and would not require so much detail and would describe the events of that day first.

"That they went downtown on an I. C. train, planted the letter.

"At two thirty called up the Yellow Cab to go to Mr. Franks and then called up Mr. Franks' residence, telling him to proceed to a certain drug store at 63rd and Blackstone. That later they went to a drug store on Stony Island Avenue and called the first drug store referred to at 63rd Street and Blackstone, inquiring for Mr. Franks. He wasn't there.

"They noticed a newspaper with the headlines on the news stand in front of the drug store, stating that a nude body had been found.

"Loeb said that they thought it was all off, but Leopold thought better of it, that they ought to try to get the money anyhow, so they made a second call at the drug store, at 63rd and Blackstone, with no result; no person by the name of Franks was there.

"Then they turned the car into the Rent-a-Car people downtown. That was their actions on Thursday that he related.

"Then he reverted to Wednesday and he stated that on Wednesday about eleven o'clock he and Leopold left the University in Leopold's red car.

"They went first to Loeb's house and then to Leopold's house, and transferred certain articles that they had in Leopold's own car to this Rent-a-Car. No, they did that later.

"They went downtown and parked Leopold's car at 14th Street and then got the Rent-a-Car and then went to Kramer's restaurant, put on the side curtains after eating lunch, and then proceeded to Leopold's house, left Leopold's car there, but transferred certain things to the Rent-a-Car they had in Leopold's car, and he named the chisel, flashlight, two rags that were used as gags, a can of ether, a bottle of acid, ropes, a lap robe.

"They went to Jackson Park and while there taped the chisel. Some discussion, then an interruption from Mr. Leopold, Mr. Leopold saying that Loeb had taped the chisel and Mr. Loeb saying that Leopold had taped it.

"At this point it was suggested by State's Attorney Crowe that Mr. Leopold make notations of any corrections he wished to make of Mr. Loeb's statement and he could present them all at once.

"He stated that after leaving Jackson Park that taping the chisel, they went to 49th and Ingleside, where they had a view of the playground of the Harvard school; that they found a couple of boys playing there; that Loeb went in and talked to two of the boys playing there, one of whom was—I think at that point—his little brother; at least, he spoke to his brother in the course of the afternoon at one of the playgrounds.

"That they went into an alley between Ellis and Ingleside; that they thought they would be noticed; and that they had better get to a more distant or remote point, so they went to Leopold's house and got a pair of field glasses, and came back so that they could have a better view of their prospects, as Loeb called them.

"They then went to another playground at 48th and Greenwood, because John Levinson, whom they had observed at the first playground, had left, and they thought he had left only for a moment, and he would come back, because Mr. Seese remained at the playground, and Mr. Seese was afterwards characterized by Mr. Loeb as a man who was a sort of playground director, or tutor—though not exactly a tutor; that he thought his first name was Eugene, but you could find out his exact name if you would go to the phone now and call up Mrs. Joseph Weisenbach, who employed Seese in some such capacity with her boy.

"That the Levinson boy did not return; that they had gone to a drug store to find the exact address on Lake Park Avenue of Levinson's people; that they went in that direction with their car and found that they did not intercept him.

"That after considerable waiting and watching at these playgrounds, and seeing some boys playing at Greenwood they were coming up Ellis Avenue and noticed Robert Franks going toward his home, south. He was just a little short of 48th Street, Mr. Loeb said.

"He said also that that was an ideal victim. He said he drove north into 48th, and made a left-hand turn, and went into great detail as to that turn, because he said that was the place where Leopold got out of the front seat and got into the back seat.

"At this point Mr. Leopold demurred, but was told to make his note. He did, however, step outside; asked Mr. Savage to step with him to the toilet, that he wanted to ask him a question, and in a moment or two they came out.

"Loeb went on with his story; that turning back into Ellis Avenue going south, he had gone just a short ways when he opened the front door, the right-hand door going south, of this car with the side curtains up, and said:

" 'Hello, Bobbie; I'll give you a lift.' The boy demurred, and said he didn't care about it, he had only a short distance to go.

"Mr. Loeb said: 'I want to ask you about the tennis racket that you had yesterday,' and then Mr. Loeb explained that a day or two prior Bobbie Franks had been playing tennis over at the Loeb home, and he had a tennis racket such as he thought would make a nice tennis racket for his, Loeb's, younger brother; that the tennis racket that Loeb's younger brother was playing with, so Loeb stated, was a heavier racket, an old one of his, and too heavy for a young boy to employ.

"With that Bobbie Franks got in on the front seat by his side.

"They turned east on 50th, and asked Franks if he would mind if they would go around the block. He said no, he wouldn't mind, or didn't care.

"Just a short distance east of Ellis on 50th, blows were struck, as Loeb said, by Leopold sitting in the back seat; several blows were struck; he did not give the number; that there was a great deal of blood, and that Leopold pulled young Franks over the back seat, dropped him on the tonneau floor, and covered him over with a rug.

"That they proceeded east on 50th Street to about Blackstone or Dorchester, he couldn't tell which, then south to the Midway, east on the Midway through the south side of Jackson Park; that he was not sure whether they went south on Jeffery or went South Shore Drive, but was pretty sure, quite positive, that it was Jeffery Avenue.

"That he remembers later of driving on Indianapolis Avenue, outside of South Chicago, and finally in a winding road, Calumet Drive, and another winding road, until they got to a blind road near a Russian Orthodox cemetery; that there they stripped the body from the waist down; took off the little pants, shoes and stockings, the belt and the buckle; that they buried certain metal portions that they knew would not burn when they tried to dispose of the other clothing. Now, there is a little matter here that I would like to speak of just before you and the attorneys, if I may, Judge, and then I can be through with that phase of it.

"It was because of this circumstance of undressing the boy just from the waist down that caused me to ask a good many questions about a certain letter that Leopold wrote to Loeb, in which it seemed to imply that there were certain homosexual practices. The natural thing, I thought, or the natural way to undress the boy is to strip his clothes off, taking his waist and other things off, but they only took the clothes off from the waist down. This letter was explained as a letter that was written out of—or as the result of a certain fellow with whom they were angry, Buckley, who had written to their fraternity over at Ann Arbor that they had taken two perverts into their fraternity, and was based on an incident that had happened at

Loeb's house at Charlevoix, when all three of them were drunk
one night, and one of them—Loeb coming back from the toilet
had gotten into bed with Leopold; that Buckley had drawn certain conclusions, and had written to Leopold's brother, or called
his attention to it, and also had written a letter to the fraternity
after they had joined over in Michigan.

"That was the occasion of my asking a great many questions
along the line of sexual perversion and homosexual practices. I
didn't want to refer to it any further here, and I simply wanted
to get rid of that phase of it.

"That it being as yet too light to make disposition of the body
of the victim, they drove around, and among other places visited
a lunch stand by the road side, and then later proceeded to the
culvert, and proceeded to carry the body in lap robe from the
car to the culvert. Loeb stated he had hold of the head and
Leopold had hold of the feet; that they carried the body, swathed
in this rug, as you would carry a stretcher; that he went first
with the head, that Leopold followed with the feet; that at the
culvert Loeb put on some hip boots; that he passed the bottle
of acid, after having first removed the cork,—he passed the bottle of acid to Leopold, who poured the acid over the face and
the eyes; that they noticed at this time that the boy was in what
Loeb styled rigor mortis; the body was stiff and the eyes were
glazed; that they let the body easily down into the culvert so
that it would not make a splash; that he went to the upper side
of the culvert where the stream or the intake flowed in, and
washed his hands, and Leopold also washed his hands; that they
came back from the culvert and proceeded to a drug store to call
up Leopold's people.

"That they made a previous call in the afternoon to a drug
store—at a drug store, the young lady who had nothing to do
with the case and her name was kept out of his statement on
that account; that Leopold made the call and when he came out

of the drug store that he said to Loeb, 'Slide over, Dick; I will drive now.' That was the first time that the word 'Dick' had been used in the course of the afternoon, as designating Loeb.

"Loeb said that he had driven all the time up to that time. That was the basis of a considerable argument to which I shall allude later when I come to Leopold's response by notes.

"That later they telephoned the Franks family, and that they mailed the letter from 55th Street in front of the substation or branch post office.

"They went to Leopold's house. That Leopold took some people, an aunt or someone else, to their home in his own car, and while there he talked with Leopold's father. That after Leopold came back they played cards a little while and they drank and then Leopold took him home.

"That covers most of the details of Wednesday. They had already recited Tuesday and Thursday.

"At this point Mr. Leopold made his first statement in the way of interruption. He stated that, 'You gentlemen will see that Loeb could not have driven the car because he could not recall to you the streets on which we drove. He stated that we were on 50th Street. He didn't know whether we turned on Dorchester, on Blackstone or Harper. But we went to the Midway and he didn't know whether we were on Jeffery or the South Shore Drive. I can tell you every street.'

"To this Loeb replied that Leopold always had a much better memory than his; that he was not concerned so much with the streets as to that particular day, but he knew all of the streets on the south side and had a general impression of them, that those were the streets, but he could not say exactly. He wanted to be positive that now he was giving an exact statement and he wanted to be right and would not mention any streets that he was not sure of.

"Leopold said that the time the blows were struck was on

50th Street, just east of Ellis, and there were exactly four blows struck.

" 'I heard them and, glancing over, saw them.' He said, 'I could not strike anybody like that on the head with a chisel. I have a certain feeling of revulsion. I deserve no special credit for it; it is an idiosyncrasy of mine, but I cannot even hit another head with a boxing glove. I have that feeling that I cannot bear to strike a human head.'

"At that point I asked him, 'Is that the only feeling of revulsion, Mr. Leopold, that you had throughout this whole transaction, bearing in mind the acid, the crime itself, and all of the details, is that the only feeling of revulsion you experienced on Wednesday?'

"He said, 'I am afraid I have to acknowledge that it is the only feeling of revulsion that I experienced.'

"He then stated that Loeb had always been a natural leader in their set. That if there were six fellows together, five of them wanted to do one thing and Loeb wanted to do the other, they always agreed in doing the thing that Loeb wanted to do. That was the result, that Loeb was a natural leader.

"At this Mr. Loeb turned and said, 'Well, I will leave it to you gentlemen to say who has the brightest mind here, I will leave it to you to judge, yourselves, from what has taken place here this afternoon as to which of the two has the brighter mind and who has the dominating mind of the two.'

"At this point Mr. Leopold started to cross-examine Mr. Loeb in some such fashion as this: 'Dick,'—and this is the second time he used the name Dick—'Dick, haven't you been always more or less interested in detective stories?' To which Mr. Loeb answered, 'Yes, and for a very good reason. The reason is this, that my studies have been along the lines of history and literature, and the outside reading that I have to do in the way of source reading in history is very tiresome, takes a lot of time, the additional reading of literature, so that when I do read for pleasure I want to read something that is entirely different, and that is the reason why I read detective stories.'

"He was then asked by Leopold if he had not been interested in a game called Detective; to which Loeb replied: 'Not always, but for the last four or five years, and I shall tell you how that came about. I have a brother nine years younger than I. Naturally he cannot enter into the same games of contests, of tennis or ball or games of that type that one of my age would indulge in, so up at Charlevoix I started the game of playing detective. We try to separate from each other and then when we would come back together each would try to tell the other how many movements of the other he had observed and witnessed, and the one who could tell the most of these movements won the game.'

"Thereupon, Leopold asked him, 'But have not you had others of us of the same age join in the same game?' He said, 'Yes, I have,' and mentioned Mr. Leopold and some others who had been in this game as a diversion.

"At this point Dr. Church turned to Leopold, and he said: 'Mr. Leopold, did you have in mind the responsibilities for your act when you kidnapped the Franks boy?' He said: 'I did,' and Dr. Church added: 'And the penalties therefor?' And Leopold said: 'I was not thinking so much of the penalty as the disgrace to my family.'

"I then asked Mr. Loeb if there was any time in the course of the plan and the transaction which culminated in the kidnapping and the murder of the boy that he could not have withdrawn from the arrangement, that he could not have backed out. He stated that he always hated a quitter, that he had no use for a coward. To a similar question Mr. Leopold made practically the same answer.

"Mr. Crowe then asked this question: 'Did you know the

difference between right and wrong when you kidnapped the Franks boy?' Mr. Loeb answered: 'Absolutely, I did.' 'Did you have the power of choice?' 'I certainly did.'

"Leopold answered in practically the same words without the use of the word 'absolutely.'

"During the course of this discussion and confession or statement of facts on these three days, as well as the six months prior, they were shown the various articles such as the shoes, the stocking, belt buckle, and identified the chisel and so on.

"After something over an hour and three quarters, an hour and a half, we proceeded to the jail yard to see the car, the rented car that had been employed, or was said to have been employed by these two defendants.

"Mr. Loeb could not or did not identify the car.

"Mr. Leopold did from an elevation in the middle of the right-hand door, a little raise with a very slight scratch.

"Loeb said that he could not do so. It was a car like that and that it had number 17 on it, but there was no number on this car.

"At this point, at the suggestion of Dr. Webster, Dr. Wesener and Dr. Hektoen, I asked Mr. Leopold whether they had used anything in scrubbing the blood or the attempt they made to scrub the blood off the car with a chemical, for the purpose of finding out whether any chemical had been used that would make it more difficult to analyze the blood stains, and asked him if they had used anything like Gold Dust or anything of that sort to cleanse off the blood stains. They said nothing, unless some gasoline may have been on the rag with which they wiped off the blood stains.

"Flashlights were set off down there, during one of which Loeb fell back or collapsed back, not to his knees, but against the wall, and was supported by the party with him, in a sort of a faint, and then he gathered himself together.

"Coming back to the State's Attorney's office, Dr. Patrick and I proceeded to make an examination, rather tersely, but an examination of these two defendants; they were both stripped.

"Inspection showed no marks or abrasions or scratches of any kind, and in the conversation they denied they had been roughly treated at any time, said the contrary, that they had been as well treated as they could be under the circumstances, that they had been allowed to communicate with their people, been allowed to have changes of linen, take a bath and so on, and they had been well treated. But I noticed one mark on Loeb's left wrist, just above the prominence of the ulna bone. It was a scab. He said that he had received it from playing baseball about ten days before the date of this examination on June 1st.

"The examination consisted of the pulse rate, examining the eyes as to their reflexes, standing with the eyes closed as to their ability to stand with the eyes closed for tremors, the protrusion of the tongue and the heart beat.

"There was absolutely no sign of any abnormality of gait or station, or anything disclosed like an organic disease of the brain, that would be disclosed by the eye reflex if it had not been normal.

"That in the main——there is a great deal more detail I could give if it was desired. I am only trying to touch on the high spots of this so-called story of the crime.

"There is a great deal I could give of that if it is desired, and if you wish it on cross examination I could give more."

"Doctor, in what light would you consider the opportunities for the examination and observation that you made in the Sate's Attorney's office on June 1st, 1924?"

"I consider them very excellent opportunities for an examination of mental condition. In certain respects they were ideal; in other respects, not so good. By being excellent, I mean they were excellent because as to the state of mind of these two defendants at the time of the examination on Sunday afternoon, they were stripped bare of all pretense, there was no posing; whatever they said and did was done spontaneously, and without any studied effort, without any defense reaction having as yet presented itself. It gave the opportunity that we seek in examining, in all mental cases, of examining a person in their most natural state of mind, just as when we are called to examine a man in business as to his mental condition, we like to take him at the most natural period instead of having him brought to an office and staged for an examination. In those respects the opportunities for learning the mental condition of these defendants were ideal."

"As a result of your examination, doctor, have you an opinion as to whether the defendant, Richard Loeb, was suffering from any mental disease on May 21st, 1924?"

"I have an opinion, yes sir."

"What is that opinion?"

"In my opinion as the result of that examination he was not suffering from any mental disease, either functional or structural, on May 21st, 1924, or on the date I examined him."

"Will you give your reasons?"

"In the first place, if we take each of the mental processes in groups, as we used to call them, faculties, sensation first, there was not any evidence or any indication of any defect of sense. Eyes, ears, all of the senses were working normally.

"With reference to memory, there was disclosed remarkable health and integrity of memory. The fact that this person could recite his fake, or alibi, story of his movements on the 21st day of May and recite it on June 1st, could recall his state of mind when he was deciding to tell the true story, that he could recall in detail the plan that had ensued from November till May 21st from the November prior, the fact that he could give not only details of the plan, details of the purchase of the different articles used in the homicide, of the place where they had each been secured and who secured them,—there was no question about memory being in any way defective or deficient.

"With reference to judgment or comparison, the comparative worth of conduct or judgment of values, judgment of situations, this man gave definite examples of having the power of judgment and comparison that was not in any wise interfered with.

"In placing himself in the front seat of the car, in his argument that the natural thing would be for him to open the front door and for the boy to get in there, he showed that he was waiting different events and making judgments as to worth or value.

"With these instances in mind of his judgment as exercised, in his recital, we know that the same judgment, the same faculty of mind, makes judgment as to other things, as to moral conditions, as to different operations, so that in these things he disclosed so many instances of a healthy judgment it shows that he has not a disease of mind affecting his judgment.

"The logical sequence of the entire story as it was related, the catching up of each thread when broken by discussion, the other party interrupting, the other party to the homicide interrupting, taking up the thread of the argument, using illustrations for the purpose of enforcing the point concerning which he made appeal to the audience, a logical sequence that is rare to find in its excellence of continuity and relations.

"Furthermore, the stream of thought flowed without any interruption or any break from within. There was not a single remark made that was beside the point. The answer to every question was responsive. There was no irresponsive answer to any question.

"There was abundant evidence that the man I have described, and I assume with reference to this answer to this question, was perfectly oriented as to time, as to place and as to his social relations. His regardfulness for the way in which it would affect his family showed that he considered those relations to his family.

"The reasoning not only was evidenced by the logical processes in which he gathered inductively certain instances and grouped them so as to bring forth a conclusion by induction processes, that he gave evidence of good reasoning by deduction.

"Not only that, there was excellence of attention; there was no diversion—diverting of his attention from the subject in hand during any part of the discussion. In fact, you take each and all of the mental faculties or the groups of mental activities as we discussed them with reference to any one, and there was not a single evidence of any defect, any disorder, any lack of development, or any disease, and by disease I mean functional as well as structural."

"And as a result of your examination on that date, have you an opinion as to whether Nathan Leopold, Jr., was suffering from any mental disease on May 21, 1924?"

"I have an opinion, yes sir."

"Will you state that opinion, please?"

"In my opinion he was not suffering from any mental disease."

The Defense Attorneys

Clarence Darrow, chief counsel for the defendants, has been practicing law for forty years. He has been identified with many prominent cases. His civil practice has been chiefly with cases against monopoly. He was chief counsel for the Anthracite Miners, in the anthracite coal strike in Pennsylvania in 1902 and 1903. He was chief counsel of Eugene V. Debs in the case of the injunction against organized labor at the time of the great railway strike in Chicago. He has always been interested on the side of organized labor. He represented the McNamara brothers in the Los Angeles Times dynamite case in 1911. He was attorney for the defendants Moyer, Haywood and Pettibone when they were tried for the murder of ex-Governor Steuneberg of Idaho. He is the author of "Farmington," a novel; "An Eye for an Eye" and various pamphlets on social, biographical and economic questions. He successfully defended Fred Lundin, indicted in Chicago for conspiracy to defraud the city, and has been connected with many other famous trials.

Benjamin Charles Bachrach was retained with Clarence Darrow and Walter Bachrach by the relatives of Richard Loeb and Nathan Leopold, Jr., the day it became known the boys had confessed.

Benjamin C. Bachrach was graduated from Notre Dame University in 1892 and afterward attended Cornell University and Columbia College, law department, in New York City. He was admitted to the bar in Chicago in June, 1896, while he was a law clerk in the office of William S. Forrest, a distinguished criminal lawyer. Though well versed in most branches of legal practice, during the last twenty years he has devoted most of his time to the practice of criminal law, especially in federal courts.

Among the important cases he has handled was that of the Rhodus brothers, who were charged in the District Court of the United States with the violation of the postal laws. Indictments were quashed by Judge Landis. In 1909 Mr. Bachrach won his first case before the Supreme Court of the United States. This was the case of Keller and Ullman, in which the Supreme Court declared the then white slave law unconstitutional.

By this decision Mr. Bachrach's clients were released from prison. In 1913 he defended Jack Johnson, champion heavyweight pugilist of the world, who was charged with the violation of the Mann act. Although there was a conviction in the District Court, the case was reversed in the United States Circuit Court of Appeals upon a writ of error brought by Mr. Bachrach. He was also attorney for Joseph Fish, an insurance adjuster, whose trial on the charge of arson lasted a long time in the Criminal Court of Cook County and finally resulted in a jury verdict of "not guilty." As the defense attorney in many criminal cases—the Kiebel, Baginski, Alderman O'Malley, Baron Curt von Biedenfeld Roder, Kracjci, Riafman, Goldberger and Morgan Breese cases—he has secured verdicts of "not guilty."

He is an able cross-examiner and has the reputation of popularity with juries. His interests in literature and philosophy are wide. His orderly mind has made him a dangerous opponent in any law suit.

Walter Bachrach is a member of the well-known law firm of Moses, Rosenthal & Kennedy, of Chicago, Illinois.

Mr. Bachrach was born in Chicago, September 13, 1885. He secured his general and legal education in the city of Chicago, and was admitted to the bar of Illinois in 1908, having previously received the degree of LL.B. He has ever since been actively engaged in the general practice of law.

For more than ten years Mr. Bachrach has made an intensive study of modern psychology, including abnormal psychology and psychiatry, and therefore is familiar with the remarkable progress of modern psychiatry. In 1921 Mr. Bachrach, with others, sponsored a visit to Chicago, of some two and a half months' duration, by Dr. Wilhelm Stekel (the internationally distinguished Viennese psychiatrist and colleague of Dr. Freud) who, by his lectures and treatments in Chicago, endeavored to make known to Americans the extraordinary progress in therapeutic methods and results obtained by renowned German and Austrian psychiatrists.

The Plea of Clarence Darrow

Your Honor, it has been almost three months since the great responsibility of this case was assumed by my associates and myself. I am willing to confess that it has been three months of great anxiety. A burden which I gladly would have been spared excepting for my feelings of affection toward some of the members of one of these unfortunate families. This responsibility is almost too great for any one to assume; but we lawyers can no more choose than the court can choose.

Our anxiety over this case has not been due to the facts that are connected with this most unfortunate affair, but to the almost unheard of publicity it has received; to the fact that newspapers all over this country have been giving it space such as they have almost never before given to any case. The fact that day after day the people of Chicago have been regaled with stories of all sorts about it, until almost every person has formed an opinion.

And when the public is interested and demands a punishment, no matter what the offense, great or small, it thinks of only one punishment, and that is death.

It may not be a question that involves the taking of human life; it may be a question of pure prejudice alone; but when the public speaks as one man it thinks only of killing.

We have been in this stress and strain for three months. We did what we could and all we could to gain the confidence of the public, who in the end really control, whether wisely or unwisely.

It was announced that there were millions of dollars to be spent on this case. Wild and extravagant stories were freely published as though they were facts. Here was to be an effort to save the lives of two boys by the use of money in fabulous amounts, amounts such as these families never even had.

We announced to the public that no excessive use of money would be made in this case, neither for lawyers nor for psychiatrists, or in any other way. We have faithfully kept that promise.

The psychiatrists, as has been shown by the evidence in this case, are receiving a per diem, and only a per diem, which is the same as is paid by the State.

The attorneys, at their own request, have agreed to take such amount as the officers of the Chicago Bar Association may think is proper in this case.

If we fail in this defense it will not be for lack of money. It will be on account of money. Money has been the most serious handicap that we have met. There are times when poverty is fortunate.

I insist, your Honor, that had this been the case of two boys of these defendants' age, unconnected with families supposed to have great wealth, there is not a State's Attorney in Illinois who would not have consented at once to a plea of guilty and a punishment in the penitentiary for life. Not one.

No lawyer could have justified any other attitude. No prosecution could have justified it.

We could have come into this court without evidence, without argument, and this court would have given to us what every judge in the City of Chicago has given to every boy in the City of Chicago since the first capital case was tried. We would have had no contest.

We are here with the lives of two boys imperiled, with the public aroused. For what?

Because, unfortunately, the parents have money. Nothing else.

I told your Honor in the beginning that never had there been a case in Chicago, where on a plea of guilty a boy under twenty-one had been sentenced to death. I will raise that age and say, never has there been a case where a human being under the age of twenty-three has been sentenced to death. And, I think I am safe in saying, although I have not examined all the records and could not—but I think I am safe in saying—that never has there been such a case in the State of Illinois.

And yet this court is urged, aye, threatened, that he must hang two boys contrary to precedents, contrary to the acts of every judge who ever held court in this state.

Why?

Tell me what public necessity there is for this.

Why need the State's Attorney ask for something that never before has been demanded?

Why need a judge be urged by every argument, moderate and immoderate, to hang two boys in the face of every precedent in Illinois, and in the face of the progress of the last fifty years?

Lawyers stand here by the day and read cases from the Dark Ages, where Judges have said that if a man had a grain of sense left and a child if he was barely out of his cradle, he could be hanged because he knew the difference between right and wrong. Death sentences for eighteen, seventeen, sixteen and fourteen years have been cited. Brother Marshall has not half done his job. He should read his beloved Blackstone again.

I have heard in the last six weeks nothing but the cry for blood. I have heard from the office of the State's Attorney only ugly hate.

I have heard precedents quoted which would be a disgrace to a savage race.

I have seen a court urged almost to the point of threats to hang two boys, in the face of science, in the face of philosophy, in the face of humanity, in the face of experience, in the face of all the better and more humane thought of the age.

Why did not my friend, Mr. Marshall, who dug up from the relics of the buried past these precedents that would bring a blush of shame to the face of a savage, read this from Blackstone:

"Under fourteen, though an infant shall be judged to be incapable of guile prima facie, yet if it appeared to the court and the jury that he was capable of guile, and could discern between good and evil, he may be convicted and suffer death."

Thus a girl thirteen has been burned for killing her mistress.

How this case would delight Dr. Krohn!

He would lick his chops over that more gleefully than over his dastardly homicidal attempt to kill these boys.

One boy of ten, and another of nine years of age, who had killed his companion were sentenced to death; and he of ten actually hanged.

Why?

He knew the difference between right and wrong. He had learned that in Sunday School.

Age does not count.

Why, Mr. Savage says age makes no difference, and that if this court should do what every other court in Illinois has done since its foundation, and refuse to sentence these boys to death, no one else would ever be hanged in Illinois.

Well, I can imagine some results worse than that. So long as this terrible tool is to be used for a plaything, without thought or consideration, we ought to get rid of it for the protection of human life.

My friend Marshall has read Blackstone by the page, as if it had something to do with a fairly enlightened age, as if it had something to do with the year 1924, as if it had something to do with Chicago, with its boys' courts and its fairly tender protection of the young.

Now, your Honor, I shall discuss that more in detail a little later, and I only say it now because my friend Mr. Savage—did you pick him for his name or his ability or his learning?—because my friend Mr. Savage, in as cruel a speech as he knew how to make, said to this court that we plead guilty because we were afraid to do anything else.

Your Honor, that is true.

It was not correct that we would have defended these boys in this court; we believe we have been fair to the public. Anyhow, we have tried, and we have tried under terribly hard conditions.

We have said to the public and to this court that neither the parents, nor the friends, nor the attorneys would want these boys released. That they are as they are. Unfortunate though it be, it is true, and those the closest to them know perfectly well that they should not be realeased, and that they should be permanently isolated from society. We have said that; and we mean it. We are asking this court to save their lives, which is the least and the most that a judge can do.

We did plead guilty before your Honor because we were afraid to submit our cause to a jury. I would not for a moment deny to this court or to this community a realization of the serious danger we were in and how perplexed we were before we took this most unusual step.

I can tell your Honor why.

I have found that years and experience with life tempers one's emotions and makes him more understanding of his fellow man.

When my friend Savage is my age, or even yours, he will read his address to this court with horror.

I am aware that as one grows older he is less critical. He is not so sure. He is inclined to make some allowance for his fellow man. I am aware that a court has more experience, more judgment and more kindliness than a jury.

Your Honor, it may be hardly fair to the court, I am aware that I have helped to place a serious burden upon your shoulders. And at that, I have always meant to be your friend. But this was not an act of friendship.

I know perfectly well that where responsibility is divided by twelve, it is easy to say:

"Away with him".

But, your Honor, if these boys hang, you must do it. There can be no division of responsibility here. You can never explain that the rest overpowered you. It must be by your deliberate, cool, premeditated act, without a chance to shift responsibility.

It was not a kindness to you. We placed this responsibility on your shoulders because we were mindful of the rights of our clients, and we were mindful of the unhappy families who have done no wrong.

Now, let us see, your Honor, what we had to sustain us. Of course, I have known your Honor for a good many years. Not intimately. I could not say that I could even guess from my experience what your Honor might do, but I did know something. I knew, your Honor, that ninety unfortunate human beings had been hanged by the neck until dead in the city of Chicago in our history. We would not have civilization except for those ninety that were hanged, and if we can not make it ninety-two we will have to shut up shop. Some ninety human being have been hanged in the history of Chicago, and of those only four have been hanged on the plea of guilty—one out of twenty-two.

I know that in the last ten years four hundred and fifty people have been indicted for murder in the city of Chicago and have plead guilty. Four hundred and fifty have pleaded guilty in the city of Chicago, and only one has been hanged!—And my friend who is prosecuting this case deserves the honor of that hanging while he was on the bench. But his victim was forty years old.

Your Honor will never thank me for unloading this responsibility upon you, but you know that I would have been untrue to my clients if I had not concluded to take this chance before a court, instead of submitting it to a poisoned jury in the city of Chicago. I did it knowing that it would be an unheard of thing for any court, no matter who, to sentence these boys to death.

And, so far as that goes, Mr. Savage is right. I hope, your Honor, that I have made no mistake.

I could have wished that the State's Attorney's office had met this case with the same fairness that we have met it.

It has seemed to me as I have listened to this case five or six times repeating the story of this tragedy, spending days to urge your Honor that a condition of mind could not mitigate, or that tender years could not mitigate, it has seemed to me that it ought to be beneath the representative of a proud state like this to invoke the dark and cruel and bloody past to affect this court and compass these boys' death.

Your Honor, I must for a moment criticize the arguments that have preceded me. I can read to you in a minute my friend Marshall's argument, barring Blackstone. But the rest of his arguments and the rest of Brother Savage's argument, I can sum up in a minute: *Cruel; dastardly; premeditated; fiendish; abandoned and malignant heart;*—sounds like a cancer—*cowardly,*—cold-blooded!

Now that is what I have listened to for three days against two minors, two children, who have no right to sign a note or make a deed.

Cowardly?

Well, I don't know. Let me tell you something that I think is cowardly, whether their acts were or not. Here is Dickie Loeb, and Nathan Leopold, and the State objects to anybody calling one "Dickie" and the other "Babe" although everybody does, but they think they can hang them easier if their names are Richard and Nathan, so, we will call them Richard and Nathan.

Eighteen and nineteen years old at the time of the homicide.

Here are three officers watching them. They are led out and in this jail and across the bridge waiting to be hanged. Not a chance to get away. Handcuffed when they get out of this room. Not a chance. Penned like rats in a trap; and for a lawyer with physiological eloquence to wave his fist in front of their faces and shout "Cowardly!" does not appeal to me as a brave act. It does not commend itself to me as a proper thing for a State's Attorney or his assistant; for even defendants not yet hanged have some rights with an official. Cold-blooded? But I don't know, your Honor. I will discuss that a little later,—whether it was cold-blooded or not.
and arranged, and fixed?

Cold-blooded? Why? Because they planned, and schemed,

Yes. But here are the officers of justice, so-called, with all the power of the State, with all the influence of the press, to fan this community into a frenzy of hate; with all of that, who for months have been planning and scheming, and contriving, and working to take these two boys' lives.

You may stand them up on the trap-door of the scaffold, and choke them to death, but that act will be infinitely more cold-blooded whether justified or not, than any act that these boys have committed or can commit.

Cold-blooded!

Let the State, who is so anxious to take these boys' lives, set an example in consideration, kindheartedness and tenderness before they call my clients cold-blooded.

I have heard this crime described; this most distressing and unfortunate homicide, as I would call it;—this cold-blooded murder, as the State would call it.

I call it a homicide particularly distressing because I am defending.

They call it a cold-blooded murder because they want to take human lives.

Call it what you will.

I have heard this case talked of, and I have heard these

lawyers say that this is the coldest-blooded murder that the civilized world ever has known. I don't know what they include in the civilized world. I suppose Illinois. Although they talk as if they did not. But we will assume Illinois. This is the most cold-blooded murder, says the State, that ever occurred.

Now, your Honor, I have been practicing law a good deal longer than I should have, anyhow, for forty-five or forty-six years, and during a part of that time I have tried a good many criminal cases, always defending. It does not mean that I am better. It probably means that I am more squeamish than the other fellows. It means neither that I am better nor worse. It means the way I am made. I can not help it.

I have never yet tried a case where the state's attorney did not say that it was the most cold-blooded, inexcusable, premeditated case that ever occurred. If it was murder, there never was such a murder. If it was robbery, there never was such a robbery. If it was a conspiracy, it was the most terrible conspiracy that ever happened since the star-chamber passed into oblivion. If it was larceny, there never was such a larceny.

Now, I am speaking moderately. All of them are the worst. Why? Well, it adds to the credit of the State's Attorney to be connected with a big case. That is one thing. They can say,—

"Well, I tried the most cold-blooded murder case that ever was tried, and I convicted them, and they are dead."

"I tried the worst forgery case that ever was tried, and I won that. I never did anything that was not big."

Lawyers are apt to say that.

And then there is another thing, your Honor: Of course, I generally try cases to juries, and these adjectives always go well with juries; bloody, cold-blooded, despicable, cowardly, dastardly, cruel, heartless,—the whole litany of the State's Attorney's office generally goes well with a jury. The twelve jurors, being good themselves, think it is a tribute to their virtue if they follow the litany of the State's Attorney.

I suppose it may have some effect with the court; I do not know. Anyway, those are the chances we take when we do our best to save life and reputation.

"Here, your clients have pleaded guilty to the most cold-blooded murder that ever took place in the history of the world. And how does a judge dare to refuse to hang by the neck until dead two cowardly ruffians who committed the coldest blooded murder in the history of the world?"

That is a good talking point.

I want to give some attention to this cold-blooded murder, your Honor.

Was it a cold-blooded murder?

Was it the most terrible murder that ever happened in the State of Illinois?

Was it the most dastardly act in the annals of crime?

No.

I insist, your Honor, that under all fair rules and measurements, this was one of the least dastardly and cruel of any that I have known anything about.

Now, let us see how we should measure it.

They say that this was a cruel murder, the worst that ever happened. I say that very few murders ever occurred that were as free from cruelty as this.

There ought to be some rule to determine whether a murder is exceedingly cruel or not.

Of course, your Honor, I admit that I hate killing, and I hate it no matter how it is done,—whether you shoot a man through the heart, or cut his head off with an axe, or kill him with a chisel or tie a rope around his neck, I hate it. I always did. I always shall.

But, there are degrees, and if I might be permitted to make my own rules I would say that if I were estimating what was the most cruel murder, I might first consider the sufferings of the victim.

Now, probably the State would not take that rule. They would say the one that had the most attention in the newspapers. In that way they have got me beaten at the start.

But I would say the first thing to consider is the degree of pain to the victim.

Poor little Bobby Franks suffered very little. There is no excuse for his killing. If to hang these two boys would bring him back to life, I would say let them go, and I believe their parents would say so, too. But:

The moving finger writes, and having writ,
Moves on; nor all your piety nor wit
Shall lure it back to cancel half a line,
Nor all your tears wash out a word of it.

Robert Franks is dead, and we cannot call him back to life. It was all over in fifteen minutes after he got into the car, and he probably never knew it or thought of it. That does not justify it. It is the last thing I would do. I am sorry for the poor boy. I am sorry for his parents. But, it is done.

Of course I cannot say with the certainty of Mr. Savage that he would have been a great man if he had grown up. At fourteen years of age I don't know whether he would or not. Savage, I suppose, is a mind reader, and he says that he would. He has a phantasy, which is hanging. So far as the cruelty to the victim is concerned, you can scarce imagine one less cruel.

Now, what else would stamp a murder as being a most atrocious crime?

First, I put the victim, who ought not to suffer; and next, I would put the attitude of those who kill.

What was the attitude of these two boys?

It may be that the State's Attorney would think that it was particularly cruel to the victim because he was a boy.

Well, my clients are boys, too, and if it would make more serious the offense to kill a boy, it should make less serious the offense of the boys who did the killing.

What was there in the conduct of these two boys which showed a wicked, malignant, and abandoned heart beyond that of anybody else, who ever lived? Your Honor, it is simply foolish.

Everybody who thinks knows the purpose of this. Counsel knows that under all the rules of the courts they have not the slightest right to ask this court to take life. Yet they urge it upon this court by falsely characterizing this as being the cruelest act that ever occurred. What about these two boys,— the second thing that would settle whether it was cruel or not?

Mr. Marshall read case after case of murders and he said: "Why, those cases don't compare with yours. Yours is worse."

Worse, why? What were those cases? Most of his cases were robbery cases,—where a man went out with a gun to take a person's money and shot him down. Some of them were cases where a man killed from spite and hatred and malice. Some of them were cases of special atrocities, mostly connected with money. A man kills someone to get money, he kills someone through hatred. What is this case?

This is a senseless, useless, purposeless, motiveless act of two boys. Now, let me see if I can prove it. There was not a particle of hate, there was not a grain of malice, there was no opportunity to be cruel except as death is cruel,—and death is cruel.

There was absolutely no purpose in it all, no reason in it all, and no motive for it all.

Now, let me see whether I am right or not.

I mean to argue this thoroughly, and it seems to me that there is no chance for a court to hesitate upon the facts in this case.

I want to try to do it honestly and plainly, and without any attempt at frills or oratory; to state the facts of this case just as the facts exist, and nothing else.

What does the State say about it?

In order to make this the most cruel thing that ever happened, of course they must have a motive. And what, do they say, was the motive?

Your Honor, if there was ever anything so foolish, so utterly futile as the motive claimed in this case, then I have never listened to it.

What did Tom Marshall say?

What did Joe Savage say?

"The motive was to get ten thousand dollars" say they.

These two boys, neither one of whom needed a cent, scions of wealthy people, killed this little inoffensive boy to get ten thousand dollars?

First let us call your attention to the opening statement of Judge Crowe, where we heard for the first time the full details of this homicide after a plea of guilty.

All right. He said these two young men were heavy gamblers, and they needed the money to pay gambling debts,—or on account of gambling.

Now, your Honor, he said this was atrocious, most atrocious, and they did it to get the money because they were gamblers and needed it to pay gambling debts.

What did he prove?

He put on one witness, and one only, who had played bridge with both of them in college, and he said they played for five cents a point.

Now, I trust your Honor knows better than I do how much of a game that would be. At poker I might guess, but I know little about bridge.

But what else?

He said that in a game one of them lost ninety dollars to the other one.

They were playing against each other, and one of them lost ninety dollars?

Ninety dollars!

Their joint money was just the same; and there is not another word of evidence in this case to sustain the statement of Mr. Crowe, who pleads to hang these boys. Your Honor, is it not trifling?

It would be trifling, excepting, your Honor, that we are dealing in human life. And we are dealing in more than that; we are dealing in the future fate of two families. We are talking of placing a blot upon the escutcheon of two houses that do not deserve it for nothing. And all that they can get out of their imagination is that there was a game of bridge and one lost ninety dollars to the other, and therefore they went out and committed murder.

What would I get if on the part of the defense we should resort to a thing like that? Could I expect anyone to have the slightest confidence in anything we have said? Your Honor knows that it is utterly absurd.

The evidence was absolutely worthless. The statement was made out of whole cloth, and Mr. Crowe felt like that policeman who came in here and perjured himself, as I will show you later on, who said that when he was talking with Nathan Leopold Jr., he told him the public were not satisfied with the motive.

I wonder if the public is satisfied with the motive? If there is any person in Chicago who under the evidence in this case would believe that this was the motive, then he is stupid. That is all I have to say for him;—just plain stupid.

But let us go further than that. Who were these two boys? And how did it happen?

On a certain day they killed poor little Robert Franks. I will not go over the paraphernalia, the letter demanding money, the ransom, because I will discuss that later in another connection. But they killed him. These two boys. They were not to get ten thousand dollars; they were to get five thousand dollars if it worked; that is, five thousand dollars each. Neither one could get more than five, and either one was risking his neck in the job. So each one of my clients was risking his neck for five thousand dollars, if it had anything to do with it, which it did not.

Did they need the money?

Why, at this very time, and a few months before, Dickie Loeb had three thousand dollars checking account in the bank. Your Honor, I would be ashamed to talk about this except that in all apparent seriousness they are asking to kill these two boys on the strength of this flimsy foolishness.

At that time Richard Loeb had a three thousand dollar checking account in the bank. He had three Liberty Bonds, one of which was past due, and the interest on each of them had not been collected for three years. I said, had not been collected; not a penny's interest had been collected,—and the coupons were there for three years. And yet they would ask to hang him on the theory that he committed this murder because he needed money, and for money.

In addition to that we brought his father's private secretary here, who swears that whenever he asked for it, he got a check, without ever consulting the father. She had an open order to give him a check whenever he wanted it, and she had sent him a check in February, and he had lost it and had not cashed it. So he got another in March.

Your Honor, how far would this kind of an excuse go on the part of the defense? Anything is good enough to dump into a pot where the public are clamouring, and where the stage is set and where loud-voiced young attorneys are talking about the sanctity of the law, which means killing people; anything is enough to justify a demand for hanging.

How about Leopold?

Leopold was in regular receipt of one hundred and twenty-five dollars a month; he had an automobile; paid nothing for board and clothes, and expenses; he got money whenever he wanted it, and he had arranged to go to Europe and had bought his ticket and was going to leave about the time he was arrested in this case.

He passed his examination for the Harvard Law School, and was going to take a short trip to Europe before it was time for him to attend the fall term. His ticket had been bought, and his father was to give him three thousand dollars to make the trip.

Your Honor, jurors sometimes make mistakes, and courts do, too. If on this evidence the court is to construe a motive out of this case, then I insist that human liberty is not safe and human life is not safe. A motive could be construed out of any set of circumstances and facts that might be imagined.

In addition to that, these boys' families were extremely wealthy. The boys had been reared in luxury, they had never been denied anything; no want or desire left unsatisfied; no debts; no need of money; nothing.

And yet they murdered a little boy, against whom they had nothing in the world, without malice, without reason, to get five thousand dollars each. All right. All right, your Honor, if the court believes it, if anyone believes it, I can't help it.

That is what this case rests on. It could not stand up a minute without motive. Without it, it was the senseless act of immature and diseased children, as it was; a senseless act of children, wandering around in the dark and moved by some emotion, that we still perhaps have not the knowledge or the insight into life to thoroughly understand.

Now, let me go on with it. What else do they claim?

I want to say to your Honor that you may cut out every expert in this case, you may cut out every lay witness in this case, you may decide this case upon the facts as they appear here alone; and there is no sort of question but what these boys were mentally diseased.

I do not know, but I do not believe that there is any man who knows this case, who does not know that it can be accounted for only on the theory of the mental disease of these two lads.

First, I want to refer to something else. Mr. Marshall argues to this court that you can do no such thing as to grant us the almost divine favor of saving the lives of two boys, that it is against the law, that the penalty for murder is death; and this court, who, in the fiction of the lawyers and the judges, forgets that he is a human being and becomes a court, pulseless, emotionless, devoid of those common feelings which alone make men; that this court as a human machine must hang them because they killed.

Now, let us see. I do not need to ask mercy from this court for these clients, nor for anybody else, nor for myself; though I have never yet found a person who did not need it.

But I do not ask mercy for these boys. Your Honor may be as strict in the enforcement of the law as you please and you cannot hang these boys. You can only hang them because back of the law and back of justice and back of the common instincts of man, and back of the human feeling for the young, is the hoarse voice of the mob which says, "Kill." I need ask nothing. What is the law of Illinois?

If one is found guilty of murder in the first degree by a jury, or if he pleads guilty before a court, the court or jury may do one of three things: he may hang; he may imprison for life; or, he may imprison for a term of not less than fourteen years. Now, why is that the law?

Does it follow from the statute that a court is bound to ascertain the impossible, and must necessarily measure the degrees of guilt? Not at all. He may not be able to do it. A court may act from any reason or from no reason. A jury may fix any one of these penalties as they separate. Why was this law passed? Undoubtedly in recognition of the growing feeling in all the forward-thinking people of the United States against capital punishment. Undoubtedly, through the deep reluctance of courts and juries to take human life.

Without any reason whatever, without any facts whatever, your Honor must make the choice, and you have the same right to make one choice as another, no matter what Mr. Justice

Blackstone says. It is your Honor's province; you may do it, and I need ask nothing in order to have you do it. There is the statute. But there is more than that in this case.

We have sought to tell this court why he should not hang these boys. We have sought to tell this court, and to make this court believe, that they were diseased of mind, and that they were of tender age. However, before I discuss that, I ought to say another word in reference to the question of motive in this case. If there was no motive, except the senseless act of immature boys, then of course there is taken from this case all of the feeling of deep guilt upon the part of these defendants.

There was neither cruelty to the deceased, beyond taking his life—which is much—nor was there any depth of guilt and depravity on the part of the defendants, for it was a truly motiveless act, without the slightest feeling of hatred or revenge, done by a couple of children for no sane reason.

But, your Honor, we have gone further than that, and we have sought to show you, as I think we have, the condition of these boys' minds. Of course it is not an easy task to find out the condition of another person's mind. These experts in the main have told you that it is impossible to ascertain what the mind is, to start with; or to tell how it acts.

I will refer later, your Honor, to the purpose of asking for the ransom which has been clearly testified to here. I simply, so far, wish to show that the money had nothing whatever to do with the homicide.

The inadequacy of it all, the risk taken for nothing, the utter lack of need, the senselessness of it all, shows that it had nothing whatever to do with this crime, and that the reason is the reason that has been given by the boys.

Now, I was about to say that it needs no expert, it needs nothing but a bare recitation of these facts, and a fair consideration of them, to convince any human being that this act was the act of diseased brains.

The state, in their usual effort to magnify and distort, to force every construction against the defendants, have spoken about this act having its inception in their going to Ann Arbor to steal a typewriter six months before.

This is on a plane par with their statement that this crime

was committed for the purpose of getting ten thousand dollars.
What is the evidence?

The getting of the typewriter in Ann Arbor had nothing to
do with this offense; not the slightest. The evidence in this
case shows that they went to Ann Arbor on the 12th day of
November. This act was committed on the 21st day of May.

They went to Ann Arbor one night, after the football game,
drove through in the night time. Nobody knew they were
going and nobody knew they had been there. They knew the
next morning that somebody had been there, because they
missed things.

They went there, under the evidence in this case, purely to
steal something from the fraternity house. I will explain the
reason for that further on. Among the rest of the things that
they took was the typewriter on which these ransom letters were
written. And yet the State with its fertile imagination says:
"Aha, these wonderful planners," who Dr. Krohn has told
you showed such great knowledge, such active brain, such consistent action, such plans and such schemes that they must be
sane. And yet a three-year-old child would not have done any
of it.

These wonderful planners foresaw that six months later they
were going to write a ransom letter to somebody, and they were
going to kill a boy; nobody knew who, or when, or where, or
how.

And in asking for a ransom they would need a machine to
write on, and so that they could not be detected they went to Ann
Arbor and stole one.

There is some evidence somewhere in this record that on
their way home from Ann Arbor they began to discuss this
question of committing a perfect crime, which had been their
phantasy for months.

The typewriter had nothing whatever to do with it, but to
make it seem that they were schemers and planners, that they
knew how to think and how to act, it is argued that they went
all the way to Ann Arbor in the night time to steal a typewriter,
instead of buying one here, or stealing one here, or getting one
here, or using their own, or advertising for one, or securing one
in any one of a hundred ways of getting a typewriter here.

Of course it is impossible on the face of it, but let us see what the evidence is. They did bring a typewriter from Ann Arbor and on that typewriter they wrote this so-called ransom letter, and after the boy had been killed they threw the type-writer into the lagoon, after twisting off the letters.

Why did they twist off the letters?

Well, I suppose anybody knows why. Because one who is fairly familiar with a typewriter knows that you can always detect the writing on almost every typewriter. There will be imperfect letters, imperfect tracking and imperfect this, that and the other, by which detection is accomplished, and probably they knew it.

But mark this: Leopold kept this typewriter in his house for six month. According to the testimony of the maid, he had written many letters on it. According to the testimony of his tutors he had written the dope sheets for his law examination on it; numbers of them. These were still in existence. The State's Attorney got them; the typewriter could be identified without the machine at all. It was identified without the machine; all that was needed was to show that the same machine that wrote the ransom letter wrote the dope sheets and wrote the other letters.

No effort was made to conceal it through all these months. All the boy's friends knew it; the maid knew it, everybody in the house knew it; letters were sent out broadcast and the dope sheets were made from it for the examination. Were they trying to conceal it? Did they take a drive in the night time to Ann Arbor, to get it, together with other stuff so that they might be tracked, or did they just get it with other stuff without any thought of this homicide that happened six months later?

The State says, in order to make out the wonderful mental processes of these two boys, that they fixed up a plan to go to Ann Arbor to get this machine, and yet when they got ready to do this act, they went down the street a few doors from their house and bought a rope; they went around the corner and bought acid; then went somewhere else nearby and bought tape; they went down to the hotel and rented a room, and then gave it up, and went to another hotel, and rented one there. And then Dick Loeb went to the hotel room, took a valise containing his library card and some books from the library, left it two days in the room, until the hotel took the valise and took the books. Then he went to another hotel and rented another room. He might just as well have sent his card with the ransom letter.

They went to the "Rent-a-Car" place and hired a car. All this clumsy machinery was gone through, without intelligence or method or rational thought. I submit, your Honor, that no one, unless he had an afflicted mind, together with youth, could possibly have done it.

But let's get to something stronger than that. Were these boys in their right minds? Here were two boys with good intellect, one eighteen and one nineteen. They had all the prospects that life could hold out for any of the young; one a graduate of Chicago and another of Ann Arbor; one who had passed his examination for the Harvard Law School and was about to take a trip in Europe,—another who had passed at Ann Arbor, the youngest in his class, with three thousand dollars in the bank. Boys who never knew what it was to want a dollar; boys who could reach any position that was given to boys of that kind to reach; boys of distinguished and honorable families, families of wealth and position, with all the world before them. And they gave it all up for nothing, for nothing! They took a little companion of one of them, on a crowded street, and killed him, for nothing, and sacrificed everything that could be of value in human life upon the crazy scheme of a couple of immature lads.

Now, your Honor, you have been a boy; I have been a boy. And we have known other boys. The best way to understand somebody else is to put yourself in his place.

Is it within the realm of your imagination that a boy who was right, with all the prospects of life before him, who could choose what he wanted, without the slightest reason in the world would lure a young companion to his death, and take his place in the shadow of the gallows?

I do not care what Dr. Krohn may say; he is liable to say anything, except to tell the truth, and he is not liable to do that. No one who has the process of reasoning could doubt that a boy who would do that is not right.

How insane they are I care not, whether medically or legally. They did not reason; they could not reason; they committed the most foolish, most unprovoked, most purposeless, most causeless act that any two boys ever committed, and they put themselves where the rope is dangling above their heads.

There are not physicians enough in the world to convince any thoughtful, fair-minded man that these boys are right. Was their act one of deliberation, of intellect, or were they driven by some force such as Dr. White and Dr. Glueck and Dr. Healy have told this court?

There are only two theories; one is that their diseased brains drove them to it; the other is the old theory of possession by devils, and my friend Marshall could have read you books on that, too, but it has been pretty well given up in Illinois.

That they were intelligent, sane, sound and reasoning is unthinkable. Let me call your Honor's attention to another thing.

Why did they kill little Bobby Franks?

Not for money, not for spite; not for hate. They killed him as they might kill a spider or a fly, for the experience. They killed him because they were made that way. Because somewhere in the infinite processes that go to the making up of the boy or the man something slipped, and those unfortunate lads sit here hated, despised, outcasts, with the community shouting for their blood.

Are they to blame for it? There is no man on earth who can mention any purpose for it all or any reason for it all. It is one of those things that happened; that happened, and it calls not for hate but for kindness, for charity, for consideration.

I heard the State's Attorney talk of mothers.

Mr. Savage is talking for the mothers, and Mr. Crowe is thinking of the mothers, and I am thinking of the mothers. Mr. Savage, with the immaturity of youth and inexperience, says that if we hang them there will be no more killing. This world has been one long slaughter house from the beginning until today, and killing goes on and on and on, and will forever. Why not read something, why not study something, why not think instead of blindly shouting for death?

Kill them. Will that prevent other senseless boys or other vicious men or vicious women from killing? No!

It will simply call upon every weak minded person to do as they have done. I know how easy it is to talk about mothers when you want to do something cruel. But I am thinking of the mothers, too. I know that any mother might be the mother of a little Bobby Franks, who left his home and went to his school, and who never came back. I know that any mother might be the mother of Richard Loeb and Nathan Leopold, just the same. The trouble is this, that if she is the mother of a Nathan Leopold or of a Richard Loeb, she has to ask herself the question,

"How came my children to be what they are? From what ancestry did they get this strain? How far removed was the poison that destroyed their lives? Was I the bearer of the seed that brings them to death?"

Any mother might be the mother of any of them. But these two are the victims. I remember a little poem that gives the soliloquy of a boy about to be hanged, a soliloquy such as these boys might make:

> "The night my father got me
>   His mind was not on me;
> He did not plague his fancy
>   To muse if I should be
>   The son you see.
>
> The day my mother bore me
>   She was a fool and glad,
> For all the pain I cost her,
>   That she had borne the lad
>   That borne she had.
>
> My father and my mother
>   Out of the light they lie;
> The warrant would not find them,
>   And here, 'tis only I
>   Shall hang so high.
>
> O let not man remember
>   The soul that God forgot,

But fetch the county sheriff
 And noose me in a knot,
 And I will rot.

And so the game is ended,
 That should not have begun.
My father and my mother
 They had a likely son,
 And I have none."

No one knows what will be the fate of the child he gets or the child she bears; the fate of the child is the last thing they consider. This weary old world goes on, begetting, with birth and with living and with death; and all of it is blind from the beginning to the end. I do not know what it was that made these boys do this mad act, but I do know there is a reason for it. I know they did not beget themselves. I know that any one of an infinite number of causes reaching back to the beginning might be working out in these boys' minds, whom you are asked to hang in malice and in hatred and injustice, because someone in the past has sinned against them.

I am sorry for the fathers as well as the mothers, for the fathers who give their strength and their lives for educating and protecting and creating a fortune for the boys that they love; for the mothers who go down into the shadow of death for their children, who nourish them and care for them, and risk their lives, that they may live, who watch them with tenderness and fondness and longing, and who go down into dishonor and disgrace for the children that they love.

All of these are helpless. We are all helpless. But when you are pitying the father and the mother of poor Bobby Franks, what about the fathers and mothers of these two unfortunate boys, and what about the unfortunate boys themselves, and what about all the fathers and all the mothers and all the boys and all the girls who tread a dangerous maze in darkness from birth to death?

Do you think you can cure it by hanging these two? Do you think you can cure the hatreds and the mal-adjustments of the world by hanging them? You simply show your ignorance and your hate when you say it. You may here and there cure hatred with love and understanding, but you can only add fuel to the flames by cruelty and hate.

What is my friend's idea of justice? He says to this court, whom he says he respects—and I believe he does—your Honor, who sits here patiently, holding the lives of these two boys in your hands:

"Give them the same mercy that they gave to Bobby Franks."

Is that the law? Is that justice? Is this what a court should do? Is this what a State's Attorney should do? If the state in which I live is not kinder, more human, more considerate, more intelligent than the mad act of these two boys, I am sorry that I have lived so long.

I am sorry for all fathers and all mothers. The mother who looks into the blue eyes of her little babe cannot help musing over the end of the child, whether it will be crowned with the greatest promises which her mind can image or whether he may meet death upon the scaffold. All she can do is to rear him with hope and trust and confidence, and to leave the rest with love and care, to watch over him tenderly, to meet life fate.

Your Honor, last night I was speaking about what is perfectly obvious in this case, that no human being could have done what these boys did, excepting through the operation of a diseased brain. I do not propose to go through each step of the terrible deed,—it would take too long. But I do want to call the attention of this court to some of the other acts of these two boys, in this distressing and weird homicide; acts which show conclusively that there could be no reason for their conduct.

I spoke about their registering at a hotel, and leaving their names behind them, without a chance to escape. I referred to these weird letters which were written and mailed after the boy was dead.

I want to come down now to the actions on the afternoon of the tragedy.

Without any excuse, without the slightest motive, not moved by money, not moved by passion or hatred, by nothing except the vague wanderings of children, they rented a machine, and about four o'clock in the afternoon started to find somebody to kill. For nothing.

They went over to the Harvard School. Dick's little brother was there, on the playground. Dick went there himself in open daylight, known by all of them, he had been a pupil there himself, the school was near his home, and he looked over the little boys.

Your Honor has been in these courts for a long time; you have listened to murder cases before. Has any such case ever appeared here or in any of the books? Has it ever come to the human experience of any judge, or any lawyer, or any person of affairs? Never once!

Ordinarily there would be no sort of question of the condition of these boys' minds. The question is raised only because their parents have money.

They first picked out a little boy named Levinson, and Dick trailed him around.

Now, of course, that is a hard story. It is a story that shocks one. A boy bent on killing, not knowing where he would go or who he would get, but seeking some victim.

Here is a little boy, but the circumstances are not opportune, and so he fails to get him.

As I think of that story of Dick trailing this little boy around, there comes to my mind a picture of Dr. Krohn; for sixteen years going in and out of the court rooms in this building and other buildings, trailing victims without regard to the name or sex or age or surroundings. But he had a motive, and his motive was cash, as I will show further. One was the mad act of a child; the other the cold, deliberate act of a man getting his living by dealing in blood.

Dick abandons that lead; Dick and Nathan are in the car, and they see Bobby Franks on the street, and they call to him to get into the car. It is about five o'clock in the afternoon, in the long summer days, on a thickly settled street, built up with homes, the houses of their friends and their companions known to everybody, automobiles appearing and disappearing, and they take him in the car—for nothing.

If there had been a question of revenge, yes; if there had been a question of hate, where no one cares for his own fate, intent only on accomplishing his end, yes. But without any motive or any reason they picked up this little boy right in sight of their own homes, and surrounded by their neighbors. They drive a little way, on a populous street, where everybody could see, where eyes might be at every window as they pass by. They hit him over the head with a chisel and kill him, and go on about their business, driving this car within half a block of Loeb's home, within the same distance of Frank's home, drive it past the neighbors that they knew, in the open highway, in broad daylight. And still men will say that they have a bright intellect, and, as Dr. Krohn puts it, can orient themselves and reason as well as he can, possibly, and it is the sane act of sane men.

I say again, whatever madness and hate and frenzy may do to the human mind, there is not a single person who reasons who can believe that one of these acts was the act of men, of brains that were not diseased. There is no other explanation for it. And had it not been for the wealth and the weirdness and the notoriety, they would have been sent to the psychopathic hospital for examination, and been taken care of, instead of the state demanding that this court take the last pound of flesh and the last drop of blood from two irresponsible lads.

They pull the dead boy into the back seat, and wrap him in a blanket, and this funeral car starts on its route.

If ever any death car went over the same route or the same kind of a route driven by sane people, I have never heard of it, and I fancy no one else has ever heard of it.

This car is driven for twenty miles. First down through thickly populated streets, where everyone knew the boys and their families, and had known them for years, till they come to The Midway Boulevard, and then take the main line of a street which is traveled more than any other street on the south side except in the loop, among automobiles that can scarcely go along on account of the number, straight down The Midway through the regular route of Jackson Park, Nathan Leopold driving this car, and Dick Loeb on the back seat, and the dead boy with him.

The slightest accident, the slightest misfortune, a bit of curiosity, an arrest for speeding, anything would bring destruction. They go down The Midway, through the park, meeting hundreds of machines, in sight of thousands of eyes, with this dead boy.

For what? For nothing! The mad acts of the fool in King Lear is the only thing I know of that compares with it. And yet doctors will swear that it is a sane act. They know better.

They go down a thickly populated street through South Chicago, and then for three miles take the longest street to go through this city; built solid with business, buildings, filled with automobiles backed upon the street, with street cars on the track, with thousands of peering eyes; one boy driving and the other on the back seat, with the corpse of little Bobby Franks, the blood streaming from him, wetting everything in the car.

And yet they tell me that this is sanity; they tell me that the brains of these boys are not diseased. You need no experts, you need no X-rays; you need no study of the endocrines. Their conduct shows exactly what it was, and shows that this court has before him two young men who should be examined in a psychopathic hospital and treated kindly and with care. They get through South Chicago, and they take the regular automobile road down toward Hammond. There is the same situation; hundreds of machines; any accident might encompass their ruin. They stop at the forks of the road, and leave little Bobby Franks, soaked with blood, in the machine, and get their dinner, and eat it without an emotion or a qualm.

Your Honor, we do not need to believe in miracles; we need not resort to that in order to get blood. If it were any other case, there could not be a moment's hesitancy as to what to do.

I repeat, you may search the annals of crime, and you can find no parallel. It is utterly at variance with every motive and every act and every part of conduct that influences normal people in the commission of crime. There is not a sane thing in all of this from the beginning to the end. There was not a normal act in any of it, from its inception in a diseased brain, until today, when they sit here awaiting their doom.

But we are told that they planned. Well, what does that mean? A maniac plans, an idiot plans; an animal plans; any brain that functions may plan; but their plans were the diseased plans of the diseased mind. Do I need to argue it? Does anybody need to more than glance at it? Is there any man with a fair intellect and a decent regard for human life, and the slightest bit of heart that does not understand this situation?

And still, your Honor, on account of its weirdness and its strangeness, and its advertising, we are forced to fight. For what? Forced to plead to this court that two boys, one eighteen and the other nineteen, may be permitted to live in silence and solitude and disgrace and spend all their days in the penitentiary. Asking this court and the State's Attorney to be merciful enough to let these two boys be locked up in a prison until they die.

I sometimes wonder if I am dreaming. If in the first quarter of the twentieth century there has come back into the hearts of men, the hate and feeling and the lust for blood which possesses the primitive savage of barbarous lands.

What do they want? Tell me, is a life time for the young boys spent behind prison bars,—is that not enough for this mad act? And is there any reason why this great public should be regaled by a hanging?

I can not understand it, your Honor. It would be past belief, excepting that to the four corners of the earth the news of this weird act has been carried and men have been stirred, and the primitive has come back, and the intellect has been stifled, and men have been controlled by feelings and passions and hatred which should have died centuries ago.

My friend Savage pictured to you the putting of this dead boy in this culvert. Well, no one can minutely describe any killing and not make it shocking. It is shocking. It is shocking because we love life and because we instinctively draw back from death. It is shocking wherever it is and however it is, and perhaps all death is almost equally shocking.

But here is the picture of a dead boy, past pain, when no harm can come to him, put in a culvert, after taking off his clothes so that the evidence would be destroyed; and that is pictured to this court as a reason for hanging. Well, your Honor, that does not appeal to me as strongly as the hitting over the head of little Robert Franks with a chisel. The boy was dead.

I could say something about the death penalty that, for some mysterious reason, the state wants in this case. Why do they want it? To vindicate the law? Oh, no. The law can be vindicated without killing anyone else. It might shock the fine sensibilities of the state's counsel that this boy was put into a culvert and left after he was dead, but, your Honor, I can think of a scene that makes this pale into insignificance. I can think, and only *think,* your Honor, of taking two boys, one eighteen and the other nineteen, irresponsible, weak, diseased, penning them in a cell, checking off the days and the hours and the minutes, until they will be taken out and hanged. Wouldn't it be a glorious day for Chicago? Wouldn't it be a glorious triumph for the State's Attorney? Wouldn't it be a glorious triumph for justice in this land? Wouldn't it be a glorious illustration of Christianity and kindness and charity? I can picture them, wakened in the gray light of morning, furnished a suit of clothes by the state, led to the scaffold, their feet tied, black caps drawn over their heads, stood on a trap door, the hangman pressing a spring, so that it gives way under them; I can see them fall through space—and—stopped by the rope around their necks.

This would surely expiate placing Bobbie Franks in the culvert after he was dead. This would doubtless bring immense satisfaction to some people. It would bring a greater satisfaction because it would be done in the name of justice. I am always suspicious of righteous indignation. Nothing is more cruel than righteous indignation. To hear young men talk glibly of justice. Well, it would make me smile if it did not make me sad. Who knows what it is? Does Mr. Savage know? Does Mr. Crowe know? Do I know? Does your Honor know? Is there any human machinery for finding it out? Is there any man can weigh me and say what I deserve? Can your Honor? Let us be honest. Can your Honor appraise yourself, and say what you deserve? Can your Honor appraise these two young men and say what they deserve? Justice must take account of infinite circumstances which a human being cannot understand.

If there is such a thing as justice it could only be administered by one who knew the inmost thoughts of the man to whom they were meting it out. Aye, who knew the father and mother and the grandparents and the infinite number of people back of him? Who knew the origin of every cell that went into the body, who could understand the structure, and how it acted? Who could tell how the emotions that sway the human being affected that particular frail piece of clay? It means more than that. It means that you must appraise every influence that moves them, the civilization where they live, and all society which enters into the making of the child or the man! If your Honor can do it—if you can do it you are wise, and with wisdom goes mercy.

No one with wisdom and with understanding, no one who is honest with himself and with his own life whoever he may be, no one who has seen himself the prey and the sport and the plaything of the infinite forces that move man, no one who has tried and who has failed,—and we have all tried and we have all failed,—no one can tell what justice is for someone else or for himself—and the more he tries and the more responsibility he takes the more he clings to mercy as being the one thing which he is sure should control his judgment of men.

It is not so much mercy either, your Honor. I can hardly understand myself pleading to a court to visit mercy on two boys by shutting them into a prison for life.

For life! Where is the human heart that would not be satisfied with that?

Where is the man or woman who understands his own life and who has a particle of feeling that could ask for more. Any cry for more, roots back to the hyena; it roots back to the hissing serpent; it roots back to the beast and the jungle. It is not a part of man. It is not a part of that feeling which, let us hope, is growing, though scenes like this sometimes make me doubt that it is growing; it is not a part of that feeling of mercy and pity and understanding of each other which we believe has been slowly raising man from his low estate. It is not a part of the finer instincts which are slow to develop; of the wider knowledge which is slow to come, and slow to move us when it comes. It is not a part of all that makes the best there is in man. It is not a part of all that promises any hope for the future and any justice for the present. And must I ask that these boys get mercy by spending the rest of their lives in prison, year following year, month following month, and day following day, with nothing to look forward to but hostile guards and stone walls? It ought not to be hard to get that much mercy in any court in the year 1924. These boys left this body down in the culvert and they came back; telephoned, first;—telephoned home that they would be too late for supper. Here, surely, was an act of consideration on the part of Leopold, telephoning home that he would be late for supper. Dr. Krohn says he must be able to think and act because he could do this. But the boy who through habit would telephone his home that he would be late for supper had not a tremor or a thought or a shudder at taking the life of little Bobby Franks for nothing, and he has not had one yet. He was in the habit of doing what he did, when he telephoned,—that was all; but in the presence of life and death, and a cruel death, he had no tremor, and no thought.

They came back. They got their dinner. They parked the bloody automobile in front of Leopold's house. They cleaned it to some extent that night and left it standing in the street in front of their home.

"Oriented," of course. "Oriented." They left it there for the night, so that anybody might see and might know. They took it into the garage the next day and washed it, and then poor little Dickie Loeb—I shouldn't call him Dickie, and I shouldn't call him poor, because that might be playing for sympathy, and you have no right to ask for sympathy in this world: You should ask for justice, whatever that may be; and only State's Attorneys know.

And then in a day or so we find Dick Loeb with his pockets stuffed with newspapers telling of the Franks tragedy. We find him consulting with his friends in the club, with the newspaper reporters; and my experience is that the last person that a conscious criminal associates with is a reporter. He even shuns them more than he does a detective, because they are smarter and less merciful. But he picks up a reporter, and he tells him he has read a great many detective stories, and he knows just how this would happen and that the fellow who telephoned must have been down on 63rd Street, and the way to find him is to go down on 63rd street and visit the drug stores, and he would go with him.

And Dick Loeb pilots reporters around the drug stores where the telephoning was done, and he talks about it, and he takes the newspapers, and takes them with him, and he is having a glorious time. And yet he is "perfectly oriented," in the language of Dr. Krohn. "Perfectly oriented." Is there any question about the condition of his mind? Why was he doing it? He liked to hear about it. He had done something that he could not boast of directly, but he did want to hear other people talk about it, and he looked around there, and helped them find the place where the telephone message was sent out.

Your Honor has had experience with criminals and you know how they act. Was any such thing as this ever heard of before on land or sea? Does not the man who knows what he is doing, who for some reason has been overpowered and commits what is called a crime, keep as far away from it as he can? Does he go to the reporters and help them hunt it out? There is not a single act in this case that is not the act of a diseased mind, not one.

Talk about scheming. Yes, it is the scheme of disease; it is the scheme of infancy; it is the scheme of fools; it is the scheme of irresponsibility from the time it was conceived until the last act in the tragedy. And yet we have to talk about it, and argue about it, when it is obvious to anyone who cares to know the truth. But they must be hanged, because everybody is talking about the case, and their people have money. Am I asking for much in this case? Let me see for a moment now. Is it custo-Attorney? Do they not give you something on a plea of guilty? mary to get anything on a plea of guilty? How about the State's How many times has your honor listened to the State's Attorney come into this court, with a man charged with robbery with a gun, which means from ten years to life, and on condition of a plea of guilty, ask to have the gun charge stricken out, and get a sentence of three to twenty years, with a chance to see daylight inside of three years? How many times? How many times has the State's Attorney himself asked consideration for everything including murder, not only for the young, but even the old? How many times have they come into this court, and into every court, not only here but everywhere, and asked for it? Your honor knows. I will guarantee that three times out of four in criminal cases, and much more than that in murder, ninety-nine times out of one hundred, and much more than that; I would say not twice in a thousand times has the state failed to give consideration to the defendant on a plea.

How many times has your honor been asked to change a sentence, and not hold a man guilty of robbery with a gun, and give him a chance on a plea of guilty—not a boy but a man?

How many times have others done it, and over and over and over again? And it will be done so long as justice is fairly administered; and in a case of a charge of robbery with a gun, coupled with larceny, how many times have both the robbery and the gun been waived, and a plea of larceny made, so that the defendant might be released in a year?

How many times has all of it been waived, and the defendant given a year in the bridewell? Many and many a time because they are boys,—and youth has terrible responsibilities, and youth should have advantages; and with sane and humane people, youth, the protection of childhood, is always one of the first concerns of the state. It is one of the first in the human heart, and it is one of the first in the human mind.

How many times has rape been changed to assault, and the defendant given a year, or even a Bridewell sentence? How many times has mercy come even from the State's Attorney's office? I am not criticizing. It should come and I am telling this court what this court knows. And yet forsooth, for some reason, here is a case of two immature boys of diseased mind, as plain as the light of day, and they say you can get justice only by shedding their last drop of blood!

Why? I can ask the question easier than I can answer it. Why? It is unheard of, unprecedented in this court, unknown among civilized men. And yet this court is to make an example or civilization will fail. I suppose civilization will survive if your Honor hangs them. But it will be a terrible blow that you shall deal. Your Honor will be turning back over the long, long road we have traveled. You will be turning back from the protection of youth and infancy. Your Honor would be turning back from the treatment of children. Your Honor would be turning back to the barbarous days which Brother Marshall seems to love, when they burned people thirteen years of age. You would be dealing a staggering blow to all that has been done in the City of Chicago in the last twenty years for the protection of infancy and childhood and youth.

And for what? Because the people are talking about it.

Nothing else. It would not mean, your Honor, that your reason was convinced. It would mean in this land of ours, where talk is cheap, where newspapers are plenty, where the most immature expresses his opinion, and the more immature the stronger, that a court couldn't help feeling the great pressure of the public opinion which they say exists in this case.

Coming alone in this court room with obscure defendants, doing what has been done in this case, coming with the outside world shut off, as in most cases, and saying to this court and counsel:

"I believe that these boys ought not to be at large, I believe they are immature and irresponsible, and I am willing to enter a plea of guilty and let you sentence them to life imprisonment," how long do you suppose your Honor would hesitate? Do you suppose the State's Attorneys would raise their voices in protest?

You know it has been done too many times. And here for the first time, under these circumstances, this court is told that you must make an example.

Let us take some other cases. How many times has a defendant come into this court charged with burglary and larceny, and because of youth or because of something else the State's Attorney has waived the burglary, and consented to a year for larceny; no more than that.

Let me ask this question.

How many times, your Honor, have defendants come into this court—and I am not speaking of your Honor's court alone; I am speaking of all the criminal courts in this country—have defendants come in charged with a burglary and larceny and been put on parole, told to go and sin no more, given another chance? It is true in almost all cases of the young, except for serious aggravation.

Can you administer law without consideration? Can you administer what approaches justice without it? Can this court or any court administer justice by consciously turning his heart to stone and being deaf to all the finer instincts which move men? Without those instincts I wonder what would happen to the human race?

If a man could judge a fellow in coldness without taking

account of his own life, without taking account of what he knows of human life, without some understanding,—how long would we be a race of real human beings? It has taken the world a long time for man to get to even where he is today. If the law was administered without any feeling of sympathy or humanity or kindliness, we would begin our long, slow journey back to the jungle that was formerly our home.

How many times has assault with intent to rob or kill been changed in these courts to assault and battery? How many times has felony been waived in assault with a deadly weapon and a man or a boy given a chance? And we are asking a chance to be shut up in stone walls for life. For life. It is hard for me to think of it, but that is the mercy we are asking from this court, which we ought not to be required to ask, and which we should have as a matter of right in this court and which I have faith to believe we will have as a matter of right.

Is this new? Why, I undertake to say that even the State's Attorney's office, and if he denies it I would like to see him bring in the records—I will undertake to say that in three cases out of four of all kinds and all degrees, clemency has been shown.

Three hundred and forty murder cases in ten years with a plea of guilty in this county. All the young who pleaded guilty —every one of them, three hundred and forty in ten years with one hanging on a plea of guilty, and that a man forty years of age. And yet they say we come here with a preposterous plea for mercy. When did any plea for mercy become preposterous in any tribunal in all the universe?

We are satisfied with justice, if the court knows what justice is, or if any human being can tell what justice is. If anybody can look into the minds and hearts and the lives and the origin of these two youths and tell what justice is, we would be content. But nobody can do it without imagination, without sympathy, without kindliness, without understanding, and I have faith that this court will take this case, with his conscience, and his judgment and his courage and save these boys' lives.

Now, your honor, let me go a little further with this. I have gone over some of the high spots in this tragedy. This tragedy has not claimed all the attention it has had on account of its atrocity. There is nothing to that. Why is it? There are two reasons, and only two that I can see. First is the reputed extreme wealth of these families; not only the Loeb and Leopold families, but the Franks family, and of course it is unusual. And next is the fact it is weird and uncanny and motiveless. That is what attracted the attention of the world. Many may say now that they want to hang these boys; but I know that giving the people blood is something like giving them their dinner. When they get it they go to sleep. They may for the time being have an emotion, but they will bitterly regret it. And I undertake to say that if these two boys are sentenced to death, and are hanged on that day there will be a pall settle over the people of this land that will be dark and deep, and at least cover every humane and intelligent person with its gloom. I wonder if it will do good. I wonder if it will help the children—and there is an infinite number like these. I marveled when I heard Mr. Savage talk. I do not criticize him. He is young and enthusiastic. But has he ever read anything? Has he ever thought? Was there ever any man who had studied science, who has read anything of criminology or philosophy,—was there ever any man who knew himself who could speak with the assurance with which he speaks?

What about this matter of crime and punishment, anyhow? I may know less than the rest, but I have at least tried to find out, and I am fairly familiar with the best literature that has been written on that subject in the last hundred years. The more men study, the more they doubt the effect of severe punishment on crime. And yet Mr. Savage tells this court that if these boys are hanged, there will be no more murder.

Mr. Savage is an optimist. He says that if the defendants are hanged there will be no more boys like these.

I could give him a sketch of punishment, punishment beginning with the brute which killed something because something hurt it; the punishment of the savage; if a person is injured in the tribe, they must injure somebody in the other tribe; it makes no difference who it is, but somebody. If one is killed his friends or family must kill in return.

You can trace it all down through the history of man. You can trace the burnings, the boilings, the drawings and quarter-

ings, the hanging of people in England at the crossroads, carving
them up and hanging them as examples for all to see.

We can come down to the last century when nearly two hundred crimes were punishable by death, and by death in every
form; not only hanging—that was too humane—but burning,
boiling, cutting into pieces, torturing in all conceivable forms.

You can read the stories of the hangings on a high hill, and
the populace for miles around coming out to the scene, that
everybody might be awed into goodness. Hanging for picking
pockets—and more pockets were picked in the crowd that went
to the hanging than had been known before. Hangings for
murder—and men were murdered on the way there and on the
way home. Hangings for poaching, hangings for everything and
hangings in public, not shut up cruelly and brutally in a jail,
out of the light of day, wakened in the night time and led
forth and killed, but taken to the shire town on a high hill, in
the presence of a multitude, so that all might see that the wages
of sin were death.

What happened? I have read the life of Lord Shaftesbury, a
great nobleman of England, who gave his life and his labors
toward modifying the penal code. I have read of the slow,
painful efforts through all the ages for more humanity of man
to his fellowman. I know what history says, I know what it
means, and I know what flows from it, so far as we can tell,
which is not with certainty.

I know that every step in the progress of humanity has been
met and opposed by prosecutors, and many times by courts. I
know that when poaching and petty larceny was punishable by
death in England, juries refused to convict. They were too
humane to obey the law; and judges refused to sentence. I
know that when the delusion of witchcraft was spreading over
Europe, claiming its victims by the millions, many a judge so
shaped his cases that no crime of witchcraft could be punished
in his court. I know that these trials were stopped in America
because juries would no longer convict. I know that every
step in the progress of the world in reference to crime has come
from the human feelings of man. It has come from that deep
well of sympathy, that in spite of all our training and all our
conventions and all our teaching, still lives in the human

breast. Without it there could be no human life on this weary old world.

Gradually the laws have been changed and modified, and men look back with horror at the hangings and the killings of the past. What did they find in England? That as they got rid of these barbarous statutes crimes decreased instead of increased; as the criminal law was modified and humanized, there was less crime instead of more. I will undertake to say, your Honor, that you can scarcely find a single book written by a student— and I will include all the works on criminology of the past— that has not made the statement over and over again that as the penal code was made less terrible, crimes grew less frequent.

Now let us see a little about the psychology of man. It is easy, your Honor. Anybody can understand it if he just looks into himself. This weird tragedy occurred on the 21st of May. It has been heralded broadcast through the world. How many attempted kidnappings have come since then? How many threatening letters have been sent out by weak minded boys and weak minded men since then? How many times have they sought to repeat again and again this same crime because of the effect of publicity upon the mind? I can point to examples of killing and hanging in the city of Chicago which have been repeated in detail over and over again, simply from the publicity of the newspapers and the public generally.

Let us take this case. Let's see whether we can guess about it. Still it is not a guess.

If these two boys die on the scaffold, which I can never bring myself to imagine,—if they do die on the scaffold, the details of this will be spread over the world. Every newspaper in the United States will carry a full account. Every newspaper of Chicago will be filled with the gruesome details. It will enter every home and every family.

Will it make men better or make men worse? I would like to put that to the intelligence of man, at least such intelligence as they have. I would like to appeal to the feelings of human beings so far as they have feelings,—would it make the human heart softer or would it make hearts harder? How many men would be colder and crueler for it? How many men would enjoy the details, and you cannot enjoy human suffering without being affected for better or for worse; those who enjoyed it would be affected for the worse.

What influence would it have upon the millions of men who will read it? What influence would it have upon the millions of women who will read it, more sensitive, more impressionable, more imaginative than men? Would it help them if your Honor should do what the state begs you to do? What influence would it have upon the infinite number of children who will devour its details as Dicky Loeb has enjoyed reading detective stories? Would it make them better or would it make them worse? The question needs no answer. You can answer it from the human heart. What influence, let me ask you, will it have for the unborn babes still sleeping in their mother's womb? And what influence will it have on the psychology of the fathers and mothers yet to come? Do I need to argue to your Honor that cruelty only breeds cruelty?—that hatred only causes hatred; that if there is any way to soften this human heart which is hard enough at its best, if there is any way to kill evil and hatred and all that goes with it, it is not through evil and hatred and cruelty; it is through charity, and love and understanding.

How often do people need to be told this? Look back at the world. There is not a man who is pointed to as an example to the world who has not taught it. There is not a philosopher, there is not a religious leader, there is not a creed that has not taught it. This is a Christian community, so-called at least it boasts of it, and yet they would hang these boys in a Christian community. Let me ask this court, is there any doubt about whether these boys would be safe in the hands of the founder of the Christian religion? It would be blasphemy to say they would not. Nobody could imagine, nobody could even think of it. And yet there are men who want to hang them for a childish, purposeless act, conceived without the slightest malice in the world.

Your Honor, I feel like apologizing for urging it so long. It is not because I doubt this court. It is not because I do not know something of the human emotions and the human heart. It is not that I do not know that every result of logic, every page of history, every line of philosophy and religion, every precedent in this court, urges this court to save life. It is not that. I have become obsessed with this deep feeling of hate and anger that has swept across this city and this land. I have been fighting it, battling with it, until it has fairly driven me mad, until I sometimes wonder whether every righteous human emotion has not gone down in the raging storm.

I am not pleading so much for these boys as I am for the infinite number of others to follow, those who perhaps cannot be as well defended as these have been, those who may go down in the storm, and the tempest, without aid. It is of them I am thinking, and for them I am begging of this court not to turn backward toward the barbarous and cruel past.

Now, your Honor, who are these two boys?

Leopold, with a wonderfully brilliant mind; Loeb, with an unusual intelligence;—both from their very youth, crowded like hot-house plants, to learn more and more and more. Dr. Krohn says that they are intelligent. In spite of that, it is true:— they are unusually intelligent. But it takes something besides brains to make a human being who can adjust himself to life.

In fact, as Dr. Church and as Dr. Singer regretfully admitted, brains are not the chief essential in human conduct. There is no question about it. The emotions are the urge that make us live; the urge that makes us work or play, or move along the pathways of life. They are the instinctive things. In fact, intellect is a late development of life. Long before it was evolved, the emotional life kept the organism in existence until death. Whatever our action is, it comes from the emotions, and nobody is balanced without them.

The intellect does not count so much. Let me call the attention of the court to two or three cases. Four or five years ago the world was startled by a story about a boy of eleven, the youngest boy ever turned out at Harvard, who had studied everything on earth and understood it; he was simply a freak. He went through Harvard much younger than anybody else. All questions of science and philosophy he could discuss with the most learned. How he got it nobody knows. It was prophesied that he would have a brilliant future. I do not know his name, and it is not necessary. In a short time the fire had burned out. He was a prodigy, with nothing but this marvelous brain power, which nobody understood or could understand. He was an intellectual freak. He never was a boy; he never will be a completed normal man. Harvard had another of the same kind some years before, unbalanced, impossible,—an intellectual machine. Nature works in mysterious ways. We have all read of Blind Tom, who was an idiot, and yet a marvelous musician. He never could understand music, and he never did understand it; he never knew anything about it; and yet he could go to the piano and play so well that people marveled and wondered. How it comes nobody can explain.

The question of intellect means the smallest part of life. Back of this are man's nerves, muscles, heart, blood, lungs— in fact, the whole organism; the brain is the least part in human development. Without the emotion-life man is nothing. How is it with these two boys? Is there any question about them?

I insist there is not the slightest question about it. All teaching and all training appeals, not only to the inellectual, but to emotional life. A child is born with no ideas of right and wrong, just with plastic brain, ready for such impressions as come to it, ready to be developed. Lying, stealing, killing are not wrong to the child. These mean nothing.

Gradually his parents and his teachers tell him things, teach him habits, show him that he may do this and he may not do that, teach him the difference between his and mine. No child knows this when he is born. He knows nothing about property or property rights. They are given to him as he goes along. He is like the animal that wants something and goes out and gets it, kills it, operating purely from instinct, without training.

The child is gradually taught, and habits are built up. These habits are supposed to be strong enough so that they will form inhibitions against conduct when the emotions come in conflict with the duties of life. Dr. Singer and Dr. Church, both of them, admitted exactly what I am saying now. The child of himself knows nothing about right and wrong, and the teachings built up give him habits, so he will be able to control certain instincts that surge upon him, and which surge upon everyone who lives. If the instinct is strong enough and the habit weak enough, the habit goes down before it. Both of these eminent men admit it. There can be no question about it. His conduct depends upon the relative strength of the instinct and the habit that has been built up.

Education means fixing these habits so deeply in the life of man that they stand him in stead when he needs them to keep him in the path,—and that is all it does mean. Suppose one sees a thousand dollar bill and nobody present. He may have the impulse to take it. If he does not take it, it will be because his emotional nature revolts at it, through habit and through training. If the emotional nature does not revolt at it he will do it. That is why people do not commit what we call crime; that, and caution. All education means is the building of habits so that certain conduct revolts you and stops you, saves you; but without an emotional nature you cannot do that. Some are born practically without it.

How about this case?

The state put on three alienists and Dr. Krohn. Two of them, Dr. Patrick and Dr. Church are undoubtedly able men. One of them, Dr. Church, is a man whom I have known for thirty years, and for whom I have the highest regard.

On Sunday, June 1st, before any of the friends of these boys or their counsel could see them, while they were in the care of the State's Attorney's office, they brought them in to be examined by these alienists. I am not going to discuss that in detail as I may later on. Dr. Patrick said this:

The only thing unnatural he noted about it was that they had no emotional reactions. Dr. Church said the same. These are their alienists, not ours. These boys could tell this gruesome story without a change of countenance, without the slightest feelings. There were no emotional reactions to it. What was the reason? I do not know. How can I tell why? I know what causes the emotional life. I know it comes from the nerves, the muscles, the endocrine glands, the vegetative system. I know it is the most important part of life. I know it is practically left out of some. I know that without it men cannot live. I know that without it they cannot act with the rest. I know they cannot feel what you feel and what I feel; that they cannot feel the moral shocks which come to men who are educated and who have not been deprived of an emotional system or emotional feelings. I know it, and every person who has honestly studied this subject knows it as well. Is Dickey Loeb to blame because out of the infinite forces that conspired to form him, the infinite forces that were at work producing him ages before he was born, that because out of these infinite combinations he was born without it? If he is, then there should be a new definition for justice. Is he to blame for what he did not have and never had? Is he to blame that his machine is imperfect? Who is to blame? I do not know. I have never in my life been interested so much in fixing blame as I have in relieving people from blame. I am not wise enough to fix it. I know that somewhere in the past that entered into him something missed. It may be defective nerves. It may be a defective heart or liver. It may be defective endocrine glands. I know it is something. I know that nothing happens in this world without a cause.

I know, your Honor, that if you, sitting here in this court, and in this case, had infinite knowledge you could lay your fingers on it, and I know you would not visit it on Dickey Loeb. I asked Dr. Church and I asked Dr. Singer whether, if they were wise enough to know, they could not find the cause, and both of them said yes. I know that they are just as they are, and that they did not make themselves. There are at least two theories of man's responsibility. There may be more. There is the old theory that if a man does something it is because he wilfully, purposely, maliciously and with a malignant heart sees fit to do it. And that goes back to the possession of man by devils. The old indictments used to read that a man being possessed of a devil did so and so. But why was he possessed with the devil? Did he invite him in? Could he help it? Very few half-civilized people believe that doctrine any more. Science has been at work, humanity has been at work, scholarship has been at work, and intelligent people now know that every human being is the product of the endless heredity back of him and the infinite environment around him. He is made as he is and he is the sport of all that goes before him and is applied to him, and under the same stress and storm, you would act one way and I act another, and poor Dickey Loeb another.

Dr. Church said so and Dr. Singer said so, and it is the truth.

Take a normal boy, your Honor. Do you suppose he could have taken a boy into an automobile without any reason and hit him over the head and killed him? I might just as well ask you whether you thought the sun could shine at midnight in this latitude. It is not a part of normality. Something was wrong. I am asking your Honor not to visit the grave and dire and terrible misfortunes of Dickey Loeb and Nathan Leopold upon these two boys. I do not know where to place it. I know it is somewhere in the infinite economy of nature, and if I were wise enough I could find it. I know it is there, and to say that because they are as they are you should hang them, is brutality and cruelty, and savors of the fang and claw.

There can be no question on the evidence in this case. Dr. Church and Dr. Patrick both testified that these boys have no emotional reactions in reference to this crime. Every one of the alienists on both sides has told this court, what no doubt this court already knew, that the emotions furnish the urge and the drive to life. A man can get along without his intellect, and most people do, but he cannot get along without his emotions. When they did make a brain for man, they did not make it good enough to hurt, because emotions can still hold sway. He eats and he drinks, he works and plays and sleeps, in obedience to his emotional system. The intellectual part of man acts only as a judge over his emotions, and then he generally gets it wrong, and has to rely on his instincts to save him.

These boys—I do not care what their mentality—that simply makes it worse—are emotionally defective. Every single alienist who has testified in this case has said so. The only person who did not was Dr. Krohn. While I am on that subject, lest I forget the eminent doctor, I want to refer to one or two things. In the first place, all these alienists that the State called came into the State's Attorney's office and heard these boys tell their story of this crime, and that is all they heard.

Now, your Honor is familiar with Chicago the same as I am, and I am willing to admit right here and now that the two ablest alienists in Chicago are Dr. Church and Dr. Patrick. There may be abler ones, but we lawyers do not know them.

And I will go further: If my friend Crowe had not got to them first, I would have tried to get them. There is no ques-

tion about it at all. I said I would have tried to; I didn't say
I would, and yet I suspect I would. And I say that, your Honor,
without casting the slightest reflection on either of them, for I
really have a high regard for them, and aside from that a deep
friendship for Dr. Church. And, I have considerable regard
for Dr. Singer. I will go no further now.

We could not get them, and Mr. Crowe was very wise, and
he deserves a great deal of credit for the industry, the research
and the thoroughness that he and his staff have used in detecting
this terrible crime.

He worked with intelligence and rapidity. If here and there
he trampled on the edges of the constitution I am not going to
talk about it here. If he did it, he is not the first one in that
office and probably will not be the last who will do it, so let
that go. A great many people in this world believe the end
justifies the means. I don't know but that I do myself. And
that is the reason I never want to take the side of the prosecution, because I might harm an individual. I am sure the State
will live anyhow.

On that Sunday afternoon before we had a chance, he got in
two alienists, Church and Patrick, and also called Dr. Krohn,
and they sat around hearing these boys tell their stories, and that
is all.

Your Honor, they were not holding an examination. They
were holding an inquest, and nothing else. It has not the slightest reference to, or earmarks of, an examination for sanity. It
was just an inquest; a little premature, but still an inquest.

What is the truth about it? What did Patrick say? He said
that it was not a good opportunity for examination. What did
Church say? I read from his own book what was necessary
for an examination, and he said that it was not a good opportunity for an examination. What did Krohn say? "Fine—a
fine opportunity for an examination," the best he had ever
heard of, or that ever anybody had, because, their souls were
stripped naked. Krohn is not an alienist. He is an orator. He
said, because their souls were naked to them. Well, if Krohn's
was naked, there would not be much to show. But Patrick and
Church said that the conditions were unfavorable for an examination, that they never would choose it, that their opportu-

nities were poor. And yet Krohn states the contrary—Krohn, who by his own admissions, for sixteen years has not been a physician, but has used a license for the sake of haunting these courts, civil and criminal, and going up and down the land peddling perjury. He has told your Honor what he has done, and there is scarcely a child on the street who does not know it, there is not a judge in the court who does not know it; there is not a lawyer at the bar who does not know it; there is not a physician in Chicago who does not know it; and I am willing to stake the lives of these two boys on the court knowing it, and I will throw my own in for good measure. What else did he say, in which the State's alienists dispute him?

Both of them say that these boys showed no adequate emotion. Krohn said they did. One boy fainted. They had been in the hands of the State's Attorney for sixty hours. They had been in the hands of policemen, lawyers, detectives, stenographers, inquisitors and newspaper men for sixty hours, and one of them fainted. Well, the only person who is entirely without emotion is a dead man. You cannot live without breathing and some emotional responses. Krohn says: "Why, Loeb had emotion. He was polite; begged our pardon; got up from his chair"; even Dr. Krohn knows better than that. I fancy if your Honor goes into an elevator where there is a lady he takes off his hat. Is that out of emotion for the lady or is it habit? You say, "Please," and "thank you," because of habit. Emotions haven't the slightest thing to do with it. Mr. Leopold has good manners. Mr. Loeb has good manners. They have been taught them. They have lived them. That does not mean that they are emotional. It means training. That is all it means. And Dr. Krohn knew it.

Krohn told the story of this interview and he told almost twice as much as the other two men who sat there and heard it. And how he told it—how he told it!

When he testified my mind carried me back to the time when I was a kid, which was some years ago, and we used to eat watermelons. I have seen little boys take a rind of watermelon and cover their whole faces with water, eat it, devour it, and have the time of their lives, up to their ears in watermelon. And when I heard Dr. Krohn testify in this case, to take the blood of these two boys, I could see his mouth water with the joy it gave him, and he showed all the delight and pleasure of myself and my young companions when we ate watermelon.

I can imagine a psychiatrist, a real one who knows the mechanism of man, who knows life and its machinery, who knows the misfortunes of youth, who knows the stress and the strain of adolescence which comes to every boy and overpowers so many, who knows the weird fantastic world that hedges around the life of a child—I can imagine a psychiatrist who might honestly think that under the crude definitions of the law the defendants were sane and know the difference between right and wrong. But if he were a real physician, whose mission is the highest that man can follow, to save life and minister to human suffering—to save life regardless of what the life is—to prevent suffering, regardless of whose suffering it is—and no mission could be higher than that—that if this was his mission, instead of testifying in court; and if he were called on for an opinion that might send his fellowman to doom, I can imagine him doing it reluctantly, carefully, modestly, timorously, fearfully, and being careful that he did not turn one hair to the right or left more than he should, and giving the advantage in favor of life and humanity and mercy, but I can never imagine a real physician who cared for life or who thought of anything excepting cash, gloating over his testimony, as Dr. Krohn did in this case.

Without any consideration of the lives and the trainings of these boys, without any evidence from experts, I have tried to make a plain statement of the facts of this case, and I believe, as I have said repeatedly, that no one can honestly study the facts and conclude that anything but diseased minds was responsible for this terrible act. Let us see how far we can account for it, your Honor.

So far we have determined whether men are diseased of mind or normal from their conduct alone. This line of conduct shows disease and that line of conduct shows normality. We have not been able with any satisfaction to peer into the brain and see its workings; to analyze the human system and see where it has gone awry. Science is doing something, but so far has done little, and we have been compelled to make up our minds from conduct as to the condition of the minds of men.

The mind, of course, is an illusive thing. Whether it exists or not no one can tell. It cannot be found as you find the brain. Its relation to the brain and the nervous system is uncertain. It simply means the activity of the body, which is co-ordinated with the brain. But when we do find from human conduct that we believe there is a diseased mind, we naturally speculate on how it came about. And we wish to find always, if possible, the reason why it is so. We may find it; we may not find it; because the unknown is infinitely wider and larger than the known, both as to the human mind and as to almost everything else in the Universe.

It has not been so very long since the insane were supposed to be possessed of devils, and since criminals were supposed to be possessed of devils, when wise men solved intricate questions by saying that devils possessed human beings. It has not been so very long since it was supposed that diseased persons were possessed of devils, which must be driven out to cure the disease. We have gone further than this. We understand that there is some connection between the workings of the mind and the working of the body. We understand something of the physical basis of life. We understand something of the intricate mechanism which may fail in some minute part and cause such serious havoc in human conduct.

I have tried to study the lives of these two most unfortunate boys. Three months ago, if their friends and the friends of the family had been asked to pick out the most promising lads of their acquaintance, they probably would have picked these two boys. With every opportunity, with plenty of wealth, they would have said that those two would succeed.

In a day, by an act of madness, all this is destroyed, until the best they can hope for now is a life of silence and pain, continuing to the end of their years.

How did it happen?

Let us take Dickie Loeb first.

I do not claim to know how it happened; I have sought to find out. I know that something, or some combination of things, is responsible for his mad act. I know that there are no accidents in nature. I know that effect follows cause. I know that, if I were wise enough, and knew enough about this case, I could lay my finger on the cause. I will do the best I can, but it is largely speculation.

The child, of course, is born without knowledge.

Impressions are made upon its mind as it goes along. Dickie Loeb was a child of wealth and opportunity. Over and over in this court your Honor has been asked, and other courts have been asked, to consider boys who have no chance; they have been asked to consider the poor, whose home had been the street, with no education and no opportunity in life, and they have done it, and done it rightfully.

But your Honor, it is just as often a great misfortune to be the child of the rich as it is to be the child of the poor. Wealth has its misfortunes. Too much, too great opportunity and advantage given to a child has its misfortunes, and I am asking your Honor to consider the rich as well as the poor (and nothing else). Can I find what was wrong? I think I can. Here was a boy at a tender age, placed in the hands of a governess, intellectual, vigorous, devoted, with a strong ambition for the welfare of this boy. He was pushed in his studies, as plants are forced in hot houses. He had no pleasures, such as a boy should have, except as they were gained by lying and cheating. Now, I am not criticising the nurse. I suggest that some day your Honor look at her picture. It explains her fully. Forceful, brooking no interference, she loved the boy, and her ambition was that he should reach the highest perfection. No time to pause, no time to stop from one book to another, no time to have those pleasures which a boy ought to have to create a normal life. And what happened? Your Honor, what would happen? Nothing strange or unusual. This nurse was with him all the time, except when he stole out at night, from two to fourteen years of age, and it is instructive to read her letter to show her attitude. It speaks volumes; tells exactly the relation between these two people. He, scheming and planning as healthy boys would do, to get out from under her restraint. She, putting before him the best books, which children generally do not want; and he, when she was not looking, reading detective stories, which he devoured, story after story, in his young life. Of all of this there can be no question. What is the result? Every story he read was a story of crime. We have a statute in this state, passed only last

Chief Justice John Caverly of the Criminal Court of Chicago
during the trial of Leopold and Loeb for the slaying of little
Robert Franks

Secret conference during the trial, during the testimony of Dr. Healy, one of the defense alienists. Below, the two slayers conferring with one of their attorneys, Walter Bachrach

year, if I recall it, which forbids minors reading stories of crime. Why? There is only one reason. Because the legislature in its wisdom felt that it would produce criminal tendencies in the boys who read them. The legislature of this state has given its opinion, and forbidden boys to read these books. He read them day after day. He never stopped. While he was passing through college at Ann Arbor he was still reading them. When he was a senior he read them, and almost nothing else.

Now, these facts are beyond dispute. He early developed the tendency to mix with crime, to be a detective; as a little boy shadowing people on the street; as a little child going out with his phantasy of being the head of a band of criminals and directing them on the street. How did this grow and develop in him? Let us see. It seems to me as natural as the day following the night. Every detective story is a story of a sleuth getting the best of it; trailing some unfortunate individual through devious ways until his victim is finally landed in jail or stands on the gallows. They all show how smart the detective is, and where the criminal himself falls down.

This boy early in his life conceived the idea that there could be a perfect crime, one that nobody could ever detect; that there could be one where the detective did not land his game; a perfect crime. He had been interested in the story of Charley Ross, who was kidnapped. He was interested in these things all his life. He believed in his childish way that a crime could be so carefully planned that there would be no detection, and his idea was to plan and accomplish a perfect crime. It would involve kidnapping, and involve murder. I might digress here just a moment, because my friend Savage spoke about two crimes that were committed here—kidnapping and murder. That is, the court should hang them twice—once for each. There are more than two committed here. There are more than two crimes committed in almost every capital act.

An attempt to extort money was committed. A conspiracy to do each one was committed. Carrying firearms was committed. I could probably mention half a dozen if I tried, but it is all one thing, and counsel knows it is all one thing.

Is this anything new in criminal practice?

Why, your Honor, we have it every day in these courts. In

almost any important crime the State's Attorney can write indictments as long as the paper lasts, not only counts, but indictments. Take a case of burning a building for insurance. (Two people.) There is the crime of arson. There is the crime of burning a building to defraud an insurance company. There is conspiracy to commit arson. There is conspiracy to burn a building to defraud an insurance company. And I might mention others, all in the one act. Burglary and larceny includes a number of crimes, especially if there are two or more persons involved. It is nothing new. This was really one offense and one only. They could have made six out of it, or one out of it, or two out of it. But it is only one thing. Just like any other important crime.

They wanted to commit a perfect crime. There had been growing in this brain, dwarfed and twisted—as every act in this case shows it to have been dwarfed and twisted—there had been growing this scheme, not due to any wickedness of Dickie Loeb, for he is a child. It grew as he grew; it grew from those around him; it grew from the lack of the proper training until it possessed him. He believed he could beat the police. He believed he could plan the perfect crime. He had thought of it and talked of it for years. Had talked of it as a child; had worked at it as a child, and this sorry act of his, utterly irrational and motiveless, a plan to commit a perfect crime which must contain kidnaping, and there must be ransom, or else it could not be perfect, and they must get the money.

The state itself in opening this case said that it was largely for experience and for a thrill, which it was. In the end the state switched it on to the foolish reason of getting cash.

Every fact in this case shows that cash had almost nothing to do with it, except as a factor in the perfect crime; and to commit the perfect crime there must be a kidnaping, and a kidnaping where they could get money, and that was all there was of it. Now, these are the two theories of this case, and I submit, your Honor, under the facts in this case, that there can be no question but that we are right. This phantasy grew in the mind of Dickie Loeb almost before he began to read. It developed as a child just as kleptomania has developed in many a person and is clearly recognized by the courts. He went from one thing to another—

in the main insignificant, childish things. Then, the utterly foolish and stupid and unnecessary thing of going to Ann Arbor to
steal from a fraternity house, a fraternity of which he was a
member. And, finally, the planning for this crime. Murder was
the least part of it; to kidnap and get the money, and kill in connection with it; that was the childish scheme growing up in these
childish minds. And they had it in mind for five or six months
—planning what? Planning where every step was foolish and
childish; acts that could have been planned in an hour or a day;
planning this, and then planning that, changing this and changing that; the weird actions of two mad brains.

Counsel have laughed at us for talking about phantasies and
hallucinations. They have laughed at us in one breath, but admitted it in another. Let us look at that for a moment, your
Honor. Your Honor has been a child. I well remember that I
have been a child. And while youth has its advantages, it has
its grievous troubles. There is an old prayer, The Heart of a
Child, 'Though I grow old in years, let me keep the heart of a
child,' with its abundant life, its disregard for consequences, its
living in the moment, and for the moment alone; its lack of responsibility, and its freedom from care.

The law knows and has recognized childhood for many and
many a long year. What do we know about childhood? The
brain of the child is the home of dreams, of castles, of visions, of
illusions and of delusions. In fact, there could be no childhood
without delusions, for delusions are always more alluring than
facts. Delusions, dreams and hallucinations are a part of the
warp and woof of childhood. You know it and I know it. I
remember, when I was a child, the men seemed as tall as the
trees, the trees as tall as the mountains. I can remember very
well when, as a little boy, I swam the deepest spot in the river
for the first time. I swam breathlessly, and landed with as much
sense of glory and triumph as Julius Cæsar felt when he led his
army across the Rubicon. I have been back since, and I can almost
step across the same place, but it seemed an ocean then. And
those men whom I thought were so wonderful were dead and
left nothing behind. I had lived in a dream. I had never
known the real world which I met, to my discomfort and despair,
and that dispelled the illusions of my youth.

The whole life of childhood is a dream and an illusion, and whether they take one shape or another shape depends not upon the dreamy boy but on what surrounds him. As well might I have dreamed of burglars and wished to be one as to dream of policemen and wished to be one. Perhaps I was lucky, too, that I had no money. We have grown to think that the misfortune is in not having it. The great misfortune in this terrible case is the money. That has destroyed their lives. That has fostered these illusions. That has promoted this mad act. And, if your honor shall doom them to die, it will be because they are the sons of the rich.

Do you suppose that if they lived up here on the Northwest Side and had no money, with the evidence as clear in this case as it is, that any human being would want to hang them? Excessive wealth is a grievous misfortune in every step in life. When I hear foolish people, when I read malicious newspapers talking of excessive fees in this case, it makes me ill. That there is nothing bigger in life, that it is presumed that no man lives to whom money is not the first concern, that human instincts, sympathy and kindness and charity and logic can only be used for cash. It shows how deeply money has corrupted the hearts of most men.

Now, to get back to Dickie Loeb. He was a child. The books he read by day were not the books he read by night. We are all of us moulded somewhat by the influences around us (and of those), to people who read, perhaps books are the greatest and the strongest.

I know where my life has been moulded by books, amongst other things. We all know where our lives have been influenced by books. The nurse, strict and jealous and watchful, gave him one kind of books; by night he would steal off and read the other influences.

Which, think you, shaped the life of Dickie Loeb? Is there any kind of question about it? A child: Was it pure maliciousness? Was a boy of five or six or seven to blame for it? Where did he get it? He got it where we all get our ideas, and these books became a part of his dreams and a part of his life, and as he grew up his visions grew to hallucinations.

He went out on the street and fantastically directed his companions, who were not there, in their various moves to complete the perfect crime. Can there be any sort of question about it?

Suppose, your Honor, that instead of this boy being here in this court, under the plea of the state that your Honor shall pronounce a sentence to hang him by the neck until dead, he had been taken to a pathological hospital to be analyzed, and the physicians had inquired into his case, what would they have said? There is only one thing that they could possibly have said. They would have traced everything back to the gradual growth of the child.

That is not all there is about it. Youth is hard enough. The only good thing about youth is that it has no thought and no care; and how blindly we can do things when we are young!

Where is the man who has not been guilty of delinquencies in youth? Let us be honest with ourselves. Let us look into our own hearts. How many men are there today—lawyers and congressmen and judges, and even state's attorneys—who have not been guilty of some mad act in youth? And if they did not get caught, or the consequences were trivial, it was their good fortune.

We might as well be honest with ourselves, your Honor. Before I would tie a noose around the neck of a boy I would try to call back into my mind the emotions of youth. I would try to remember what the world looked like to me when I was a child. I would try to remember how strong were these instinctive, persistent emotions that moved my life. I would try to remember how weak and inefficient was youth in the presence of the surging, controlling feelings of the child. One that honestly remembers and asks himself the question and tries to unlock the door that he thinks is closed, and calls back the boy, can understand the boy.

But, your Honor, that is not all there is to boyhood. Nature is strong and she is pitiless. She works in her own mysterious way, and we are her victims. We have not much to do with it ourselves. Nature takes this job in hand, and we play our parts. In the words of old Omar Khayyam, we are only

"Impotent pieces in the game He plays
  Upon this checkerboard of nights and days,

> Hither and thither moves, and checks, and slays,
> And one by one back in the closet lays."

What had this boy to do with it? He was not his own father; he was not his own mother; he was not his own grandparents. All of this was handed to him. He did not surround himself with governesses and wealth. He did not make himself. And yet he is to be compelled to pay.

There was a time in England, running down as late as the beginning of the last century, when judges used to convene court and call juries to try a horse, a dog, a pig, for crime. I have in my library a story of a judge and jury and lawyers trying and convicting an old sow for lying down on her ten pigs and killing them.

What does it mean? Animals were tried. Do you mean to tell me that Dickie Loeb had any more to do with his making than any other product of heredity that is born upon the earth?

At his period of life it is not enough to take a boy—your Honor, I wish I knew when to stop talking about this question that always has interested me so much—it is not enough to take a boy filled with his dreams and his phantasies and living in an unreal world, but the age of adolescence comes on him with all the rest.

What does he know? Both these boys are in the adolescent age; both these boys, as every alienist in this case on both sides tells you, are in the most trying period of the life of a child; both these boys, when the call of sex is new and strange; both these boys, at a time seeking to adjust their young lives to the world, moved by the strongest feelings and passions that have ever moved men; both these boys, at the time boys grow insane, at the time crimes are committed; all of this is added to all the rest of the vagaries of their lives. Shall we charge them with full responsibility that we may have a hanging? That we may deck Chicago in a holiday garb and let the people have their fill of blood; that you may put stains upon the heart of every man, woman and child on that day, and that the dead walls of Chicago will tell the story of the shedding of their blood?

For God's sake, are we crazy? In the face of history, of every line of philosophy, against the teaching of every religionist and seer and prophet the world has ever given us, we are still doing what our barbaric ancestors did when they came out of the caves and the woods.

From the age of fifteen to the age of twenty or twenty-one, the child has the burden of adolescence, of puberty and sex thrust upon him. Girls are kept at home and carefully watched. Boys without instruction are left to work the period out for themselves. It may lead to excess. It may lead to disgrace. It may lead to perversion. Who is to blame? Who did it? Did Dickie Loeb do it?

Your Honor, I am almost ashamed to talk about it. I can hardly imagine that we are in the 20th Century. And yet there are men who seriously say that for what Nature has done, for what life has done, for what training has done, you should hang these boys.

Now, there is no mystery about this case, your Honor. I seem to be criticising their parents. They had parents who were kind and good and wise in their way. But I say to you seriously that the parents are more responsible than these boys. And yet few boys had better parents.

Your Honor, it is the easiest thing in the world to be a parent. We talk of motherhood, and yet every woman can be a mother. We talk of fatherhood, and yet every man can be a father. Nature takes care of that. It is easy to be a parent. But to be wise and far seeing enough to understand the boy is another thing; only a very few so wise and so far seeing as that. When I think of the light way nature has of picking out parents and populating the earth, I cannot hold human beings to the same degree of responsibility that young lawyers hold them when they are enthusiastic in a prosecution. I know what it means. I know there are no better citizens in Chicago than the fathers of these poor boys.

I know there were no better women than their mothers. But I am going to be honest with this court, if it is at the expense of both. I know that one of two things happened to Richard Loeb; that this terrible crime was inherent in his organism, and came from some ancestor, or that it came through his education and his training after he was born. Do I need to prove it? Judge Crowe said at one point in this case, when some witness spoke about their wealth, that "probably that was responsible."

To believe that any boy is responsible for himself or his early training is an absurdity that no lawyer or judge should be guilty of today. Somewhere this came to this boy. If his failing came from his heredity, I do not know where or how. None of us are bred perfect and pure, and the color of our hair, the color of our eyes, our stature, the weight and fineness of our brain, and everything about us could, with full knowledge, be traced with absolute certainty to somewhere; if we had the pedigree it could be traced just the same in a boy as it could be in a dog, a horse or cow.

I do not know what remote ancestors may have sent down the seed that corrupted him, and I do not know through how many ancestors it may have passed until it reached Dickie Loeb.

All I know is that it is true, and there is not a biologist in the world who will not say that I am right.

If it did not come that way, then I know that if he was normal, if he had been understood, if he had been trained as he should have been it would not have happened. Not that anybody may not slip, but I know it and your Honor knows it, and every school house and every church in the land is an evidence of it. Else why build them?

Every effort to protect society is an effort toward training the youth to keep the path. Every bit of training in the world proves it, and it likewise proves that it sometimes fails. I know that if this boy had been understood and properly trained—properly for him—and the training that he got might have been the very best for someone else; but if it had been the proper training for him he would not be in this court room today with the noose above his head. If there is responsibility anywhere, it is back of him; somewhere in the infinite number of his ancestors, or in his surroundings, or in both. And I submit, your Honor, that under every principle of natural justice, under every principle of conscience, of right, and of law, he should not be made responsible for the acts of someone else.

I say this again, without finding fault with his parents, for whom I have the highest regard, and who doubtless did the best they could. They might have done better if they had not had so much money. I do not know. Great wealth often curses all who touch it.

This boy was sent to school. His mind worked; his emotions were dead. He could learn books, but he read detective stories. There never was a time since he was old enough to move back and forth, according to what seemed to be his volition, when he was not haunted with these phantasies.

The state made fun of Dr. White, the ablest and, I believe, the best psychiatrist in America today, for speaking about this boy's mind running back to the Teddy bears he used to play with, and in addressing somebody he was wont to say, "You know, Teddy——"

Well, your Honor, it is nothing but the commonplace action of the commonplace child or the ordinary man? A set of emotions, thoughts, feelings take possession of the mind and we find them recurring and recurring over and over again.

I catch myself many and many a time repeating phrases of my childhood, and I have not quite got into my second childhood yet. I have caught myself doing this while I still could catch myself. It means nothing. We may have all the dreams and visions and build all the castles we wish, but the castles of youth should be discarded with youth, and when they linger to the time when boys should think wiser things, then it indicates a diseased mind. "When I was young I thought as a child, I spoke as a child, I understood as a child; but now I have put off childish things," said the Psalmist twenty centuries ago. It is when these dreams of boyhood, these phantasies of youth still linger, and the growing boy is still a child—a child in emotion, a child in feeling, a child in hallucinations—that you can say that it is the dreams and the hallucinations of childhood that are responsible for his conduct. There is not an act in all this horrible tragedy that was not the act of a child, the act of a child wandering around in the morning of life, moved by the new feelings of a boy, moved by the uncontrolled impulses which his teaching was not strong enough to take care of, moved by the dreams and the hallucinations which haunt the brain of a child. I say, your Honor, that it would be the height of cruelty, of injustice, of wrong and barbarism to visit the penalty upon this poor boy.

Your Honor, again I want to say that all parents can be criticized; likewise grandparents and teachers. Science is not so much interested in criticism as in finding causes. Some time education will be more scientific. Some time we will try to know the boy before we educate him and as we educate him. Some time we will try to know what will fit the individual boy, instead of putting all boys through the same course, regardless of what they are.

This boy needed more of home, more love, more directing. He needed to have his emotions awakened. He needed guiding hands along the serious road that youth must travel. Had these been given him, he would not be here today. Now, your Honor, I want to speak of the other lad, Babe.

Babe is somewhat older than Dick, and is a boy of remarkable mind—away beyond his years. He is a sort of freak in this direction, as in others; a boy without emotions, a boy obsessed of philosophy, a boy obsessed of learning, busy every minute of his life.

He went through school quickly; he went to college young; he could learn faster than almost everybody else. . His emotional life was lacking, as every alienist and witness in this case excepting Dr. Krohn has told you. He was just a half boy, an intellect, an intellectual machine going without balance and without a governor, seeking to find out everything there was in life intellectually; seeking to solve every philosophy, but using his intellect only.

Of course his family did not understand him; few men would. His mother died when he was young; he had plenty of money; everything was given to him that he wanted. Both these boys with unlimited money; both these boys with automobiles; both of these boys with every luxury around them and in front of them. They grew up in this environment.

Babe took to philosophy. I call him Babe, not because I want it to affect your Honor, but because everybody else does. He is the youngest of the family and I suppose that is why he got his nickname. We will call him a man. Mr. Crowe thinks it is easier to hang a man than a boy, and so I will call him a man if I can think of it.

He grew up in this way. He became enamoured of the philosophy of Nietzsche.

Your Honor, I have read almost everything that Nietzsche ever wrote. He was a man of a wonderful intellect; the most original philosopher of the last century. A man who probably has made a deeper imprint on philosophy than any other man within a hundred years, whether right or wrong. More books have been written about him than probably all the rest of the philosophers in a hundred years. More college professors have talked about him. In a way he has reached more people, and still he has been a philosopher of what we might call the intellectual cult. Nietzsche believed that some time the superman would be born, that evolution was working toward the superman.

He wrote one book, "Beyond Good and Evil," which was a criticism of all moral codes as the world understands them; a treatise holding that the intelligent man is beyond good and evil; that the laws for good and the laws for evil do not apply to those who approach the superman. He wrote on the will to power. He wrote some ten or fifteen volumes on his various philosophical ideas. Nathan Leopold is not the only boy who has read Nietzsche. He may be the only one who was influenced in the way that he was influenced.

I have just made a few short extracts from Nietzsche, that show the things that Nathan read and which no doubt influenced him. These extracts are short and taken almost at random.

It is not how this would affect you. It is not how it would affect me. The question is how it did affect the impressionable, visionary, dreamy mind of a boy.

At seventeen, at sixteen, at eighteen, while healthy boys were playing baseball or working on the farm, or doing odd jobs, he was reading Nietzsche, a boy who never should have seen it, at that early age. Babe was obsessed of it, and here are some of the things which Nietzsche taught:

"Why so soft, oh, my brethren? Why so soft, so unresisting and yielding? Why is there so much disavowal and abnegation in your heart? Why is there so little fate in your looks? For all creators are hard, and it must seem blessedness unto you to press your hand upon milleniums and upon wax. This new table, oh, my brethren, I put over you: Become hard. To be obsessed by moral consideration presupposes a very low grade of intellect. We should substitute for morality the will to our own end, and consequently to the means to accomplish that.

"A great man, a man that nature has built up and invented in a grand style, is colder, harder, less cautious and more free from the fear of public opinion. He does not posses the virtues which are compatible with respectability, with being respected, nor any of those things which are counted among the virtues of the hard."

Nietzsche held a contemptuous, scornful attitude to all those things which the young are taught as important in life; a fixing of new values which are not the values by which any normal child has ever yet been reared—a philosophical dream, containing more or less truth, that was not meant by anyone to be applied to life.

Again he says:

"The morality of the master class is irritating to the taste of the present day because of its fundamental principle that a man has obligation only to his equals; that he may act to all of lower rank and to all that are foreign, as he pleases."

In other words, man has no obligations; he may do with all other men and all other boys, and all society, as he pleases—the superman was a creation of Nietzsche, but it has permeated every college and university in the civilized world.

Again, quoting from a professor of a university:

"Although no perfect superman has yet appeared in history, Nietzsche's types are to be found in the world's great figures—Alexander, Napoleon—in the wicked heroes such as the Borgias, Wagner's Siegfried and Ibsen's Brand—and the great cosmopolitan intellects such as Goethe and Stendahl. These were the gods of Nietzsche's idolatry."

The superman-like qualities lie not in their genius, but in their freedom from scruple. They rightly felt themselves to be above the law. What they thought was right, not because sanctioned by any law, beyond themselves, but because they did it. So the superman will be a law unto himself. What he does will come from the will and superabundant power within him.

Your Honor, I could read for a week from Nietzsche, all to the same purpose, and the same end.

Counsel have said that because a man believes in murder that does not excuse him.

Quite right. But this is not a case like the anarchists case, where a number of men, perhaps honestly believing in revolution and knowing the consequences of their act and knowing its illegal character, were held responsible for murder.

Of course the books are full of statements that the fact that a man believes in committing a crime does not excuse him.

That is not this case, and counsel must know that it is not this case. Here is a boy at sixteen or seventeen becoming obsessed with these doctrines. There isn't any question about the facts. Their own witnesses tell it and every one of our witnesses tell it. It was not a casual bit of philosophy with him; it was his life. He believed in a superman. He and Dickie Loeb were the supermen. There might have been others, but they were two, and two chums. The ordinary commands of society were not for him.

Many of us read this philosophy but know that it has no actual application to life; but not he. It became a part of his being. It was his philosophy. He lived it and practiced it; he thought it applied to him, and he could not have believed it excepting that it either caused a diseased mind or was the result of a diseased mind.

Now let me call your attention hastily to just a few facts in connection with it. One of the cases is a New York case, where a man named Freeman became obsessed in a very strange way of religious ideas. He read the story of Isaac and Abraham and he felt a call that he must sacrifice his son. He arranged an altar in his parlor. He converted his wife to the idea. He took his little babe and put it on the altar and cut its throat. Why? Because he was obsessed of that idea. Was he sane? Was he normal? Was his mind diseased? Was this poor fellow responsible? Not in the least. And he was acquitted because he was the victim of a delusion. Men are largely what their ideas make them. Boys are largely what their ideas make them.

Here is a boy who by day and by night, in season and out, was talking of the superman, owing no obligations to anyone; whatever gave him pleasure he should do, believing it just as another man might believe a religion or any philosophical theory.

You remember that I asked Dr. Church about these religious cases and he said "yes, many people go to the insane asylum on account of them," that "they place a literal meaning on parables and believe them thoroughly." I asked Dr. Church, whom I again say I believe to be an honest man, and an intelligent man —I asked him whether the same thing might be done or might come from a philosophical belief, and he said, "if one believed it strongly enough."

And I asked him about Nietzsche. He said he knew something of Nietzsche, something of his responsibility for the war, for which he perhaps was not responsible. He said he knew something about his doctrines. I asked him what became of him, and he said he was insane for fifteen years just before the time of his death. His very doctrine is a species of insanity.

Here is a man, a wise man—perhaps not wise, but brilliant— a thoughtful man who has made his impress upon the world. Every student of philosophy knows him. His own doctrines made him a maniac. And here is a young boy, in the adolescent age, harassed by everything that harasses children, who takes this philosophy and believes it literally. It is a part of his life. It is his life. Do you suppose this mad act could have been done by him in any other way? What could he have to win from this homicide?

A boy with a beautiful home, with automobiles, a graduate of college, going to Europe, and then to study law at Harvard; as brilliant in intellect as any boy that you could find; a boy with every prospect that life might hold out to him; and yet he goes out and commits this weird, strange, wild, mad act, that he may die on the gallows or live in a prison cell until he dies of old age or disease.

He did it, obsessed of an idea, perhaps to some extent influenced by what has not been developed publicly in this case— perversions that were present in the boy. Both signs of insanity, both, together with this act, proving a diseased mind.

Is there any question about what was responsible for him?

What else could be? A boy in his youth, with every promise that the world could hold out before him—wealth and position and intellect, yes, genius, scholarship, nothing that he could not obtain, and he throws it away, and mounts the gallows or goes into a cell for life. It is too foolish to talk about. Can your Honor imagine a sane brain doing it? Can you imagine it coming from anything but a diseased mind? Can you imagine it is any part of normality? And yet, your Honor, you are asked to hang a boy of his age, abnormal, obsessed of dreams and visions, a philosophy that destroyed his life, when there is no sort of question in the world as to what caused his downfall.

Now, I have said that, as to Loeb, if there is anybody to blame it is back of him. Your Honor, lots of things happen in this world that nobody is to blame for. In fact, I am not very much for settling blame myself. If I could settle the blame on somebody else for this special act, I would wonder why that somebody else did it, and I know if I could find that out, I would move it back still another peg.

I know, your Honor, that every atom of life in all this universe is bound up together. I know that a pebble cannot be thrown into the ocean without disturbing every drop of water in the sea. I know that every life is inextricably mixed and woven with every other life. I know that every influence, conscious and unconscious, acts and reacts on every living organism, and that no one can fix the blame. I know that all life is a series of infinite chances, which sometimes result one way and sometimes another. I have not the infinite wisdom that can fathom it, neither has any other human brain. But I do know that if back of it is a power that made it, that power alone can tell, and if there is no power, then it is an infinite chance, which man cannot solve.

Why should this boy's life be bound up with Frederick Nietzsche, who died thirty years ago, insane, in Germany? I don't know.

I only know it is. I know that no man who ever wrote a line that I read failed to influence me to some extent. I know that every life I ever touched influenced me, and I influenced it; and that it is not given to me to unravel the infinite causes and say, "this is I, and this is you." I am responsible for so much; and you are responsible for so much. I know—I know that in the infinite universe everything has its place and that the smallest particle is a part of all. Tell me that you can visit the wrath of fate and chance and life and eternity upon a nineteen-year-old-boy! If you could, justice would be a travesty and mercy a fraud.

I might say further about Nathan Leopold—where did he get this philosophy?—at college? He did not make it, your Honor. He did not write these books, and I will venture to say there are at least ten thousand books on Neitzsche and his philosophy. I never counted them, but I will venture to say that there are that many in the libraries of the world.

No other philosopher ever caused the discussion that Nietzsche has caused. There is no university in the world where the professors are not familiar with Nietzsche; not one. There is not an intellectual man in the world whose life and feelings run to philosophy, who is not more or less familiar with the Nietzschien philosophy. Some believe it, and some do not believe it. Some read it as I do, and take it as a theory, a dream, a vision, mixed with good and bad, but not in any way related to human life. Some take it seriously. The universities perhaps do not all teach it, for perhaps some teach nothing in philosophy; but they give the boys the books of the masters, and tell them what they taught, and discuss the doctrines.

There is not a university in the world of any high standing where the professors do not tell you about Nietzsche, and discuss it, or where the books can not be found.

I will guarantee that you can go down to the University of Chicago today—into its big library—and find over a thousand volumes on Nietzsche, and I am sure I speak moderately. If this boy is to blame for this, where did he get it? Is there any blame attaches because somebody took Nietzsche's philosophy seriously and fashioned his life on it? And there is no question in this case but what it is true. Then who is to blame? The university would be more to blame than he is. The scholars of the world would be more to blame than he is. The publishers of the world—and Nietzsche's books are published by one of the biggest publishers in the world—are more to blame than he. Your Honor, it is hardly fair to hang a nineteen-year-old boy for the philosophy that was taught him at the university.

Now, I do not want to be misunderstood about this. Even for the sake of saving the lives of my clients, I do not want to be dishonest, and tell the court something that I do not honestly

Palatial Chicago homes of the two slayers. Above, home of Albert
H. Loeb. Below is that of Nathan Leopold. The Loeb home is
diagonally across the street from the Franks home

A view of the entrance and two interiors of the palatial summer
home of the Loeb family at Charlevoix, Michigan, where "Dickie"
spent his summers

think in this case. I do not believe that the universities are to blame. I do not think they should be held responsible, I do think, however, that they are too large, and that they should keep a closer watch, if possible, upon the individual. But, you cannot destroy thought because, forsooth, some brain may be deranged by thought. It is the duty of the university, as I conceive it, to be the great storehouse of the wisdom of the ages, and to let students go there, and learn, and choose. I have no doubt but that it has meant the death of many; that we cannot help. Every changed idea in the world has had its consequences. Every new religious doctrine has created its victims. Every new philosophy has caused suffering and death. Every new machine has carved up men while it served the world. No railroad can be built without the destruction of human life. No great building can be erected but that unfortunate workmen fall to the earth and die. No great movement that does not bear its toll of life and death; no great ideal but does good and harm, and we cannot stop because it may do harm.

I have no idea in this case that this act would ever have been committed or participated in by him excepting for the philosophy which he had taken literally, which belonged to older boys and older men, and which no one can take literally and practice literally and live. So, your Honor, I do not mean to unload this act on that man or this man, or this organization or that organization. I am trying to trace causes. I am trying to trace them honestly. I am trying to trace them with the light I have. I am trying to say to this court that these boys are not responsible for this; and that their act was due to this and this, and this and this; and asking this court not to visit the judgment of its wrath upon them for things for which they are not to blame.

There is something else in this case, your Honor, that is stronger still. There is a large element of chance in life. I know I will die. I don't know when; I don't know how; I don't know where; and I don't want to know. I know it will come. I know that it depends on infinite chances. Do I live to myself? Did I make myself? And control my fate? Can I fix my death unless I suicide—and I cannot do that because the will to live is too strong; I know it depends on infinite chances.

Take the rabbit running through the woods; a fox meets him
at a certain fence. If the rabbit had not started when it did,
it would not have met the fox and would have lived longer.
If the fox had started later or earlier it would not have met
the rabbit and its fate would have been different.

My death will depend upon chances. It may be by the taking
in of a germ; it may be a pistol; it may be the decaying of my
faculties, and all that makes life; it may be a cancer; it may
be any one of an indefinite number of things, and where I am at
a certain time, and whether I take in that germ, and the condition of my system when I breathe is an accident which is sealed
up in the book of fate and which no human being can open.

These boys, neither one of them, could possibly have committed this act excepting by coming together. It was not the act
for one; it was the act of two. It was the act of their planning,
their conniving, their believing in each other; their thinking
themselves supermen. Without it they could not have done it.
It would not have happened. Their parents happened to meet,
these boys happened to meet; some sort of chemical alchemy
operated so that they cared for each other, and poor Bobby
Franks' dead body was found in the culvert as a result. Neither
of them could have done it alone.

I want to call your attention, your Honor, to the two letters
in this case which settle this matter to my mind conclusively;
not only the condition of these boys' minds, but the terrible fate
that overtook them.

Your Honor, I am sorry for poor Bobby Franks, and I think
anybody who knows me knows that I am not saying it simply
to talk. I am sorry for the bereaved father and the bereaved
mother, and I would like to know what they would do with
these poor unfortunate lads who are here in this court today.
I know something of them, of their lives, of their charity, of
their ideas, and nobody here sympathizes with them   more
than I.

On the 21st day of May poor Bobby Franks, stripped and
naked, was left in a culvert down near the Indiana line. I know
it came through the mad act of mad boys. Mr. Savage told us
that Franks, if he had lived, would have been a great man and
have accomplished much. I want to leave this thought with your

Honor now. I do not know what Bobby Franks would have been had he grown to be a man. I do not know the laws that control one's growth. Sometimes, your Honor, a boy of great promise is cut off in his early youth. Sometimes he dies and is placed in a culvert. Sometimes a boy of great promise stands on a trap door and is hanged by the neck until dead. Sometimes he dies of diphtheria. Death somehow pays no attention to age, sex, prospects, wealth or intellect.

It comes, and perhaps, I can only say perhaps, for I never professed to unravel the mysteries of fate, and I cannot tell; but I can say—perhaps, the boy who died at fourteen did as much as if he had died at seventy, and perhaps the boy who died as a babe did as much as if he had lived longer. Perhaps, somewhere in fate and chance, it might be that he lived as long as he should.

And I want to say this, that the death of poor little Bobby Franks should not be in vain. Would it mean anything if on account of that death, these two boys were taken out and a rope tied around their necks and they died felons? Would that show that Bobby Franks had a purpose in his life and a purpose in his death? No, your Honor, the unfortunate and tragic death of this weak young lad should mean something. It should mean an appeal to the fathers and the mothers, an appeal to the teachers, to the religious guides, to society at large. It should mean an appeal to all of them to appraise children, to understand the emotions that control them, to understand the ideas that possess them, to teach them to avoid the pitfalls of life.

Society, too, should assume its share of the burdens of this case, and not make two more tragedies, but use this calamity as best it can to make life safer, to make childhood easier, and more secure, to do something to cure the cruelty, the hatred, the chance, and the wilfulness of life.

I have discussed somewhat in detail these two boys separately. Their coming together was the means of their undoing. Your Honor is familiar with the facts in reference to their association. They had a weird, almost impossible relationship. Leopold, with his obsession of the superman, had repeatedly said that Loeb was his idea of the superman. He had the attitude toward him that one has to his most devoted friend, or that a man has to a lover. Without the combination of these two, nothing of this sort probably could have happened. It is not necessary for us, your Honor, to rely upon words to prove the condition of these boys' minds, and to prove the effect of this strange and fatal relationship between these two boys.

It is mostly told in a letter which the state itself introduced in this case. Not the whole story, but enough of it is shown, so that I take it that no intelligent, thoughtful person could fail to realize what was the relation between them and how they had played upon each other to effect their downfall and their ruin. I want to read this letter once more, a letter which was introduced by the state, a letter dated October 9th, a month and three days before their trip to Ann Arbor, and I want the court to say in his own mind whether this letter was anything but the products of a diseased mind, and if it does not show a relationship that was responsible for this terrible homicide. This was written by Leopold to Loeb. They lived close together, only a few blocks from each other; saw each other every day; but Leopold wrote him this letter:

October 9, 1923.

Dear Dick:

In view of our former relations, I take it for granted that it is unnecessary to make any excuse for writing you at this time, and still I am going to state my reasons for so doing, as this may turn out to be a long letter, and I don't want to cause you the inconvenience of reading it all to find out what it contains if you are not interested in the subjects dealt with.

First, I am enclosing the document which I mentioned to you today, and which I will explain later. Second, I am going to tell you of a new fact which has come up since our discussion. And third, I am going to put in writing what my attitude toward our present relations, with a view of avoiding future possible misunderstandings, and in the hope (though I think it rather vain) that possibly we may have misunderstood each other, and can yet clear this matter up.

Now, as to the first, I wanted you this afternoon, and still want you, to feel that we are on an equal footing legally, and therefore, I purposely committed the same tort of which you were guilty, the only difference being that in your case the facts would be harder to prove than in mine, should I deny them.

The enclosed document should secure you against changing my mind in admitting the facts, if the matter should come up, as it would prove to any court that they were true.

As to the second. On your suggestion I immediately phoned Dick Rubel, and speaking from a paper prepared beforehand (to be sure of the exact wording) said:

"Dick, when we were together yesterday, did I tell you that Dick (Loeb) had told me the things which I then told you, or that it was merely my opinion that I believed them to be so?"

I asked this twice to be sure he understood, and on the same answer both times (which I took down as he spoke) felt that he did understand.

He replied:

"No, you did not tell me that Dick told you these things, but said that they were in your opinion true."

He further denied telling you subsequently that I had said that they were gleaned from conversation with you, and I then told him that he was quite right, that you never had told me. I further told him that this was merely your suggestion of how to settle a question of fact that he was in no way implicated, and that neither of us would be angry with him at his reply. (I imply your assent to this.)

This of course proves that you were mistaken this afternoon in the question of my having actually and technically broken confidence, and voids my apology, which I made contingent on proof of this matter.

Now, as to the third, last, and most important question. When you came to my home this afternoon I expected either to break friendship with you or attempt to kill you unless you told me why you acted as you did yesterday.

You did, however, tell me, and hence the question shifted to the fact that I would act as before if you persisted in thinking me treacherous, either in act (which you waived if Dick's opinion went with mine) or in intention.

Now, I apprehend, though here I am not quite sure, that you said that you did not think me treacherous in intent, nor ever have, but that you considered me in the wrong and expected such a statement from me. This statement I unconditionally refused to make until such time as I may become convinced of its truth.

However, the question of our relation I think must be in your hands (unless the above conceptions are mistaken), inasmuch as you have satisfied first one and then the other requirement, upon which I agreed to refrain from attempting to kill you or refusing to continue our friendship. Hence I have no reason not to continue to be on friendly terms with you, and would under ordinary conditions continue as before.

The only question, then, is with you. You demand me to perform an act, namely, state that I acted wrongly. This I refuse. Now it is up to you to inflict the penalty for this refusal—at your discretion, to break friendship, inflict physical punishment, or anything else you like, or on the other hand to continue as before.

The decision, therefore, must rest with you. This is all of my opinion on the right and wrong of the matter.

Now comes a practical question. I think that I would ordinarily be expected to, and in fact do expect to continue my attitude toward you, as before, until I learn either by direct words or by conduct on your part which way your decision has been formed. This I shall do.

Now a word of advice. I do not wish to influence your decision either way, but I do want to warn you that in case you deem it advisable to discontinue our friendship, that in both our interests extreme care must be had. The motif of "A falling out of ————" would be sure to be popular, which is patently undesirable and forms an irksome but unavoidable bond between us.

Therefore, it is, in my humble opinion, expedient, though our breech need be no less real in fact, yet to observe the conventionalities, such as salutation on the street and a general appearance of at least not unfriendly relations on all occasions when we may be thrown together in public.

Now, Dick, I am going to make a request to which I have perhaps no right, and yet which I dare to make also for "Auld Lang Syne." Will you, if not too inconvenient, let me know your answer (before I leave tomorrow) on the last count? This, to which I have no right, would greatly help my peace of mind in the next few days when it is most necessary to me. You can if you will merely call up my home before 12 noon and leave a message saying, "Dick says yes," if you wish our relations to continue as before, and "Dick says no," if not.

It is unnecessary to add that your decision will of course have no effect on my keeping to myself our confidences of the past, and that I regret the whole affair more than I can say.

Hoping not to have caused you too much trouble in reading this, I am (for the present), as ever

"BABE."

Now, I undertake to say that under any interpretation of this case, taking into account all the things your Honor knows, that have not been made public, or leaving them out, nobody can interpret that letter excepting on the theory of a diseased mind, and with it goes this strange document which was referred to in the letter.

"I, Nathan F. Leopold, Jr., being under no duress or compulsion, do hereby affirm and declare that on this, the 9th day of October, 1923, I for reasons of my own locked the door of the room in which I was with one Richard A. Loeb, with the intent of blocking his only feasible mode of egress, and that I further indicated my intention of applying physical force upon the person of the said Richard A. Loeb if necessary to carry out my design, to-wit, to block his only feasible mode of egress."

There is nothing in this case, whether heard alone by the court or heard in public that can explain these documents, on the theory that the defendants were normal human beings.

I want to call your attention then to an extract from another letter by Babe, if I may be permitted to call him Babe, until you hang him.

On October 10th, this is written by Leopold on the 20th Century train, the day after the other letter was written, and in it he says:

" . . . now, that is all that is in point to our controversy."

But I am going to add a little more in an effort to explain my system of the Nietzschian philosophy with regard to you.

"It may not have occurred to you why a mere mistake in judgment on your part should be treated as a crime when on the part of another it should not be so considered. Here are the reasons. In formulating a superman he is, on account of certain superior qualities inherent in him, exempted from the ordinary laws which govern ordinary men. He is not liable for anything he may do, whereas others would be, except for the one crime that it is possible for him to commit—to make a mistake.

"Now obviously any code which conferred upon an individual or upon a group extraordinary privileges without also putting on him extraordinary responsibility, would be unfair and bad. Therefore, the superman is held to have committed a crime every time he errs in judgment—a mistake excusable in others. But you may say that you have previously made mistakes which I did not treat as crimes. This is true. To cite an example, the other night you expressed the opinion, and insisted, that Marcus Aurelius Antonius was practically the founder of Stoicism. In so doing you committed a crime. But it was a slight crime, and I chose to forgive it. I have, and had before that, forgiven the crime which you committed in committing the error in judgment which caused the whole train of events. I did not and do not wish to charge you with crime, but I feel justified in using any of the consequences of your crime for which you are held responsible, to my advantage. This and only this I did, so you see how careful you must be."

Is that the letter of a normal eighteen-year-old boy, or is it the letter of a diseased brain?

Is that the letter of boys acting as boys should, and thinking as boys should, or is it the letter of one whose philosophy has taken possession of him, who understands that what the world calls a crime is something that the superman may do—who believes that the only crime the superman can commit is to make a mistake? He believed it. He was immature. It possessed him. It was manifest in the strange compact that the court already knows about between these two boys, by which each was to yield something and each was to give something. Out of that compact and out of these diseased minds grew this terrible crime.

Tell me, was this compact the act of normal boys, of boys who think and feel as boys should—boys who have the thoughts and emotions and physical life that boys should have? There is nothing in all of it that corresponds with normal life. There is a weird, strange, unnatural disease in all of it which is responsible for this deed.

I submit the facts do not rest on the evidence of these boys alone. It is proven by the writings; it is proven by every act. It is proven by their companions, and there can be no question about it.

We brought into this courtroom a number of their boy friends, whom they had known day by day, who had associated with them in the club house, were their constant companions, and they tell the same stories. They tell the story that neither of these two boys was responsible for his conduct.

Maremont, whom the State first called, one of the oldest of the boys, said that Leopold had never had any judgment of any sort. They talked about the superman. Leopold argued his philosophy. It was a religion with him. But as to judgment of things in life he had none. He was developed intellectually, wanting emotionally, developed in those things which a boy does not need and should not have at his age, but absolutely void of the healthy feelings, of the healthy instincts of practical life that are necessary to the child.

We called not less than ten or twelve of their companions and all of them testified the same: Dickie Loeb was not allowed by his companions the privileges of his class because of his child-ishness and his lack of judgment. Nobody denies it, and yet the State's Attorney makes a play here on account of this girl whose testimony was so important, Miss Nathan. What did the State's Attorney do in this matter? Before we ever got to these defendants these witnesses were called in by subpoenas of the Grand Jury, and then taken into the office of the State's Attorney; they were young boys and girls, taken just when this story broke. Without any friends, without any counsel, they were questioned in the State's Attorney's office, and they were asked to say whether they had seen anything strange or insane about these boys. Several of them said no. Not one of them had any warning, not one of them had any chance to think, not one of them knew what it meant, not one of them had a chance to recall the lives of both and they were in the presence of lawyers and policemen and officers, and still they seek to bind these young people by those statements.

Miss Nathan is quoted as saying that she never noticed any mental disease in them, and yet she said the lawyers refused to put down all she said and directed the reporter not to take all she said; that she came in there from a sick bed without any notice; she had no time to think about it; and then she told this court of her association with Dickie Loeb, and the strange, weird, childish things he did.

One other witness, a young man, and only one other, was called in and examined by the State's Attorney on the day that this confession was made; and we placed him on the stand and he practically tells the same story; that he was called to the State's Attorney's office; he had no chance to think about it; he had no chance to consider the conduct of these boys; he was called in immediately and the questions were put to him; and when he was called by us and had an opportunity to consider it and know what it meant he related to this court what has been related by every other witness in this case.

As to the standing of these boys amongst their fellows—that they were irresponsible, that they had no judgment, that they were childish, that their acts were strange, that their beliefs were impossible for boys—is beyond question in this case.

And what did they do on the other side?

It was given out that they had a vast army of witnesses. They called three. A professor who talked with Leopold only upon his law studies, and two others who admitted all that we said, on cross examination, and the rest were dismissed. So it leaves all of this beyond dispute and admitted in this case.

Now both sides have called alienists and I will refer to that for a few moments. I shall only take a little time with the alienists.

The facts here are plain; when these boys had made the confession on Sunday afternoon before their counsel or their friends had any chance to see them, Mr. Crowe sent out for four men. He sent out for Dr. Patrick, who is an alienist; Dr. Church, who is an alienist; Dr. Krohn, who is a witness, a testifier; and Dr. Singer, who is pretty good—I would not criticise him but I would not class him with Patrick and with Church.

I have said to your Honor that in my opinion he sent for the two ablest men in Chicago as far as the public knows them, Dr. Church and Dr. Patrick. I have said to your Honor that if Judge Crowe had not got to them first I would have tried to get them. I not only say I would have tried, but I say I would have succeeded. You heard Dr. Church's testimony. Dr. Church is an honest man though an alienist. Under cross examination he admitted every position which I took. He admitted the failure of emotional life in these boys; he admitted its importance; he admitted the importance of beliefs strongly held in human conduct; he said himself that if he could get at all the facts he would understand what was back of this strange murder. Every single position that we have claimed in this case Dr. Church admitted.

Dr. Singer did the same. The only difference between them was this, it took but one question to get Dr. Church to admit it, and it took ten to a dozen to get Dr. Singer. He objected and hedged and ran and quibbled. There could be no mistake about it, and your Honor heard it in this court room.

He sought every way he could to avoid the truth, and when it came to the point that he could not dodge any longer, he admitted every proposition just exactly the same as Dr. Church admitted them: The value of emotional life; its effect on conduct; that it was the ruling thing in conduct, as every person knows who is familiar with psychology and who is familiar with the human system.

Could there be any doubt, your Honor, but what both those witnesses, Church and Singer, or any doubt but what Patrick would have testified for us? Now what did they do in their examination? What kind of a chance did these alienists have? It is perfectly obvious that they had none. Church, Patrick, Krohn went into a room with these two boys who had been in the possession of the State's Attorney's office for sixty hours; they were surrounded by policemen, were surrounded by guards and detectives and State's Attorneys; twelve or fifteen of them, and here they told their story. Of course this audience had a friendly attitude toward them. I know my friend Judge Crowe had a friendly attitude because I saw divers, various and sundry pictures of Prosecutor Crowe taken with these boys.

When I first saw them I believed it showed friendship for the boys, but now I am inclined to think that he had them taken just as a lawyer who goes up in the country fishing has his picture taken with his catch.

The boys had been led doubtless to believe that these people were friends. They were taken there, in the presence of all this crowd. What was done? The boys told their story, and that was all.

Of course, Krohn remembered a lot that did not take place— and we would expect that of him; and he forgot much that did take place—and we would expect that of him, too. So far as the honest witnesses were concerned, they said that not a word was spoken excepting a little conversation upon birds and the relation of the story that they had already given to the State's Attorney; and from that, and nothing else, both Patrick and Church said they showed no reaction as ordinary persons should show it, and intimated clearly that the commission of the crime itself would put them on inquiry as to whether these boys were mentally right; both admitted that the conditions surrounding them made the right kind of examination impossible; both admitted that they needed a better chance to form a reliable opinion.

The most they said was that at this time they saw no evidence of insanity.

Now, your Honor, no experts, and no alienists with any chance to examine, have testified that these boys were normal.

Singer did a thing more marvelous still. He never saw these boys until he came into this court, excepting when they were brought down in violation of their constitutional rights to the office of Judge Crowe, after they had been turned over to the jailer, and there various questions were asked them, and to all of these the boys replied that they respectfully refused to answer on advice of counsel. And yet that was enough for Singer.

Your Honor, if these boys had gone to the office of any one of these eminent gentlemen, had been taken by their parents or gone by themselves, and the doctors had seriously tried to find out whether there was anything wrong about their minds, how would they have done it? They would have taken them patiently and carefully. They would have sought to get their confidence. They would have listened to their story. They would have listened to it in the attitude of a father listening to his child. You know it. Every doctor knows it. In no other way could they find out their mental condition. And the men who are honest with this question have admitted it.

And yet Dr. Krohn will testify that they had the best chance in the world, when his own associates, sitting where they were, said that they did not.

Your Honor, nobody's life or liberty or property should be taken from them upon an examination like that. It was not an examination. It was simply an effort to get witnesses, regardless of facts, who might at some time come into court and give their testimony, to take these boys' lives.

Now, I imagine that in closing this case Judge Crowe will say that our witnesses mainly came from the East. That is true. And he is responsible for it. I am not blaming him, but he is responsible for it. There are other alienists in Chicago, and the evidence shows that we had the boys examined by numerous ones in Chicago. We wanted to get the best. Did we get them?

Your Honor knows that the place where a man lives does not affect his truthfulness or his ability. We brought the man who stands probably above all of them, and who certainly is far superior to anybody called upon the other side. First of all, we called Dr. William A. White. And who is he? For many years he has been superintendent of the Government Hospital for the insane in Washington; a man who has written more books, delivered more lectures and had more honors and knows this subject better than all of their alienists put together; a man who plainly came here not for money, and who receives for his testimony the same per diem as is paid by the other side; a man who knows his subject, and whose ability and truthfulness must have impressed this court.

It will not do, your Honor, to say that because Dr. White is not a resident of Chicago that he lies. No man stands higher in the United States, no man is better known than Dr. White, his learning and intelligence was obvious from his evidence in this case.

Who else did we get? Do I need to say anything about Dr. Healy? Is there any question about his integrity? A man who seldom goes into court except upon the order of the court.

Your Honor was connected with the Municipal Court. You know that Dr. Healy was the first man who operated with the courts in the City of Chicago to give aid to the unfortunate youths whose minds were afflicted and who were the victims of the law.

No man stands higher in Chicago than Dr. Healy. No man has done as much work in the study of adolescence. No man has either read or written or thought or worked as much with the young. No man knows the adolescent boy as well as Dr. Healy.

Dr. Healy began his research and his practice in the City of Chicago, and was the first psychiatrist of the boys' court. He was then made a director of the Baker Foundation of Boston and is now carrying on his work in connection with the courts of Boston.

His books are known wherever men study boys. His reputation is known all over the United States and in Europe. Compare him and his reputation with Dr. Krohn. Compare it with any other witness that the state called in this case.

Dr. Glueck, who was for years the alienist at Sing Sing, and connected with the penal institutions in the State of New York; a man of eminent attainments and ripe scholarship. No-one is his superior.

And Dr. Hulbert, a young man who spent nineteen days in the examination of these boys, together with Dr. Bowen, an eminent doctor in his line from Boston. These two physicians spent all this time getting every detail of these boys' lives, and structures; each one of these alienists took all the time they needed for a thorough examination, without the presence of lawyers, detectives and policemen. Each one of these psychiatrists tells this court the story, the sad, pitiful story, of the unfortunate minds of these two young lads.

I submit, your honor, that there can be no question about the relative value of these two sets of alienists; there can be no question of their means of understanding; there can be no question but that White, Glueck, Hulbert and Healy knew what they were talking about, for they had every chance to find out. They are either lying to this court, or their opinion is good.

On the other hand, not one single man called by the State had any chance to know. He was called in to see these boys, the same as the state would call a hangman: "Here are the boys; officer, do your duty." And that is all there was of it.

Now, your Honor, I shall pass that subject. I think all of the facts of this extraordinary case, all of the testimony of the alienists, all that your Honor has seen and heard, all their friends and acquaintances who have come here to enlighten this court—I think all of it shows that this terrible act was the act of immature and diseased brains, the act of children.

Nobody can explain it in any other way.

No one can imagine it in any other way.

It is not possible that it could have happened in any other way. And, I submit, your Honor, that by every law of humanity, by every law of justice, by every feeling of righteousness, by every instinct of pity, mercy and charity, your Honor should say that because of the condition of these boys' minds, it would be monstrous to visit upon them the vengeance that is asked by the State.

I want to discuss now another thing which this court must consider and which to my mind is absolutely conclusive in this case. That is, the age of these boys.

I shall discuss it more in detail than I have discussed it before, and I submit, your Honor, that it is not possible for any court to hang these two boys if he pays any attention whatever to the modern attitude toward the young, if he pays any attention whatever to the precedents in this county, if he pays any attention to the humane instincts which move ordinary men.

I have a list of executions in Cook County beginning in 1840, which I presume covers the first one, because I asked to have it go to the beginning. Ninety poor unfortunate men have given up their lives to stop murder in Chicago. Ninety men have been hanged by the neck until dead, because of the ancient superstition that in some way hanging one man keeps another from committing a crime. The ancient superstitition, I say, because I defy the state to point to a criminologist, a scientist, a student, who has ever said it. Still we go on, as if human conduct was not influenced and controlled by natural laws the same as all the rest of the Universe is the subject of law. We treat crime as if it had no cause. We go on saying, "Hang the unfortunates, and it will end." Was there ever a murder without a cause? Was there ever a crime without a cause? And yet all punishment proceeds upon the theory that there is no cause; and the only way to treat crime is to intimidate every one into goodness and obedience to law. We lawyers are a long way behind.

Crime has its cause. Perhaps all crimes do not have the same cause, but they all have some cause. And people today are seeking to find out the cause. We lawyers never try to find out. Scientists are studying it; criminologists are investigating it; but we lawyers go on and on and on, punishing and hanging and thinking that by general terror we can stamp out crime.

It never occurs to the lawyer that crime has a cause as certainly as disease, and that the way to rationally treat any abnormal condition is to remove the cause.

If a doctor were called on to treat typhoid fever he would probably try to find out what kind of milk or water the patient drank, and perhaps clean out the well so that no one else could get typhoid from the same source. But, if a lawyer was called on to treat a typhoid patient, he would give him thirty days in jail, and then he would think that nobody else would ever dare to take it. If the patient got well in fifteen days, he would be kept until his time was up; if the disease was worse at the end of thirty days, the patient would be released because his time was out.

As a rule, lawyers are not scientists. They have learned the doctrine of hate and fear, and they think that there is only one way to make men good, and that is to put them in such terror that they do not dare to be bad. They act unmindful of history, and science, and all the experience of the past.

Still, we are making some progress. Courts give attention to some things that they did not give attention to before.

Once in England they hanged children seven years of age; not necessarily hanged them, because hanging was never meant for punishment; it was meant for an exhibition. If somebody committed crime, he would be hanged by the head or the heels, it didn't matter much which, at the four cross roads, so that everybody could look at him until his bones were bare, and so that people would be good because they had seen the grewsome result of crime and hate.

Hanging was not necessarily meant for punishment. The

culprit might be killed in any other way, and then hanged—yes. Hanging was an exhibition. They were hanged on the highest hill, and hanged at the cross-ways, and hanged in public places, so that all men could see. If there is any virtue in hanging, that was the logical way, because you cannot awe men into goodness unless they know about the hanging. We have not grown better than the ancients. We have grown more squeamish; we do not like to look at it; that is all. They hanged them at seven years; they hanged them again at eleven and fourteen.

We have raised the age of hanging. We have raised it by the humanity of courts, by the understanding of courts, by the progress in science which at last is reaching the law; and in ninety men hanged in Illinois from its beginning, not one single person under twenty-three was ever hanged upon a plea of guilty—not one. If your Honor should do this, you would violate every precedent that had been set in Illinois for almost a century. There can be no excuse for it, and no justification for it, because this is the policy of the law which is rooted in the feelings of humanity, which are deep in every human being that thinks and feels. There have been two or three cases where juries have convicted boys younger than this, and where courts on convictions have refused to set aside the sentence because a jury had found it.

First, I want to call your attention, your Honor, to the cases on pleas of guilty in the State of Illinois. Back of the year 1896 the record does not show ages. After that, which is the large part, probably sixty out of ninety—all show the age. Not the age at which they are hanged, as my friend Marshall thought, but the age at the time of the verdict or sentence as is found today.

In all the history of Illinois—I am not absolutely certain of it back of 1896, but there are so many of them that I know about from the books and otherwise, that I feel I am safe in saying there is no exception to the rule—but since 1896 everyone is recorded. The first hanging in Illinois—on a plea of guilty, was May 15, 1896, when a young colored man, 24 years old, was sentenced to death by Judge Baker.

Judge Baker I knew very well; a man of ability, a fine fellow, but a man of moods. I do not know whether the court remembers him; but that was the first hanging on a plea of guilty to the credit of any man in Illinois—I mean in Chicago. I have not obtained the statistics from the rest of the state, but I am satisfied they are the same, and that boy was colored, and twenty-four, either one of which should have saved him from death, but the color probably had something to do with compassing his destruction.

The next was Julius Mannow. Now, he really was not hanged on a plea of guilty, though the records so show. I will state to your Honor just what the facts are. Joseph Windreth and Julius Mannow were tried together in 1896 on a charge of murder with robbery. When the trial was nearly finished, Julius Mannow withdrew his plea of guilty. He was defended by Elliott, whom I remember very well, and probably your Honor does. And under what he supposed was an agreement with the court he plead this man guilty, after the case was nearly finished.

Now, I am not here to discuss whether there was an agreement or not. Judge Horton who tried this case did not sentence him, but he waited for the jury's verdict on Windreth, and they found him guilty and sentenced him to death, and Judge Horton followed that sentence. Had this case come into that court on a plea of guilty, it probably would have been different; perhaps not; but it really was not a question of a plea of guilty; and he was twenty-eight or thirty years old.

I might say in passing as to Judge Horton—he is dead. I knew him very well. In some ways I liked him. I tried a case for him after he had left the bench. But I will say this: He was never noted in Chicago for his kindness and his mercy, and anybody who remembers knows that I am stating the truth.

The next man who was hanged on a plea of guilty was Daniel McCarthy, twenty-nine years old, in 1897, by Judge Stein. Well, he is dead. I am very careful about being kind to the dead, so I will say that he never knew what mercy was, at least while he lived. Whether he does now, I cannot say. Still he was a good lawyer. That was in 1897.

It was twenty-two years, your Honor, before anybody else was hanged in Cook County on a plea of guilty, old or young, twent-two years before a judge had either the old or young walk into his court and throw himself on the mercy of the court and get the rope for it; and a great many men have been tried for murder, and a great many men have been executed, and a great many men have plead guilty and have been sentenced, either to a term of years or life imprisonment, over three hundred in that twenty-two years, and no man, old or young, was executed.

But twenty-two years later, in 1919, Thomas Fitzgerald, a man about forty years old, was sentenced for killing a little girl, plead guilty before my friend Judge Crowe, and he was put to death. And that is all. In the history of Cook County that is all that have been put to death on a plea of guilty. That is all.

Your Honor, what excuse could you possibly have for putting these boys to death? You would have to turn your back on every precedent of the past. You would have to turn your back on the progress of the world. You would have to ignore all human sentiment and feeling, of which I know the court has his full share. You would have to do all this if you would hang boys of eighteen and nineteen years of age who have come into this court and thrown themselves upon your mercy.

I might do it, but I would want good reason for it, which does not exist and cannot exist in this case, unless publicity, worked-up feeling, and mad hate, is a reason, and I know it is not.

Since that time one other man has been sentenced to death on a plea of guilty. That was James H. Smith, twenty-eight years old, sentenced by Judge Kavanagh. But we were spared his hanging. That was in January, 1923. I could tell you why it was, and I will tell you later. It is due to the cruelty that has paralyzed the hearts of men growing out of the war. We are accustomed to blood, your Honor. It used to look mussy, and make us feel squeamish. But we have not only seen it shed in buckets full, we have seen it shed in rivers, lakes and oceans, and we have delighted in it; we have preached it, we have worked for it, we have advised it, we have taught it to the young, encouraged the old, until the world has been drenched in blood, and it has left its stains upon every human heart and upon every human mind, and has almost stifled the feelings of pity and charity that have their natural home in the human breast.

I do not believe that Judge Kavanagh would ever have done this except for the great war which has left its mark on all of us, one of the terrible by-products of those wretched years.

This man was reprieved, but James Smith was twenty-eight years old; he was old enough to vote, he was old enough to make contracts, he needed no guardian, he was old enough to do all the things that an older man can do. He was not a boy; a boy that is the special ward of the state, and the special ward of the court, and who cannot act except in special ways because he is not mature. He was twenty-eight and he is not dead and will not die. His life was saved, and you may go over every hanging, and if your Honor shall decorate the gallows with these two boys, your honor will be the first in Chicago who has even done such a deed. And, I know you will not.

Your Honor, I must hasten along, for I will close tonight. I know I should have closed before. Still there seems so much that I would like to say. I will spend a few more minutes on this record of hangings. There was one boy nineteen years old, Thomas Schultz, who was convicted by a jury and executed. There was one boy who has been referred to here, eighteen, Nicholas Vianni, who was convicted by a jury and executed. No one else under twenty-one, your honor, has been convicted by a jury and sentenced to death. Now, let me speak a word about these.

Schultz was convicted in 1912. Viani was convicted in 1920. Of course, I believe it should not have happened, but your Honor knows the difference between a plea of guilty and a verdict. It is easy enough for a jury to divide the responsibility by twelve. They have not the age and the experience and the charity which comes from age and experience. It is easy for some State's Attorneys to influence some juries. I don't know who defended the poor boy, but I guarantee that it was not the best lawyers at the bar,—but doubtless a good lawyer prosecuted him, and when he was convicted the court said that he had rested his fate with the jury, and he would not disturb the verdict.

I do not know whether your Honor, humane and considerate as I believe you to be, would have disturbed a jury's verdict in this case, but I know that no judge in Cook County ever himself upon a plea of guilty passed judgment of death in a case below the age of twenty-three, and only one at the age of twenty-three was ever hanged on a plea of guilty.

Viani I have looked up, and I don't care who did it or how it was done, it was a shame and a disgrace that an eighteen year old boy should be hanged, in 1920, or a nineteen year old boy should be hanged, in 1920, and I am assuming it is all right to hang somebody, which it is not. I have looked up the Viani case because my friend Marshall read a part where it said that Viani pleaded guilty. He did not say it positively, because he is honest, and he knew there might be a reason. Vianni was tried and convicted—I don't remember the name of the judge,—in 1920.

There were various things working against him. It was in 1920, after the war. Most anything might have happened after the war, which I will speak of later, and not much later, for I am to close tonight. He was convicted in 1920. There was a band of Italian desperadoes, so-called. I don't know. Sam Cardinelli was the leader, a man forty years of age. But their records were very bad.

This boy should have been singled out from the rest. If I had been defending him, and he had not been, I never would have come into court again. But he was not. He was tried with the rest. I have looked up the records, and I find that he was in the position of most of these unfortunates; he did not have a lawyer.

Your Honor, the question of whether a man is convicted or acquitted does not always depend on the evidence or entirely on the judge or entirely on the jury. The lawyer has something to do with it. And the State always has—always has at least moderately good lawyers. And the defendants have, if they can get the money; and if they cannot, they have nobody. Vianni, who was on trial with others for his life, had a lawyer appointed by the court. Ed Raber, if I am rightly informed, prosecuted. He had a fine chance, this poor Italian boy, tried with three or four others. And prosecuted by one of the most relentless prosecutors Chicago has ever known. This boy was defended by somebody whose name I never heard, who was appointed by the court.

Your Honor, if in this court a boy of eighteen and a boy of nineteen should be hanged on a plea of guilty, in violation of every precedent of the past, in violation of the policy of the law to take care of the young, in violation of all the progress that has been made and of the humanity that has been shown in the care of the young; in violation of the law that places boys in reformatories instead of prisons,—if your Honor in violation of all that and in the face of all the past should stand here in Chicago alone to hang a boy on a plea of guilty, then we are turning our faces backward toward the barbarism which once possessed the world. If your Honor can hang a boy eighteen, some other judge can hang him at seventeen, or sixteen, or fourteen. Some day, if there is any such thing as progress in the world, if there is any spirit of humanity that is working in the hearts of men, some day men would look back upon this as a barbarous age which deliberately set itself in the way of progress, humanity and sympathy, and committed an unforgivable act.

Yet your honor has been asked to hang, and I must refer here for a minute to something which I dislike to discuss. I hesitated whether to pass it by unnoticed or to speak of it, but feel that I must say something about it, and that was the testimony of Gortland, the policeman. He came into this court, the only witness who said that young Leopold told him that he might get into the hands of a friendly judge and succeed. Your Honor, that is a blow below the belt. There isn't a word of truth in his statement, as I can easily prove to your Honor. It was carved out of the air, to awe and influence the court, and place him in a position where if he saved life someone might be malicious enough to say that he was a friendly judge, and, if he took it, the fear might invade the community that he did not dare to be merciful.

I am sure that your Honor knows there is only one way to do in this case, and I know you will do it. You will take this case, with your judgment and your conscience, and settle it as you think it should be settled. I may approve or I may disapprove, or Robert Crowe may approve or disapprove, or the public may approve or disapprove, but you must satisfy yourself and you will.

Now, let me take Gortland's testimony for a minute; and I am not going over the record. It is all here. He swore that on the night after the arrest of these two boys, Nathan Leopold told him, in discussing the case, that a friendly judge might save him. He is the first man who testified for the State that any of us cross examined, if you remember. They called witness after witness to prove something that did not need to be proved under a plea of guilty. Then this came, which to me was a poisoned piece of perjury, with a purpose, and I cross examined him:

"Did you make any record?"
"Yes, I think I did."
"Where is it?"
"I think I have it."
"Let me see it."
"Yes."
There was not a word or a syllable upon that paper.
"Did you make any other?"
"Yes."
"When did you make it?"
"Within two or three days of the occurrence."
"Let me see that."
He said he would bring it back later.
"Did you make another?"
"Yes."
"What was it?"
"A complete report to the chief of police."
"Is it in there?"
"I think so."
"Will you bring that?"
"Yes."

He brought them both into this court. They contained, all these reports, a complete or almost a complete copy of everything that happened, but not one word on this subject. He deliberately said that he made that record within a few days of the time it occurred, and that he told the office about it within a few days of the time it occurred. And then what did he say? Then he came back in answer to my cross examination, and said that he never told Judge Crowe about it until the night before Judge Crowe made his opening statement in this case. Six weeks after he heard it, long after the time he said that he made a record of it, and there was not a single word or syllable about this matter in any report he made.

I am sorry to discuss it; I am sorry to embarrass this court, but what can I do? I want your Honor to know that if in your judgment you think these boys should hang, we will know it is your judgment. It is hard enough, for a court to sit where you sit, with the eyes of the world upon you, in the fierce heat of public opinion, for and against. It is hard enough, without any lawyer making it harder. I assure you it is with deep regret that I even mention the evidence, and I will say no more about it, excepting that this statement was a deliberate lie, made out of whole cloth, and his own evidence shows it.

Now, your honor, I have spoken about the war. I believed in it. I don't know whether I was crazy or not. Sometimes I think perhaps I was. I approved of it; I joined in the general cry of madness and despair. I urged men to fight. I was safe because I was too old to go. I was like the rest. What did they do? Right or wrong, justifiable or unjustifiable—which I need not discuss today—it changed the world. For four long years the civilized world was engaged in killing men. Christian against Christian, barbarians uniting with Chrstians to kill Christians; anything to kill. It was taught in every school, aye in the Sunday schools. The little children played at war. The toddling children on the street. Do you suppose this world has ever been the same since then? How long, your Honor, will it take for the world to get back the humane emotions that were daily growing before the war? How long will it take the calloused hearts of men before the scars of hatred and cruelty shall be removed?

We read of killing one hundred thousand men in a day. We read about it and we rejoiced in it—if it was the other fellows who were killed. We were fed on flesh and drank blood. Even down to the prattling babe. I need not tell your honor this, because you know; I need not tell you how many upright, honorable young boys have come into this court charged with murder, some saved and some sent to their death, boys who fought in this war and learned to place a cheap value on human life. You know it and I know it. These boys were brought up in it. The tales of death were in their homes, their playgrounds, their schools; they were in the newspapers that they read; it was a part of the common frenzy—what was a life? It was nothing. It was the least sacred thing in existence and these boys were trained to this cruelty.

It will take fifty years to wipe it out of the human heart, if ever. I know this, that after the Civil War in 1865, crimes of this sort increased, marvelously. No one needs to tell me that crime has no cause. It has as definite a cause as any other disease, and I know that out of the hatred and bitterness of the Civil War crime increased as America had never known it before. I know that growing out of the Napoleonic wars there was an era of crime such as Europe had never seen before. I know that Europe is going through the same experience today; I know it has followed every war; and I know it has influenced these boys so that life was not the same to them as it would have been if the world had not been made red with blood. I protest against the crimes and mistakes of society being visited upon them. All of us have our share in it. I have mine. I cannot tell and I shall never know how many words of mine might have given birth to cruelty in place of love and kindness and charity.

Your Honor knows that in this very court crimes of violence have increased growing out of the war. Not necessarily by those who fought but by those that learned that blood was cheap, and human life was cheap, and if the State could take it lightly why not the boy? There are causes for this terrible crime. There are causes, as I have said, for everything that happens in the world. War is a part of it; education is a part of it; birth is a part of it; money is a part of it,—all these conspired to compass the destruction of these two poor boys.

Has the court any right to consider anything but these two boys? The State says that your Honor has a right to consider the welfare of the community, as you have. If the welfare of the community would be benefited by taking these lives, well and good. I think it would work evil that no one could measure. Has your Honor a right to consider the families of these two defendants? I have been sorry, and I am sorry for the bereavement of Mr. and Mrs. Franks, for those broken ties that cannot be healed. All I can hope and wish is that some good may come from it all. But as compared with the families of Leopold and Loeb, the Franks are to be envied,— and everyone knows it.

I do not know how much salvage there is in these two boys. I hate to say it in their presence, but what is there to look forward to? I do not know but what your Honor would be merciful if you tied a rope around their necks and let them die; merciful to them, but not merciful to civilization, and not merciful to those who would be left behind. To spend the balance of their days in prison is mighty little to look forward to, if anything. Is it anything? They may have the hope that as the years roll around they might be released. I do not know. I do not know. I will be honest with this court as I have tried to be from the beginning. I know that these boys are not fit to be at large. I believe they will not be until they pass through the next stage of life, at forty-five or fifty. Whether they will be then, I cannot tell. I am sure of this; that I will not be here to help them. So far as I am concerned, it is over.

I would not tell this court that I do not hope that some time, when life and age has changed their bodies, as it does, and has changed their emotions, as it does,—that they may once more return to life. I would be the last person on earth to close the door of hope to any human being that lives, and least of all to my clients. But what have they to look forward to? Nothing. And I think here of the stanzas of Housman:

> "Now hollow fires burn out to black,
>   And lights are fluttering low:
> Square your shoulders, lift your pack
>   And leave your friends and go.
> O never fear, lads, naught's to dread,
>   Look not left nor right:
> In all the endless road you tread
>   There's nothing but the night."

I care not, your Honor, whether the march begins at the gallows or when the gates of Joliet close upon them, there is nothing but the night, and that is little for any human being to expect.

But there are others to be considered. Here are these two families, who have led honest lives, who will bear the name that they bear, and future generations must carry it on.

Here is Leopold's father,—and this boy was the pride of his life. He watched him, he cared for him, he worked for him; the boy was brilliant and accomplished, he educated him, and he thought that fame and position awaited him, as it should have awaited. It is a hard thing for a father to see his life's hopes crumble into dust.

Should he be considered? Should his brothers be considered? Will it do society any good or make your life safer, or any human being's life safer, if it should be handed down from generation to generation, that this boy, their kin, died upon the scaffold?

And Loeb's, the same. Here is the faithful uncle and brother, who have watched here day by day, while Dickie's father and his mother are too ill to stand this terrific strain, and shall be waiting for a message which means more to them than it can mean to you or me. Shall these be taken into account in this general bereavement?

Have they any rights? Is there any reason, your Honor, why their proud names and all the future generations that bear them shall have this bar sinister written across them? How many boys and girls, how many unborn children will feel it? It is bad enough as it is, God knows. It is bad enough, however it is. But it's not yet death on the scaffold. It's not that. And I ask your honor, in addition to all that I have said, to save two honorable families from a disgrace that never ends, and which could be of no avail to help any human being that lives.

Now, I must say a word more and then I will leave this with you where I should have left it long ago. None of us are unmindful of the public; courts are not, and juries are not. We placed our fate in the hands of a trained court, thinking that he would be more mindful and considerate than a jury. I cannot say how people feel. I have stood here for three months as one might stand at the ocean trying to sweep back the tide. I hope the seas are subsiding and the wind is falling, and I believe they are, but I wish to make no false pretense to this court. The easy thing and the popular thing to do is to hang my clients. I know it. Men and women who do not think will applaud. The cruel and the thoughtless will approve. It will be easy today; but in Chicago, and reaching out over the length and breadth of the land, more and more fathers and mothers, the humane, the kind and the hopeful, who are gaining an understanding and asking questions not only about these poor boys, but about their own,—these will join in no acclaim at the death of my clients. These would ask that the shedding of blood be stopped, and that the normal feelings of man resume their sway. And as the days and the months and the years go on, they will ask it more and more. But, your Honor, what they shall ask may not count. I know the easy way. I know your Honor stands between the future and the past. I know the future is with me, and what I stand for here; not merely for the lives of these two unfortunate lads, but for all boys and all girls; for all of the young, and as far as possible, for all of the old. I am pleading for life, understanding, charity, kindness, and the infinite mercy that considers all. I am pleading that we overcome cruelty with kindness and hatred with love. I know the future is on my side. Your Honor stands between the past and the future. You may hang these boys; you may hang them by the neck until they are dead. But in doing it you will turn your face toward the past. In doing it you are making it harder for every other boy who in ignorance and darkness must grope his way through the mazes which only childhood knows. In doing it you will make it harder for unborn children. You may save them and make it easier for every child that some time may stand where these boys stand. You will make it easier for every human being with an aspiration and a vision and a hope and a fate. I am pleading for the future; I am pleading for a time when hatred and cruelty will not control the hearts of men. When we can learn by reason and judgment and understanding and faith that all life is worth saving, and that mercy is the highest attribute of man.

I feel that I should apologize for the length of time I have taken. This case may not be as important as I think it is, and I am sure I do not need to tell this court, or to tell my friends that I would fight just as hard for the poor as for the rich. If I should succeed in saving these boys' lives and do nothing for the progress of the law, I should feel sad, indeed. If I can succeed, my greatest reward and my greatest hope will be that I have done something for the tens of thousands of other boys, for the countless unfortunates who must tread the same road in blind childhood that these poor boys have trod,—that I have done something to help human understanding, to temper justice with mercy, to overcome hate with love.

I was reading last night of the aspiration of the old Persian poet, Omar Khayyam. It appealed to me as the highest that I can vision. I wish it was in my heart, and I wish it was in the hearts of all.

> "So I be written in the Book of Love,
> I do not care about that Book above.
> Erase my name or write it as you will,
> So I be written in the Book of Love."

The State's Case

Thomas Marshall, Assistant State's Attorney, gave the opening argument on behalf of the people, beginning August 19th, 1924.

"There is in this case but one question before the court, and one question only. That is, what punishment is proportionate to the turpitude of the offense or, in other words, what punishment under the law fits the crime committed?

"In discussing the legal phases of the case—the facts will be discussed by Mr. Savage—I want to state at the outset of the position of the prosecution. The position of the State is that there is but one penalty that is proportionate to the turpitude of this crime. Only one penalty applies to this crime, and that is the extreme penalty—death. Under the facts and circumstances establishing premeditated, carefully planned and deliberate murder of a helpless fourteen-year-old school boy, Robert Franks. Penalty under the laws of the State of Illinois for aggravated, deliberate murder, is death.

"The statute, it is true, ranges from fourteen years to the death penalty, and the court has a duty to fix a penalty proportionate to the turpitude, that is to say, to the depravity and viciousness of the crime committed."

Mr. Marshall took the rest of the day allotted to him to cite cases where the judge, given judicial discretion, had pronounced the extreme penalty.

Mr. Joseph P. Savage, Assistant State's Attorney, presented the State's arguments, August twentieth, reviewing the facts of the case, as they had been brought out in the trial. He went

306

over the testimony of each of the eighty witnesses who had been
called by the State's Attorney to prove the crime against the boys.

At the beginning of his argument, he recalled the statement
made by one of the State's witnesses that Leopold believed with
nihilists of Russia that he was himself above the law, that, if
he thought it right to commit a murder, there was no reason why
he would not do so.

In his argument, Mr. Savage laid much emphasis upon the
alleged philosophy of Leopold and cited many cases in states'
and federal courts wherein communists holding views which he
declared were similar to Leopold's had been visited with heavy
penalties. Using this sympathy with communistic ideas, which
had been attributed to Leopold, as the basis of his charge against
the boy, Mr. Savage presented Leopold and his associate, Loeb,
as enemies to society, not only because of their crime but also
because of their beliefs.

He cited also several cases in which phantasy and delusions
of the defendants had been an element of their trial. These
cases, which he cited, had been assessed the death penalty.

The real burden of the State's case against the defendants,
Nathan F. Leopold, Jr., and Richard Loeb, was presented by
the State's Attorney, Mr. Crowe, who took the greater part of
three days to present his plea before the judge.

So heated did the State's Attorney become, near the conclusion of his plea, when he cited a remark attributed to Nathan
Leopold, Jr., "If we can secure a friendly judge," that Judge
Caverly severely rebuked him and ordered that portion of the
State's Attorney's words stricken from the record. It had been
testified by a policeman that Leopold, soon after his confession,
said, "Why couldn't a man with the millions of my father behind me, before a friendly judge, beat this case?"

This remark was disputed and denied by the defense, but Mr.
Crowe, in the climax of his address, brought out this alleged

statement and hurled it at the judge, as one more reason why the two boys should hang.

For the first time during the trial Judge Caverly showed a flash of passion. Several times he had to stop the case to quell wrangling between the attorneys. Once he had ordered the courtroom cleared of all women, when certain testimony was presented on the witness stand. When Clarence Darrow started his great speech, pleading for the lives of the two defendants, the crowd became so dense that they rushed the guards and packed the courtroom and corridors. Judge Caverly was unruffed as he ordered extra police, had the corridors cleared and from his bench brought order out of the chaos of the seething pandemonium of the hundreds fighting to hear Clarence Darrow.

But when the State's Attorney began his statements of the boast attributed to Leopold, Judge Caverly lost his calm. Such a statement in the record, he declared, whether true or false, reflected upon the integrity of the court. The State's Attorney endeavored to explain his reasons for mentioning the matter of Leopold's alleged boast, but the court did not allow him to proceed.

Robert E. Crowe, the State's Attorney, was born in Peoria, Illinois, and has lived in Chicago for the past 40 years.

He is a graduate of Yale university, and was admitted to the bar in October, 1901.

He was Assistant State's Attorney for five years and later Assistant Corporation Counsel until November, 1916, when he was elected Judge of the Circuit Court, becoming Chief Justice in 1917. Mr. Crowe was Chief Justice of the Criminal Court in 1920, and in November of that year was elected State's Attorney.

The address of the State's Attorney follows:

The Argument of the State's Attorney

"Before going into a discussion of the merits of the case, there is a matter that I would like to refer to. The distinguished gentleman whose profession it is to protect murder in Cook County, and concerning whose health thieves inquire before they go to commit crime, has seen fit to abuse the State's Attorney's office, and particularly my assistants, Mr. Marshall and Mr. Savage, for their conduct in this case. He has even objected to the State's Attorney referring to two self-confessed murderers, who have pleaded guilty to two capital offenses, as criminals.

"And he says that Marshall has no heart or if he has a heart that it must be a heart of stone; and that Savage was probably selected on account of his name and not on account of his attainments. That they have dared to tell your Honor that this is a cold-blooded murder; they have violated all the finer sensibility of this distinguished attorney whose profession it is to protect murder in this community, by representing this crime as a dastardly, cruel, premeditated crime.

"It is their business, if they refer to this case at all; but Bachrach in his closing argument said that I haven't any right after a plea of guilty has been entered and the evidence presented,—I haven't any right to talk to your Honor. That this case should be taken under advisement by you. With merely the plea of the defense the State's Attorney ought to go back to his office; he has no business to argue on behalf of the people of the State of Illinois at all. Their arguments must go uncontradicted and without a reply.

"We ought not to refer to these two young men, the poor sons of multimillionaires, with any coarse language.

"Savage and Marshall should have come up here and tried them with kindness and with consideration.

"I can imagine when this case was called for trial and your Honor began to warn these two defendants of the consequences of their plea, and when you said we may impose the death penalty, Savage and Marshall both rushing up and saying,

" 'Now, Judge, now, Judge, not so fast. We don't intend to be cruel in this case. We don't intend to be harsh. We want to try these boys, these kiddies, with kindness and consideration.'

"Your Honor ought not to shock their ears by such a cruel reference to the laws of the State, to the penalty of death. Why, don't you know that one of them has to shave every day of the week, and that is a bad sign. The other one only has to shave twice a week and that is a bad sign. One is short and one is tall, and it is equally a bad sign in both of them. When they were children they played with Teddy bears. One of them has three moles on his back. One is over developed sexually and the other not quite so good.

"My God, if one of them had a hare lip I suppose Darrow would want me to apologize for having had them indicted.

"Can you imagine Savage and Marshall making a plea of that sort to your Honor, and saying:

" 'Instead of sending these two mad boys, who are wandering around in the dark, instead of sending them for life to prison, parole them to us. Marshall will take Dickie and Savage will take Babe. And we will try to get them out of this phantasy life. We will try to wake them up, out of their dreams?'

"I know what your Honor would have said if they had pursued that line of conduct. You would have said,

" 'Mr. Sheriff, search these men, find out how much money they have in their pockets.'

"And if they had any money in their pockets your Honor would tell the sheriff to take them out to the psychopathic hospital and you would send for me and say,

" 'My God, Crowe, send up somebody who has got some brains to prosecute a murder case in my court room.'

"We are cold-blooded, we have planned according to Mr. Darrow for three months, and we have conspired to take the lives of two little boys who are wandering around in dreamland. We have been held up to the world as men who desire blood, who have no kindly instincts within our hearts at all. I do not believe that is fair to Tom Marshall. Tom Marshall has lived in this community for years. He is a kindly man in private life; he is a man of family; he enjoys the respect and confidence of every person who has been fortunate enough to know him.

"Joe Savage is a decent man, a clean living man, a man of kindly instincts. He is a man of family also, and he enjoys the confidence and respect of everybody in this community. I do not believe that even Mr. Darrow, who has known me for years, or any other person who knows me, would tell you that Bob Crowe is a cruel, vicious, heartless monster. I am a man of family; I love my children, four of them, and I love my wife, and I believe they love me. I have never been cruel or vicious to any living person in my life.

"I have never prosecuted any person for any wrong that he did me personally, and I have been grievously wronged in the past. I have never sued any person for any debt he owed me, although I have many debts now owing to me. I believe in God, —and that is a fault in this case, a fault not only to the two murderers, but a fault to the master pleader whose profession it is to protect murder in this county. I believe in the laws of this State. There is nothing personal in this prosecution with me. If I were not a State's Attorney or if I were not on the bench, I would have absolutely no feeling in my heart against these two as individuals. When they were in my care and custody, where it was a matter of man to man, I treated them with kindness and consideration. That is the sworn testimony in this case, that while they were in my custody they were treated with kindness and consideration.

"When I first got Leopold's name as a possible owner of these glasses, when I got the name of a lady of this community of respectability and refinement, when I got the name of a prominent lawyer, who might have been the owner of these glasses, I treated all three of them with kindness and consideration. I did not bring them into the State's Attorney's office, so that their names would be headlined across the newspapers, connected with this terrible crime, where they would have their pictures taken by every newspaper in the country. I brought them over to the La Salle Hotel, so that if none of them had any connection with this case, no disgrace or no notoriety would have attached to them. I think the State's Attorney of this county is just as kindly a man as the paid humanitarian, the man who believes in doing his fellow citizens good,—after he has done them good and plenty. But when I had fastened this crime upon these defendants, then I had a duty to perform, a sworn duty to perform the same as your Honor has.

"I have a right to forgive those who trespass against me, as I do, in the hopes that I in the hereafter will be forgiven my trespasses; as a private citizen I have that right, and as a private citizen I live that religion.

"But, as a public official selected by the people, charged with the duty of enforcing the laws of my country, I have no right to forgive those who violate their country's laws.

"It is my duty to prosecute them.

"Your Honor has no right to forgive those who trespass against the State of Illinois.

"You have a right, and I know you do forgive those who trespass against John R. Caverly, but sitting here as the Chief Justice of this great court, you have no right to forgive anybody who violates the law. You have got to deal with him as the law prescribes.

"All I want to say to you, your Honor, in this case, with the mass of evidence presented by the State, if a jury were sitting in that box and they returned a verdict and did not fix the punishment at death, every person in this community, including your Honor and myself, would feel that that verdict was founded on corruption.

"And I will tell you why. I have taken quite a trip during the last four or five weeks. I thought I was going to be kept in Chicago all summer trying this case, and that most of my time would be spent in the criminal court building. And I find I have been mistaken. I did come up to your Honor's court room five weeks ago, and after I was there a little while Old Doc Yak—is that his name?—the man from Washington—oh, Dr. White,—Dr. White took me by the hand and led me into the nursery of two poor, rich young boys, and he introduced me to a Teddy bear. Then he told me some bedtime stories, and after I got through listening to them, he took me into the kindergarten and he presented to me little Dickie and Babe, and he wanted to know if I had any objection to calling them that, and I said no, if he had no purpose.

"And after he had wandered between the nursery and the

kindergarten for quite a while, I was taken in hand by the Bachrach brothers and taken to a psychopathic laboratory, and there I received quite a liberal education in mental diseases, and particularly what certain doctors did not know about them.

"The three wise men from the east, who came on to tell your Honor about these little babes, and being three wise men brought on from the east, they wanted to make the picture a little more perfect, and one of them was sacrilegious enough to say this pervert, this murderer, this kidnaper, thought that he was the Christ child and that he thought that his mother was the Madonna, without a syllable of evidence any place to support the blasphemous and sacrilegious statement.

"Who said that this young pervert ever thought he was the Christ child?

"He has proclaimed since he was eleven years of age that there is no God.

" 'The fool in his heart hath said there is no God.'

"I wonder now, Nathan, whether you think there is a God or not.

"I wonder whether you think it is pure accident that this disciple of Nietzschian philosophy dropped his glasses or whether it was an act of Divine Providence to visit upon your miserable carcasses the wrath of God in the enforcement of the laws of the State of Illinois.

"Well, if your Honor please, after the Bachrachs had completed my education in the psychopathic laboratories, then my good friend, Clarence Darrow, took me an a Chautauqua trip with him, and, visiting various towns, we would go to social settlements, such as the Hull House, and Clarence would expound his peculiar philosophy of life, and we would meet with communists and anarchists, and Clarence would regale them with his philosophy of the law, which means there ought not to be any law and there ought not to be any enforcement of the law.

"And he even took me to Springfield, where he argued before the legislature that you ought to abolish capital punishment in the State of Illinois.

"I don't know whether the fact that he had a couple of rich clients who were dangerously close to the gallows prompted that trip or not. I know when he was a member of the legislature he hid not abolish it or introduce a bill for that purpose.

"Yes, and he even on this tour criticized the State's Attorney of this county severely because he, in a humane way wanted to correct the law so that men of this sort could be dealt with before somebody lay cold in death, and that the children of this community might be protected.

"If your Honor please, when I occupied the position that your Honor graces, I had an unfortunate man come before me. He was a man of my own race, of my own faith. I don't know whether his pineal gland was calcified or ossified. I don't know whether he had club feet or not, and I did not inspect his back to find out whether he had a couple of moles on him.

"I don't know whether he developed sexually at fourteen or at sixteen.

"I knew under the law he had committed a dastardly crime; he had taken a little six-year old girl, a daughter of the poor, and he was a poor man and he outraged her and he took her into the basement and he covered her over with coal.

"He did not even have the decency or the heart to put a handkerchief over that little dead face as he heaped the coal on it.

"The law says in extreme cases death shall be the penalty.

"If I were in the legislature I might vote against such a law. I don't know. But as a judge, I have no right to set aside that law. I have no right to defeat the will of the people, as expressed by the legislature of Illinois. I have no right to be a judicial anarchist, even if Clarence Darrow is an anarchistic advocate. He says that hanging does not stop murder. I think he is mistaken. From the time Thomas Fitzgerald expiated his crime upon the gallows, I have not heard of any little tot in Chicago who met a like fate to that which Janet Wilkinson met.

"He says hanging does not stop murder. I will direct your Honor's attention to the year 1920, when Judge Kavanagh, Judge Brentano, Judge Barrett and Judge Scanlon came over here at my request and from the fifth day of May until the first day of July tried nothing but murder cases. In addition to the many men that they sent to the penitentiary for manslaughter or a term of years for murder, in that brief period of less than sixty days, fifteen men were sentenced to death in the criminal court of Cook County. The records of the police department, the records of the Chicago Crime Commission, show that as the result of that, murder fell fifty-one per cent in Cook County during the year 1920. We had a time here when every night in every newspaper there was a column devoted to the number of automobiles stolen. We established an automobile court, and I presided in it, and after we had sent several hundred to penal institutions for stealing automobiles, the Rolls Royce became just as safe as the flivver on the streets of Chicago.

"We had a reign of terror inaugurated here for years by criminals who dominated labor unions. They were above and beyond the law. They laughed at it, and spat in its face, just the same as these two poor young sons of multimillionaires. Forty-one of them were convicted in the courts of Cook County. The building industry, that had been strangled for years, began to revive and take on life, and we have not heard anything more of the Maders, or the Murphys, or the Walshes since. Punishment in jail does not deter crime? Why are there so few violations of the laws of the United States? When a man files his income schedule, why does he hire an auditor to see that he makes no mistake? And yet he goes over on his personal property before the Board of Assessors and Board of Review and conceals millions. Why? Because when you get into the United States court, your Honor, where, having violated the laws of the United States, if you are guilty, no plea of mercy, however eloquent or by whom delivered, will cheat the law there.

"You have heard a lot about England. Well, I was never enthusiastic about England myself. This is due to heredity in me. I never had any liking or respect for her laws as they applied to my ancestors and people in an adjoining isle; but I have learnt to have a wholesome respect for the manner in which they enforce the laws of England in England.

"There murder is murder; it is not a phantasy. There, justice is handed out swiftly and surely, and as a result there are less murders in the entire Kingdom of Great Britain yearly than there are in the City of Chicago.

"The police of England do not carry weapons. What would happen to the Chicago police if after giving notice, they all went out one night without a weapon?

"We have heard considerable about split personalities in this case, and I was somewhat surprised to learn that my old friend, the humanitarian, who has acted as the kindly old nurse in this case for the two babes who are wandering in dreamland, also possessed a split personality.

"I have heard so much about the milk of human kindness that ran out in streams from his large heart, that I was somewhat surprised to know that he had so much poison in his system also. Is it wrong, if your Honor please, for the State's Attorney and his two assistants to refer to these two perverts, these two atheists, these two murderers, in language that they can understand?

"We ought to treat them with kindness, we ought to treat them with consideration. But it is all right for Mr. Darrow to take an honorable physician, who has for years enjoyed the confidence of the people of the community, who has enjoyed the confidence of all the judges and the various State's Attorneys in the past and characterize him without a shred of evidence, without the slightest foundation, as a peddler of perjury, and herald that cruel charge broadcast over this land.

"Where is there anything in this case that warrants Clarence Darrow in making such an infamous charge against Dr. Krohn?

"I would suggest that if they want mercy and charity, they practice a little bit of it.

"Treat them with kindness and consideration?

"Call them babes, call them children?

"Why, from the evidence in this case they are as much entitled to the sympathy and mercy of this court as a couple of rattlesnakes, flushed with venom, coiled and ready to strike.

"They are entitled to as much mercy at the hands of your Honor as two mad dogs are entitled to.

"They are no good to themselves. The only purpose that they use themselves for is to debase themselves.

"They are a disgrace to their honored families and they are a menace to this community.

"The only useful thing that remains for them now in life

is to go out of this life and go out of it as quickly as possible under the law.

"As I said, we have been traveling considerable since this trial began. We have been through dreamland; we have been through the nursery. When I came into this case, I thought the playthings of these two perverts, their play toys were bloody chisels, robes and gags, guns and acid.

"And one of these wise men from the east told me I was mistaken, that their play toys are teddy bears, soldiers' uniforms, policemen's uniforms, and the toys that all healthy minded children delight to play with.

"We have been in psychopathic laboratories, we have been in hospitals, we have been before the legislature, and we have been addressing meetings of communists and expounding a doctrine as dangerous as the crime itself.

"I think it is about time we got back into the criminal court. I think it is about time that we realize that we are before the chief justice of this court, and that we are engaged, not in experimenting, not in philosophical discussions, but we are back here trying the murder case of the age, a case, the very details of which not only astonishes, but fills you with horror.

"'Oh,' but Mr. Darrow says, 'these poor little sons of multimillionaires; it is their wealth that is their misfortune; if it was not for their wealth there would be no interest in this case.'

"And yet fifty years ago Charlie Ross was kidnaped, not the son of a multimillionaire. He was never found, and yet we all, even those of us born many years after, still talk about the case of Charlie Ross.

"There is something in the nature of the crime itself that arrests the attention of every person in the land. A child is stolen.

"The heart of every father, the heart of every mother, the heart of every man who has a heart, goes out to the parents of the child.

"Bobby Franks was kidnaped, and when we had not the slightest notion of who was guilty of the dastardly crime, the papers were full of it.

"It was the only topic of conversation.

"It remained the only topic of conversation for a week before the State's Attorney of this County called in Nathan Leopold, Jr.

"Their wealth in my judgment has not anything to do with this, except it permits a defense here seldom given to men in the criminal court.

"Take away the millions of the Loebs and the Leopolds, and Clarence Darrow's tongue is as silent as the tomb of Julius Caesar.

"Take away their millions, and the wise men from the east would not be here, to tell you about phantasies and Teddy bears and bold, bad boys who have their pictures taken in cowboy uniforms.

"Take away their money, and what happens?

"The same thing that has happened to all the other men who have been tried in this building, who had no money.

"A plea of guilty, a police officer sworn, a coroner's physician sworn, the parents of the murdered boy sworn, and a sentence.

"I used to wonder what the poet Grey meant when he talked about the simple mantles of the poor.

"Clarence Darrow once said that a poor man on trial here was disposed of in fifteen minutes, but if he was rich and committed the same crime and he got a good lawyer, his trial would last twenty-one days.

"Well, they got three lawyers and it has lasted just a little bit longer, in addition to the three wise men from the east.

"What are we trying here, if your Honor please, a murder case?

"And what is the evidence presented by the State upon which they seek a verdict?

"A murder as the result of a drunken brawl, a murder committed in hot blood to avenge some injury, either real or fancied?

"A man shooting down another because he debauched his wife and destroyed his home?

"A murder, the result of impulse or passion?

"No. One of the most carefully planned murder cases that your Honor or I in all our long experience have ever heard about.

"A murder committed by some young gamin of the streets whose father was a drunkard and his mother loose; who was denied every opportunity, brought up in the slums; never had a decent example set before him?

"No.

"But a murder committed by two super-intellects coming from the homes of the most respected families in Chicago.

"Every advantage that love, money and wealth and position could give them was theirs.

"A man's conduct, I believe, your Honor, depends upon his philosophy of life.

"Those who want to grow up to be respected citizens in the community, to be useful citizens, they have got a correct philosophy of life.

"Those who want to excel in crime, those who want to tear down instead of build up, they select the wrong philosophy in life. That is all there is to this.

"They had the power of choice, and they deliberately chose to adopt the wrong philosophy, and to make their conduct correspond with it.

"These two defendants were perverts, Loeb the victim and Leopold the aggressor, and they quarreled.

"Then they entered into a childish compact,—a childish compact, Dr. Healy says; a compact between these two so that these unnatural crimes might continue.

"Dr. Healy says that that is a childish compact.

"I say if Dr. Healy is not ashamed of himself, he ought to be.

"My God, I was a grown man before I knew of such depravity. They talk about what lawyers will do for money, but my God, I am glad that I do not know of any lawyer who would get on the witness stand and under oath characterize an unnatural agreement between these two perverts as a childish compact, and Darrow and Bachrach say that, that is an evidence of insanity.

"The statutes of Illinois say that crimes against nature are crimes punishable by imprisonment in the penitentiary.

"It is not a defense to a murder charge.

"Mitigation! Mitigation!

"I have heard so many big words and foreign words in this case that I sometimes thought that perhaps we were letting error creep into the record, so many strange, foreign words were being used here, and the constitution provides that these trials must be conducted in the English language; I do not know; maybe I have got aggravation and mitigation mixed up.

"Away back in November, if your Honor please, when this crime first began to take form, a kidnaping for ransom, it was necessary to write some letters.

"These two little boys, wandering around in dreamland, knew what very few boys and very few men know except those engaged in work such as we are engaged in, that it is possible to take a typewritten document and tell what kind of a machine it was written on.

"So they go to Ann Arbor and they steal a typewriter, a portable typewriter, for the purpose of writing those letters on it, and in order to divert suspicion from themselves or any other student, because if nothing but a typewriter was stolen, the belief would be prevalent that it was the work of some student, some member of the fraternity, they stole watches and jewelry and other things to divert suspicion.

"They go along working out the details of this crime.

"Mr. Darrow says that there is no motive, that it is a senseless crime; that the ten thousand dollars had absolutely nothing to do with it.

"I will undertake to prove, not by argument, but by sworn testimony, that the ten thousand dollars had everything to do with it.

"I will show that this was not the crime of diseased minds, but this was the crime planned in all its minuteness by more than ordinary intellects.

"I have wondered, when I heard these doctors say that you could not make a complete and adequate examination in less than twenty or thirty days, whether the fact that they were working on a per diem of two hundred and fifty dollars a day did not enter into the matter. If they were paid by the job instead of by the day, I think they could have answered all the questions here in the three or four hours that our alienists employed, from two thirty until six thirty.

"What opportunity, if your Honor please, have the State's alienists in the ordinary murder case to make an examination at all?

"The State's Attorney generally doesn't know what the defense is going to be until the case is four or five months old and is brought to trial.

"By that time the defendant has had a lawyer and he has been advised that the only way to save his neck is to appear insane, and if the State's Attorney sends a doctor over to the county jail to act as insane as it is possible for him to act while he is there.

"The State was peculiarly fortunate in this case that we took time by the forelock.

"Mr. Bachrach, Jr., was guileless enough to believe that after I had gotten their confessions, and corroborated them in every detail, that I had a suspicion in my mind that these two young perverts and murderers were insane.

"Mr. Darrow knows me a little longer and he is not quite as guileless as the younger Bachrach, and he guessed that maybe after I knew they had no defense on the facts, I knew how much money they had, that I might have thought that they were going to put in some kind of a fancy insanity defence.

"And that is the reason why I sent for the four best alienists in the city of Chicago while I still had these young egotistical smart alecks,—that is all they are.

"They are not supermen; they are not men of superior intelligence; they are just a couple of spoiled smart alecks, spoiled by the pampering and the petting of their folks and by the people who fawn upon them on account of the wealth.'

"They repeat parrot-like things that they have remembered and assume the solemn expression of an owl and pass for supermen.

"In one breath one of these wise men from the east will tell you that they still believe in Santa Claus, and then in the next breath Mr. Darrow will tell you that they do not even believe in God.

"What better opportunity, in God's world, has the State ever had in an examination, than they had in this?

"From two thirty until six thirty, when these two young smart alecks were telling their story and boasting of their depravity, before they had been advised to invent phantasies, before they had been advised to answer certain questions in certain ways, and before they had been advised to withhold even from the wise men from the east certain information that might be detrimental to the defense in this case.

"Yes, as Dr. Krohn said, their souls were bared. They were telling everything they knew, with no effort made to hide, no effort made to lie. And every incident that they told me about, I put a witness on the stand to prove.

"Every detail of their confession has been corroborated by sworn testimony and by exhibits offered in evidence.

"And our alienists examined them.

"Now, if your Honor please, I do not think that there are a lot of things that we have to have alienists for. I do not think it is necessary in a majority of cases for you or for me or for men experienced in the practice of criminal law, to call in an alienist to find out whether John Jones, the author of this handwriting, also wrote that.

"In a great many cases we can tell by looking at it whether it was written by the same person or not.

"I am not the physician that the younger Bachrach is, nor the philosopher that the senior counsel is, but I think that if I talk to a man for four hours consecutively, and he is insane, I am going to have a pretty good suspicion of it.

"And I think if your Honor watches a man for thirty days, day in and day out, and he is a lunatic, you are going to have a well-defined suspicion of it.

"If he is insane, we may not know the cause of that insanity, we may not know the extent of it, or we may not know the name of it, and we will have to call in a doctor to advise us on those matters, but if he is insane, we know it, and if he is sane, we know it.

"And after these learned doctors had talked to these men from half past two in the afternoon until six thirty that night, I think that they made an examination.

"I have sometimes thought that we were dreaming here, when the learned doctors got on the stand who had been employed to find out just how crazy these two fellows were.

"'Just make them crazy enough so that they won't hang, and don't make them crazy enough to make it necessary to put this up to twelve men, because twelve men are not going to be fooled by your twaddle. Just make them insane enough so that it will make a mitigating circumstance that we can submit to the court.'

"One of these wise men got up on the stand, and he had been employed to examine into the mental condition of Leopold. He is asked:

" 'Doctor, do you know that Leopold has written a great deal upon the subject of ornithology, that he is one of the authorities upon that subject in the United States, that he has lectured before the students of Harvard University upon that subject?'

" 'Yes sir, I do.'

" 'Did you see his works?'

" 'Yes.'

" 'Did you read them?'

" 'No.'

" 'You were employed to examine his mind, were you not?'

" 'Yes.'

" 'What did you do?'

" 'I examined his urine.'

" 'Don't you think you could get a better idea of his mental condition by reading the things that he wrote, the produce of his brain, than you could by examining his urine?'

"And the doctor says:

" 'I don't know.'

"Probably he just wanted to find out how much sugar he could discover, to lay a foundation for an argument by Clarence Darrow that these two boys are too sweet for your Honor to treat roughly, as you would the ordinary criminal."

. . . .

"I was discussing the testimony of the four state alienists, concededly the four best alienists in Chicago, and the reason why the State's Attorney in his effort to enforce the law intelligently and effectively called them in on Sunday, before the defendants were taken out of his custody and turned over to their lawyers and the sheriff.

"For the same reason and to prevent a perjured defense by their friends and associates and servants I called in every person that I understood knew either one of these boys at once and placed them under oath and asked them what they knew about the mental condition of the two defendants. If I had not, the defense in this case would have been insanity, and not a mental disease that goes all around insanity in order to avoid a jury trial. Instead of having one witness perjure himself, as Miss Nathan did, we would have had a flock of them called in to perjure themselves.

"Supposing the State's Attorney had not talked to Miss Nathan and had not had her statements that Loeb was a perfectly normal, rational boy, one of the manliest boys she had ever met, a perfect gentleman at all times? How could I have destroyed her on the stand if I had not had that statement? I do not wonder that the senior counsel, with all his wisdom, gained through many years of practice, made the proposition to the State when he found out what the State had done in the way of preparation, 'Don't you call any of your lay witnesses, and I won't call any of mine.'

"And I told him: 'Bring on your lay witnesses; the law is fortified.'

"And after he got through with Miss Nathan he was through with all the rest he had subpoenaed. Do not lose sight of the fact, if your Honor please, that all of the findings in that famous Bowman-Hulbert report were not testified to before your Honor by Dr. Hulbert.

"I suppose he thought that the State's Attorney would not read it.

"Well, in the discharge of my duty, and in an effort to protect the People of Cook County, I have to do a lot of disagreeable things, so I decided I would read his report.

"It has gotten to be quite a famous report; I do not know but what it rivals in fame the jokebook of Joe Miller, that we heard about when I was a boy.

"Why did not the State call more lay witnesses?

"Why did I not call the brothers of the defendants?

"Why did I not call Loeb's valet, whose statement I got down in the State's Attorney's office?

"Why did not I call the employes of both families, and all their fraternity brothers, in addition to those that I did call?

"Well, I would expect Walter Bachrach, who is not as ex-

perienced in the trial of criminal cases as Clarence Darrow is
to ask that question. Clarence Darrow knows why I didn't
call them, because if I put them on the stand, if I would put Miss
Nathan on the stand I was bound by her perjury. They are my
witnesses.

"I vouch for their truthfulness when I put them on, and I
knew they had all been up in Clarence Darrow's office, as Miss
Nathan had.

"I knew that he would not call them, because I could destroy
them.

"Your Honor could not call them, because under the law, the
only witness you can call as a court's witness is a person who has
seen the crime committed, an eye witness.

"That is why I didn't ask your Honor to call them, because
under the law you could not.

" 'But why, if these men have disordered and diseased minds,
if they have indulged in phantasies, why wasn't the old nurse
put on the stand to tell about it?

"She came all the way from Boston to help Dick, because she
loved him.

"I will read you some of the things she told Dr. Hulbert that
he didn't tell you, and after she got through talking to them they
knew that she would not stand for an insanity defense.

"Don't overlook the fact that every one of the State's alienists says in addition to all the matters and things that they
learned, they took into consideration every bit of Dr. Hulbert's
report, just the same as the three wise men from the east did.

"Not only that, they took into consideration all the testimony
of these three wise men. They did not overlook a word.

"They did not overlook the fact that one shaved every day
and the other only shaved twice a week. They even considered
little Teddy and the cowboy suit.

"The only explanation I can give of the testimony of Dr.
White is that he is in his second childhood. I would hate to
think a man of his attainments would prostitute his profession
and prostitute his learning to tell the story that he told your
Honor.

"One of the very significant and distinguishing things, the
eminent doctor says, was the fact that little Dickie had his pic-

ture taken in a cowboy's uniform when he was four years of age, and that is a distinguishing thing and stamps him as a man of diseased mind with homicidal tendency; and I saw a shudder go through every woman in the courtroom that has a kid four or five years of age, and I began to think of my poor kids; and the other doctors to relieve the tension and the worry—I suppose Marshall Field's sale in cowboy suits must have fallen off at least a hundred thousand since that doctor testified and the other doctors saw how ridiculous and silly it all was, and they said they paid no attention to it, and one by one each doctor discarded all this silly bosh that the preceding doctor had testified to as distinguishing matters; and finally the grand old man of the defense, Clarence Darrow, seeing how absolutely absurd it all was, discarded all their testimony, and substituted as a defense in this case his peculiar philosophy of life, of which we will talk more at length later on.

"Having taken into consideration everything that the doctors for the defense had testified to, having taken into consideration everything contained in the Hulbert report, Dr. Church, Dr. Patrick, Dr. Singer and Dr. Krohn said that there was absolutely nothing to indicate mental disease in either one of these defendants.

"Finding nothing in their mental condition that would justify a suspicion of insanity or a suspicion of disease, they put on Dr. Hulbert, to testify about certain glands, ductless and otherwise.

"Your Honor heard an eminent authority upon that subject, Dr. Woodyatt, and he says there is so little known about the pineal gland and about these other matters and things that this doctor testified to so glibly,—there is so little known about it that nobody knows what effect they would have upon the mind of a person; that a calcified gland existed in a sane, sound mind the same as it did in a diseased mind.

"And all of the testimony of Hulbert upon that proposition was as illuminating, and should be given the same serious consideration, as Old Doc Yak's Teddy bears and Buffalo Bill suits.

"If these men are insane, I ask your Honor why they were instructed not to let our alienists examine further."

"May it please your Honor, when I left off last night I was talking about the State alienists and the three wise men from the east who came on here to testify that the little "Babe" or the little Babes, rather, were suffering from a diseased mind.

"Now, when the body is sick, the ordinary practitioner can generally tell you what kind of a disease you have, and I do not think there is any man who pretends to be a specialist who will admit that he cannot tell you what is the matter with you after he examines you.

"He may guess wrong, but he is going to make some kind of a guess.

"He may tell you you have one kind of a fever, when in reality you have another, but he is going to give it some kind of a name.

"You know, the doctors have it on us lawyers. When we make mistakes they are discovered, when a doctor makes a mistake he is safe, because dead men tell no tales.

"If these two defendants are suffering from a mental disease, what is the name of it?

"No one has gone on the stand that has been able to give this mental disease a name. And yet, everyone who got on for the defendants pretended to know all that there was in the books and a great deal that never got into the books.

"I was surprised that old Doc White wasn't able to name the peculiar mental disease he says exists here, because he in the past has been able to invent names for diseases which didn't exist.

"In all probability the present mental disease of these two defendants would disappear very rapidly if the causes for its existence were removed. If the glasses had never been found, if the State's Attorney had not fastened the crime upon these two defendants, Nathan Leopold would be over in Paris or some other of the gay capitals of Europe, indulging his unnatural lust with the five thousand dollars he had wrung from Jacob Franks.

"If they were to be discharged today, through some technicality in the law, this present disturbance would all disappear very rapidly, if the causes for its existence were removed.

"Now, if your Honor please, we will go back of this defense, and see whether it is an honest defense or not, to see whether these mental disturbances came on as suddenly as they would disappear if the causes of them were removed.

"Your Honor will recollect that while doctors employed by the defense were sitting in the courtroom witnesses were put on to testify to fainting spells.

"Now, what was the purpose of that?

"The purpose of that was to lay a foundation, in my judgment, for some doctor to later take the stand and testify that Loeb was suffering from epilepsy, and it would be argued that having epilepsy, his mind was diseased.

"Dr. Hulbert in his report, as I will show you later, says that there were not any evidences of fainting in Loeb, except one fainting spell that he had during initiation, and yet witness after witness was put on, and they testified that he fainted, that he was rigid, that his eyes were glassy, and that he frothed at the mouth.

"But cross-examination showed that he was merely drunk; he was not rigid, but he was stiff, his frothing at the mouth was a drunken vomit, and after he got through he wanted to lick a couple of waiters.

"The evidence also showed that these other fainting spells were due to the fact that, in one case, seven or eight large boys jumped upon him, and he fainted as the result of injuries.

"He fainted again in the hospital after he had been in an automobile accident, and the doctor who waited upon him said that the fainting spells were due entirely, in his judgment, to the accident.

"Then the doctor who had been employed to take the stand and testify to epilepsy was dismissed.

"If these lay witnesses had stood up, and had not broken down under cross examination, that doctor would have testified to epilepsy.

"I submit that this defense is not an honest defense.

"This is a defense built up to meet the needs of the case.

"If the State only had half of the evidence that it did have, or a quarter of the evidence that it had, we would have had a jury in the box, and a plea of not guilty. But trapped like a couple of rats, with no place to escape except through an insanity defense, they proceed to build it up.

"A weird, uncanny crime?

"The crime is not half as weird or uncanny as the defense that is put in here.

"Let us see what Dr. Hulbert said in his report. That is in evidence, introduced by the defense, so I do not suppose there will be any objection to my reading from that.

"I am glad that the defendants' lawyers concede me some few rights in this courtroom, although they argue that I ought to be down in the office, after a plea of guilty, and that I have no business up here at all.

" 'Personal history, Richard Loeb. Mother's health; during pregnancy she was not very sick.

" 'Her fever was not remarkable, although there was much morning sickness.'

"The doctor did not testify to that on direct examination, your Honor. He did not think this report would ever get into the hands of the State's Attorney, and he said he did not. He created the impression by his direct examination that here was something wrong at the time of this boy's birth.

"What does he say in his report? He was a perfect baby. Oh! He developed a little late sexually, and at the age of fifteen Dr. Hulbert in his report said he had gonorrhea.

"On page nine, "There is no history of fainting attacks except that once during an initiation ceremony at school, he fainted.'

"In other words, after considering the Teddy bears and the Buffalo Bill suits, and all this other trash that was testified to by these wise men from the east, counsel or somebody decided that they had to add something more to it to make it stand even as a mitigating circumstance, and while their report said there was no history of fainting attacks except once, they tried to prove a dozen in order to build up a foundation for epilepsy.

"And your Honor recollects that on cross examination every one of them either developed into being knocked unconscious by accident, or else it was a drunken stupor brought on by debauchery.

"Then this nurse; the nurse who according to the testimony of the defense knew more about Richard Loeb up until the time he was fourteen years of age, than any living person. They tried to create the impression that she was insane, and that Dick caught his insanity from her, the same as one boy catches measles from another. They had her here in Chicago and she is not produced as a witness.

"A letter was read to indicate that she was insane, and if I ever read a letter that more clearly demonstrated sanity than the letter written by that nurse, I don't remember it.

"It was a kindly, loving letter, sent by a woman to a boy she loved, filled with motherly advice, advice that it develops is so sadly needed in this case by these two young perverts.

"A picture was introduced of her to show that she was some terribly hideous creature.

"Let me see what Dr. Hulbert says about her.

"She is supposed to have given information in reference to Dick because these people would think he had a diseased mind when he was a child:

" 'She returned to Chicago after the arrest of young Richard to help him in any way she could, and through the attorneys, arrangements were made for an interview.'

" 'She is very reserved, quiet and strict; her memory is good. She is a woman of attractive appearance, modestly and carefully dressed.'

" 'She denied any imperfections in herself while she was a nurse, and she denied any imperfections with the boy during her stay with the family.'

" 'She said that he was quite all right at fifteen years of age, at the time she left the house.'

" 'She said he was a lazy boy, but a bright student. He was lazy until he got along in several grades of school where he found that he could graduate in one year's less time than he expected, if he would study, and so began to study hard.'

" 'She would not say—she denied that he ever had any fears or any disorders in his sleep,' and if anybody would know about the day dreams or the night dreams of Richard Loeb, I submit that this woman would know about it; and we are told about the weird, uncanny dreams he had both waking and asleep.

" 'She denied that he ever had fears or any disorder in his sleep. She would not say anything which might reflect on the boy, even though she was plainly told that a complete understanding of this boy was essential for an accurate diagnosis.'

"She came on here as Dr. Hulbert said to do anything within her power to help the boy, short of perjury; and although she was told that a complete understanding of the boy was essential for a correct diagnosis, which means for a defense in this case, she would not say anything that might reflect upon him, because she intended to tell the truth, and that is why she was sworn as a witness before these alienists, but was not brought into court and sworn before your honor.

" 'Her general viewpoint is a conventional one. She was quite unaware of the fact that he had become a petty thief and played detective.'

"A woman, that they claim until he was fifteen years of age, never let him out of her sight day or night, was quite unaware that he was a petty thief or played detective.

"If she did not know it, who in God's name would know it?

"If she says he wasn't a thief and didn't play detective, will you take her word for it, or will you take Dr. Hulbert's word?

"What information has he got?

"He talked to Richard Loeb and he talked to the nurse, the one that they claim was with him every hour of the day, and because he was constantly tied to her apron strings, he is now here charged with murder, and she gives the lie to this.

"It has been argued here that because Richard Loeb told the doctors that he had no ambition in life, that he hadn't selected or thought of any profession, that is an indication he is mentally unbalanced, and because the other defendant had a definite ambition in life he is also mentally unbalanced.

"A happy philosophy of medicine, especially when you are testifying in a guilty case, and trying to cheat the gallows.

"It is too bad that they have two defendants here.

"It would be much easier to prove one insane, because anything you found in him could be a bad sign.

"But when you have two, and they are not exactly alike, when one has broken arches and the other has a high arch, why, then it has got to be a bad sign in one and a bad sign in the other.

"And if one has to shave every day, that is a bad sign; and if the other does not have to shave but twice a week that is a bad sign.

"It was a bad sign that Richard Loeb did not have any definite aim or purpose in life; and it was also a bad sign because Leopold wanted to study law and ornithology.

"Well, let us see what Dr. Hulbert says about this: 'When the patient'—that is Loeb—'—was asked what use he expected to make of his education, and what were his ambitions, he stated he expected to study law the next year. He said he had always intended to study law.'

"And yet, when they were putting on their defense, everybody was testifying that he had not any ambition in life.

"He was just wandering around like a ship without a rudder, and did not know what port he was going to put into.

"'When the patient was asked what use he expected to make of his education, and what were his ambitions, he stated he expected to study law the next year. He said he had always intended to study law. At one time he had thought of teaching history, but he felt that he was not of the scholarly type. Asked why, he replied that he was always lazy, and that he could never sit down and apply himself. As a boy, he poisoned his mind by reading detective stories.'

"Well, there is a whole lot of us in the same fix. I remember crawling under the bed to read Nick Carter. After I got through reading Nick Carter I began to read Gaboriau's French Detective Stories, and when I was a student at Yale I paid more attention to Raffles than I did to real property.

"I think that is the experience of most normal, healthy-minded people.

"Let us see what the doctor says about it.

"'It was observed that he read good books, Dickens and Thackeray, but not the Alger books, although he did read Little Lord Fauntleroy. He spent all his time in day dreams.'

"Now, that is what your Honor has been told—day dreams and the reading of detective stories.

"What does the doctor say about it?

"'He was rarely observed day dreaming.'

"That is the information he got from the nurse, because I read what the nurse said:

"'He was never haunted by fears or dreams,' is what she said.

"And Drs. Hulbert and Bowman, under another heading, in another chapter, giving information that they got from other people, say he was rarely observed day dreaming.

"And here Hulbert and Bowman, under another heading, in

another chapter, giving information that they got from other people, say, he was rarely observed day dreaming, night dreams were very rare.

"Sometimes he would talk or laugh in his sleep, but not often; he slept soundly and was hard to waken.

"Oh, the only reason that Dickie committed this slight delinquency of murdering little Bobby Franks was that he desired the thrill, all his life he craved for thrills.

"What do Bowman and Hulbert say about it?

" 'He never appeared to crave a thrill or excitement, but was rather quiet in his conduct; after Miss Struthers left that home he seemed to be much the same as before, quiet, rather affectionate, extremely polite and respectful.'

"That is what the friends and members of the family must have told the doctor.

"Here is what the patient told the doctor himself:

" 'THE PATIENT'S ESTIMATE OF HIMSELF.'

" 'While also at times he had a tremendous output of energy and physically does not tire easily. He is rather inclined to be a leader in athletics and games which he enjoys.'

" 'Why, the whole trouble with him is that he never led the natural life that boys lead.'

"He was always kept in the house with his nose buried in some serious, solemn volume. That is what we were told.

"And the only time he had any boys was when Doc White could put some interpretation upon those boys which would lead to the conclusion of a diseased mind. That is why we heard about the Teddy bears and these various suits of his.

"He never went out and played as boys play baseball, marbles and other things, and yet when he is talking to the doctor and the doctor reports to the three wise men from the east, he says he is inclined to be a leader in athletics, which he enjoys.

" 'He makes friends very easily and feels quite at ease with strangers. He is inclined to be a leader and likes to dominate his environments.'

"Well, isn't that natural in a healthy-minded person?

"Everybody desires to strive to succeed and to lead.

"But the doctor adds:

" 'But can fit himself easily into any sort of a situation, so that he does not become bothered or upset if someone else happens to be dominating the particular situation and he is compelled to assume a minor role.'

"And as a boy he did not have judgment enough to plan, a boy who had no will, to do or not to do, and yet he tells the doctor:

" 'While the patient often acts without reflection and is quite impulsive, he nevertheless plans a great deal and works out consistent schemes for the future.'

"He plans a great deal and works out consistent schemes for the future, in this mad brain of this mad boy.

" 'He is open and frank with others as long as he feels there is nothing he wants to conceal.'

"Dr. White said he couldn't lie to him.

" 'Nobody can lie to me. I can read their minds just the same as or look into it just the same as a doctor can look into the human body with an X-ray.'

"Well, I don't suppose he thinks he knows more than the Lord does, but I don't believe that he would concede that the Lord knew any more than he did when the Lord was his age.

" 'But if he feels that it is to his interest to hold anything back he does so. He therefore gives an appearance of great frankness, which is not true. The patient says that he will tell a lie with no compunction whatever, and that he is completely dishonest.

"Let us see whether he lied to these doctors and withheld information, the same as they lied to your Honor.

"Here again the doctor says, talking about his being tied to the apron strings of an old nurse and never being allowed to play as other boys played, page 41:

" 'He has always been fond of athletics and outdoor sports such as tennis, swimming, hockey, skating and so forth, always been fond of bridge. While he plays some other card games, he has not been particularly interested in them. He is considered an extremely good bridge player and has spent a great deal of time playing it. He is fond of dancing and mixed society. He has used alcohol considerably since he was fifteen and gotten drunk a number of times.'

"Oh, another interesting thing that leads these wise men to think that they are demented and stark mad is that over in jail, while he is preparing his defense, he wants to wear an old, ragged coat.

" 'He has always been careful of his personal appearance and neat and clean about his person and has liked to appear well dressed.'

"I have never seen him any other way.

" 'He has always had a pleasant consciousness of his own body.'

"And again I find in Doctor Hulbert's report:

" 'He has always been interested in camping, motor boating and outdoor life in general. This has never been linked with any intellectual pursuit, such as botany, zoology or the like.'

"Tennis, swimming, hockey, skating, bridge, dancing—all of the sports every healthy, natural young boy would like to indulge in, but a great many of which we were not able to indulge in, because we happened to be the rich boys of poor parents and not the poor boys of multimillionaires.

"They didn't lie when questioned by their alienists. It would not have done them any good to lie to Doc White anyhow, but they did not lie to any of them; and they all testified that if they had lied, an impossible thing, and the things that they had told them were false and they had held back certain things that were material and did not tell them, that would have changed their opinion.

"Oh, undoubtedly if the facts were not as they are, we would come to a different conclusion. But these boys were collaboratting with us while we were planning this weird and uncanny defense for them. They didn't lie and they didn't withhold anything.

"Well, let's see what Dr. Hulbert says and Dr. Bowman says in this report which Dr. Hulbert says,

" 'I never expected to fall into your hands, Mr. Crowe.'

"During the examination on page sixty-six: 'During the examination and his recitation of his criminal career, he was not quite frank. Without any indication facially or otherwise he would lie or repress certain instances, unless he imagined that the doctor was previously aware of those instances.'

"When questioned about this later he said he had failed to

mention certain things because he thought it advisable not to mention them or because he had been advised not to mention them. After some guileless attorney, studied in the medicine and grounded in it, probably more than he is in the practice of the criminal law, some doctor or some member of the family had gotten those two smart alecks and had trained and prepared them and told them what to tell the doctors and what not to tell them, then they brought on these doctors and say,

" 'Now, go on in and listen to that story and if after you listen to the story they tell you, you don't think they are crazy, then you must be crazy.'

"He failed to mention certain things because he either thought it advisable not to mention them, he himself, or because he had been advised not to mention them. So obviously there are gaps in his history of the development of crime.

" 'His oldest brother Allan does not know of these untold stories, but the patient says he will not tell them unless Allan advises him so to do.'

"What are these untold stories? The case is closed, and we have not heard a word of it. They were not going to lie in order to fool the doctors, so that the doctors could fool your Honor. No. They were perfectly frank. As Dr. White said,

" 'They didn't lie to me, and they wouldn't lie to a man as smart as I am.'

"They had no thought when they were talking to the doctors as to their defense in this case, none whatever. They might as a result of a childish phantasy murder little Bobby Franks as they wandered along in the dark, but God forbid that they should attempt to fool your Honor in an effort to save their worthless lives.

"But let us continue from the Hulbert-Bowman report.

" 'On the other hand, there is a certain legal advantage.

"This is not a carefully prepared examination for the purpose of putting in a crooked and silly defense, in an effort to fool your Honor, according to the witnesses when they are under oath or on the stand. But when they are making a report for the lawyers and a report for the wise men from the east to base an opinion on, Drs. Hulbert and Bowman say,

" 'On the other hand, there is a certain legal advantage in

minimizing the broadcasting of his episodes, even keeping them secret from the attorneys, examiners or relatives.'

"Here are doctors who want to make your Honor believe that their only interest is in finding out what the truth is, and telling it to you regardless, and they give their reason for not insisting on all of the facts in the following language:

" 'On the other hand, there is a certain legal advantage in minimizing the broadcasting of his episodes, even keeping them secret from his attorneys, examiners or relatives. Consequently no great effort should be made to bring forth details which he wilfully suppresses.'

"This is Dr. Bowman and Dr. Hulbert advising Dr. White, Dr. Glueck and Dr. Healy, that there is a certain legal advantage not to bring these matters out, and no effort should be made by them to bring forth details which he wilfully suppresses.

"I quite agree with Dr. Hulbert, that when he wrote this report he never thought it was going to be read by the State's Attorney, or the contents of it would ever be told to your Honor.

" 'His phantasies usually occur between the time of retiring and the time sleep comes over him. He estimates that this period was on an average of half an hour's duration.'

"Not wandering around all day, Mr. Darrow, in a day dream and indulging in phantasies, walking up and down the street, snapping fingers, pointing out buildings, waving the gang here and there; not a phantasy that became a part of his life.

"Dr. Hulbert and Dr. Bowman said that the phantasies usually occur a half hour before he goes to sleep. That is the time your Honor and I and everybody else phantasy. When we get into bed we dream dreams of what we are going to accomplish, and we scheme and plan and that is exactly what Dickie Loeb did.

"And all this other stuff that we have been regaled with is perjury, pure and simple; perjury for a purpose.

"From Philip Drunk to Philip Sober, from the lying alienists on the stand to a report made by the alienists that they did not think would come to light.

" 'On their way back from Ann Arbor'—on page 98,—'the plan of kidnaping a boy coupled with the idea of ransom was first broached by the patient.'

"That is, that is the first time that Loeb talked to Leopold about kidnaping for ransom. Not a thrill, but ransom.

"And I will demonstrate that money was the motive here. I will demonstrate that they gambled and they played for such high stakes that even their millionaire companions could not play with them.

"I will demonstrate they had money they cannot account for.

" 'The patient had a definite boy in mind at that time; the patient did not like this boy or his family.'

"A crime by mad boys, without a purpose, without any thought of revenge, without any thought of money? Let's see.

"The first boy they contemplated killing was a boy he did not like.

"Hatred, revenge, was the motive in his mind at that time; but their desire for money overcame that.

" 'The patient did not like this boy nor his family,'—the details of which were not brought out. Why not?

"Because the details might show that the hate and the anger were strong enough to impel him to kill him; but he does tell you that the first boy was one he did not like, and he did not like his family.

" 'He was the patient's own age, rather large for his age. Patient's idea was to get hold of this boy when he was coming back from a party and lure him into an automobile.

" 'He could not figure any safe way of getting the money, and because he could not figure any safe way of getting them money, he brushed aside his hate and his desire for revenge upon his enemy.'

"Money is the motive in this case, and I will prove it repeatedly by their own evidence.

"He could not figure any safe way of getting the money.

" 'The patient and his companion discussed this idea quite frequently. Neither of them, however, could think of any simple and certain method of securing the money.'

"All through this case it is money, money, money—blood.

" 'Neither of them, however, could think of any simple or certain way of securing the money. They continued to discuss the matter, weighing the pros and cons, suggesting methods only to pick flaws in them.'

" 'In March, 1924, the patient conceived the idea of securing'
—what? The thrill? The excitement? No.

" 'Conceived the idea of securing the money by having it
thrown off a moving train. This idea was discussed in great
detail, and gradually developed into a carefully systematized
plan.'

"But Mr. Darrow disagrees with the doctor. This was not
carefully discussed and gone into in great detail, and gradually
developed into a carefully systematized plan. This was just
the mad act of mad boys, wandering around in the dark, looking
for a Teddy bear.

"It was figured out first that the money shall be thrown
off a moving train when it was dark, somewhere in the country.
He and his companion spent 'many uncomfortable afternoons'—

"I really sympathize with you, dear little boys, for all of the
discomfort you suffered on those afternoons.

"It is too bad that in this weird, uncanny scheme of yours,
of murder, you had to spend many uncomfortable afternoons—
'going over the Illinois Central tracks looking for suitable loca-
tions.'

" 'Finally his companion'—that is Leopold, your Honor—
'suggested the idea of settling upon a certain brick factory on
the left side of the track as a landmark. There was considerable
discussion as to what car to use. Both the patient and his companion felt that it was not safe to use either of their own cars.'

"Mad boys in the dark and dreamland, doing a mad act without any thought of the consequences of it, and least of all not
considering their personal safety at all?

"To crazy to know that it was wrong, and too crazy to care
whether they were caught?

" 'They both felt that it was not safe to use either of their
own cars. The patient developed an intense interest in the plan,
and found also that it gave him a very pleasant topic of conversation when he and his companion were together, drinking
or driving about.'

"When he and his companion were drinking they would
gloat over the perfection of their plan to murder, and murder
for money.

"I used to think that the most impelling motive in life was

passion. But in this case passion and a desire for revenge is swept aside for money.

"Money is the controlling motive in this case. If they merely wanted to kill for a thrill, if they merely wanted to kill to satisfy his anger and hate toward this companion of his, he would have been the victim; but they could not figure out how they could safely get the money.

" 'Patient's companion suggested that they rent a car, so they went to the Morrison Hotel and registered under the name of Ballard. An elaborate'—a crime without a purpose?

"A mad act of mad boys without any purpose, without any thought either in its planning or its execution according to Mr. Darrow, but the doctor says:

" 'An elaborate plan for building up an identification was worked out. Letters were sent to Mr. Ballard at the hotel, and a bank account was opened in his name.'

"Here is a man who has no emotion; all intellect and no emotion.

"His nurse says he was kind and affectionate, obedient and respectful.

"Isn't that emotion?

"Isn't love one of the greatest emotions that surges through your heart?

"Kind and affectionate, loving.

"What does the doctor say?

" 'The bank account was opened in his name,' and then the doctor adds in parentheses:

" 'When the patient came to this point in the narrative he looked decidedly interested, drew up his chair, talked almost in a dramatic whisper with considerable tension; his eyes constantly roaming the room.'

"In fact he showed what?

"Lack of emotion?

"No.

"In fact he showed intense emotional reaction. Herein the repetition of that which he said had been very thrilling to him.

"Who are you going to believe?

"The doctor, after he has been coached, taking the stand and saying he has not any emotion, or the doctor in the first instance when he is making a report, that he does not expect you or me to see, and he stated on the stand he did not, and he says, in fact, he showed intense emotional reactions.

" 'On May 9th, patient's companion went to the Rent-a-Car company and said he wished to rent a car.'

"Well, I will pass that. Your Honor knows it.

" 'Mitigation,'—and this document is offered in mitigation of this crime. As I said yesterday, probably I have been confused by the use of all these learned terms in a strange, foreign language that I did not understand or learn. But if this is mitigation, my God, I would like to know what is aggravation.

" 'The patient's companion'—that is Leopold—'first suggested that they get a girl.'

"Then they considered half a dozen boys, any one of them would do. That they were physically small enough to be easily handled. That is the first reason.

" 'They didn't want to take a boy that might put up a fight and get the best of it.'

"That was one reason why they discarded the first boy, who was bigger than they were, and the second reason was the difficulty of getting the money.

" 'One who was physically small enough to be easily handled, and their parents were extremely wealthy and who would have no difficulty or disinclination to pay ransom money.'

"What is the motive?

"All the way through this report, all the way through the confession—money, ransom, wealth.

"These boys' identities were not sought other times, when the doctors are not anxious to get all of the facts.

"Now, continuing on page 102, your Honor:

" 'Since they planned to kidnap a boy who was known to them, because it would be easy to lure him into their automobile, they felt that it was necessary to kill him at once.'

"Why? For the thrill? For the excitement?

"The only reason that Mr. Darrow can assign for this mad act of mad boys, that they did it for thrill or excitement?

"Oh, no.

"This is what they told the doctor: 'A boy who was known to them,' etc., 'they felt it was necessary to kill him at once, to avoid any possible identification of themselves by the victim, should he escape, or their plans go awry.'

"That is the motive here.

"The kidnaping was planned for ransom. They wanted the money first, and they were going to kidnap a boy to get the money. Then to make sure they were picking the right fellow, whose folks were wealthy, and who could pay the ransom, they had to pick a boy they knew and who knew them. Then the motive for the murder was their own self preservation.

"You do not have to take my word for it. Take the word of the doctors hired by the alienists, who say the boys told them that themselves.

" 'It was necessary to kill him at once, to avoid any possible identification by the victim should he escape, or their plans go awry.'

"Was this killing done, as we have been led to believe by the defense, merely for the thrill, your Honor, or the excitement?

"What does the doctor further say on that?

" 'The patient'—Loeb—'did not anticipate the actual killing with any pleasure.'

"It was not for the thrill or the excitement. The original crime was the kidnaping for money. The killing was an afterthought, to prevent their identification, and their subsequent apprehension and punishment. He said he did not anticipate the killing with any pleasure. It was merely necessary in order to get the money.

"Motive?"

" 'The killing apparently has no other significance'—

"Now, this is not my argument, your Honor, but on page 103 of their own report, their own evidence—'the killing apparently has no other significance than being an inevitable part of a perfect crime in covering one possible trace of identification.' Drs. Hulbert and Bowman were told by these defendants, as I told your Honor, that the killing had no significance here except to prevent their being apprehended and convicted if the victim escaped.

"That is the motive for the murder, self-preservation, the same as a thief at night in your house, when suddenly surprised, shoots to kill. "Why?

"He did not go into your house to kill; he went in to rob. The killing had no significance, except he did not want to be apprehended; the desire, the urge of self-preservation.

"And that is the only significance that the murder in this case has; not the thrill; as we have been told; not a desire for excitement, but they killed for exactly the same reason that the burglar caught at night kills for, exactly the same reason that Krauser killed when he was robbing the Atlantic & Pacific Tea Store. He went in with greed, just as they went into this kidnaping. He killed because he did not want to be apprehended.

"See whether they took delight and pleasure in this killing for the mere wantonness of killing. See whether the mere wantonness of killing gave them the thrill that they tried to make you believe. 'They anticipated a few unpleasant minutes.' Not pleasant minutes; not the thrill and the delight and the fast beating hearts that they tell you that Dickie Loeb has, if he has got a heart at all 'They anticipated a few unpleasant minutes in strangling him.'

"And I might tell you at this point, your Honor, and will develop later, that the original plan of Loeb was not to kill him with the chisel, but they were to strangle him to death with the ropes that they procured.

"He was to pull one end and Leopold the other; and the reason he wanted that done was, as I will demonstrate as we go on, Leopold had something on him.

" 'They anticipated a few unpleasant minutes in strangling him,' and then the doctor says in parenthesis: 'The patient's face registered the expression of disgust.' No emotions.

"No, his emotions were split off from his intellect.

"And again the doctor says he showed emotion; he showed disgust at the plot to strangle that boy.

" 'And they planned for each of them, namely, the patient and his associate, to have hold of one end of the strangling rope and they would pull at the same time so that both would be equally guilty of murder. They did not seem to think that this would give them a closer tie in their friendship.' No thrill. No delight. It was the sharing of culpability.

" 'It was not anticipated that the blow on the back of the head with the taped chisel would be fatal'

" 'The patient stated that he thinks that during the last week preceding the crime that he had less pleasure in his anticipations.'

"He didn't take the same pleasure in thinking of getting ten thousand dollars by kidnaping the last week, because the murder end began to worry him, and he was going to make Leopold share the guilt equally of the murder. This man, who does not believe in God, and certainly does not believe in the laws of the State of Illinois, who has no emotions or no heart, might be surprised to know that it was his own conscience bothering him the last week.

" 'He did not want to back out because of their extensive plans, because of the time spent, because of the trouble they had gone to, and because of his associate being in it with him, and he was afraid of what the associate would think should he not go ahead. They decided to get any young boy they knew.'

"Any young boy they knew! Is that all? Page 104:

" 'They decided to get any young boy they knew to be of a wealthy family.'

"Money didn't enter into it.

"Again on page 104: 'They had also perfected the plan for securing'—what? The thrill? The excitement? No. 'They had also perfected the plan for securing the money. The victim's father was to be told to put the money in a cigar box,' etc. I won't go on with that because your Honor is familiar with the details.

"Again, and this is three times in this report as to this boy who had no emotions and on account of lack of emotions in a mad frenzy and in a dream committed this unthinkable crime, on page 107 the doctors say, continuing with Loeb: 'We got the boy and disposed of him as planned on Wednesday;' then I will skip some. 'So we made our escape without waiting for the train.' What I skipped is merely the details about sending the cab, and so on.

" 'We returned the car to the agency at 4:30;' and the doctors remark in parenthesis, 'At this point he choked up.' His emotions overcame him. 'He choked up and he wiped his nose with his fingers.' He wiped away the tears.

"The other fellow hasn't any emotions either, your Honor, none at all. He drove them all out when he was seven or eight or nine or ten years of age, at the same time he passed God out of his heart. Well let's see what Dickie says about it. 'I had quite a time quieting down my associate.' This is during the murder, if your Honor please. It follows immediately after, 'He was hit over the head with a chisel,' and so on.

" 'I had quite a time quieting down my associate.' On page 108: 'I cooled him down in five minutes, after we got him into the back seat, thinking he was alive. I got calmer, while quieting my associate. He was hit on the head several times (referring to Franks). My associate says, "This is terrible, this is terrible." '

"Emotion or totally devoid of emotion? When he saw Loeb knocking out the life of this boy it took Loeb five minutes to quiet him down. He said, 'This is terrible, this is terrible.' I will tell your Honor, if you don't think they have emotions, of another instance. Some of us didn't think that Harvey Church had. He told his story with the air of a braggadocio, and he gloated apparently while he was telling the authorities how tough a fellow he was. But when he was told to begin his march to the gallows they carried him there in a stupor. And if it is the fate of these two perverts that they must pay the penalty of this crime upon the gallows, when they realize it, you will find that they have got emotion and you will find they have got fear, and you will find these cowardly perverts will have to be carried to the gallows.

" 'This is terrible, this is terrible. I told him it was all right, and talked and laughed to calm him.' To calm him? No. 'I told him it was all right, and joked and laughed, possibly to calm myself, too.'

"He did not have any emotions. He first told the doctor, in accordance with his own ideas or his training, that he got a kick out of the whole thing; and then he began to get a little more truthful to the doctor.

"On page 110: 'He first stated that he got more of a kick in discussing it with his own family, but later changed his statement and said he felt he got a little less kick because he had some slight remorse. His mother said that whoever did it should be tarred and feathered.'

"What does that mean? A mob ought to take him. We have

heard Mr. Darrow talk repeatedly of the hoarse cry of the angry mob. There is no danger or no fear of us hearing the hoarse cry of the angry mob if the extreme penalty is visited here. I am not so sure otherwise.

" 'On the other hand the patient was a little worried.' Well, what is worry? Worry is an emotion the same as fear, the same as love. 'Worried by the attitude of his father.'

"Now, let us find out how he has acted in jail. On page 114, your Honor: 'He has shown nothing unusual in his behavior in jail.' Acts just like a normal, sane person.

"Of course, after this report had been given to the lawyers and the doctors from the East they had to add to it a little bit, just as they did about the epilepsy, and Doc White brought in a lot of things that are not in this report, and someone else brought the unusual conduct of the defendant while he was in jail, wearing an old coat and so on.

"But these two doctors, when the defense was young and had not matured, say he showed nothing unusual in his behavior in jail; his life is quiet and well ordered. He eats and sleeps well; even going to sleep while his associate was being examined in the same room.

"Dr. Krohn has been criticized for saying that these defendants were correctly oriented in all three manners. Let us see what these three doctors say. 'He is correctly oriented in the three spheres.' He knows his name, he knows where he is, he knows what is going on. 'He takes a lively interest in the jail routine, and in the affairs of other prisoners, speaking of their crimes and their prospects in the usual jail phraseology, such as "I think so and so 'will get the rope' " or, "I think so and so 'will get the street.' " ' Is there anything in his conduct in the jail that these doctors discovered, to indicate a mad boy who wants to do a mad act?

"Or is it just the conduct of normal people, people who are responsible to the law for their violations of it?

"I just want to call your attention to one or two little things which show that this was not a purposeless crime of mad boys traveling around in a dream.

"On page 105 of the Hulbert-Bowman report, the doctors say:

" 'The boys arranged to have their rented car, with a black cloth over the license plate, backed up to the tracks, at the place where the box would be thrown. They had timed the train, they had arranged that if the train was late, it probably meant that there had been some flaw in their plans, and that the father had sought aid, whereupon they would drive away in the car, and not wait for the train.'

"Planning, deliberating, working out the most minute details, they were perfectly assured that their plans were so perfect that they themselves would never be suspected, and, of course, would never be apprehended. And nothing, in my judgment, but an act of God, an act of Providence, is responsible for the unraveling of this terrible crime.

"I think that when the glasses that Leopold had not worn for three months, glasses that he no longer needed, dropped from his pocket at night, the hand of God was at work in this case. He may not have believed in a God. But, if he has listened and paid attention and thought as the evidence was unfolded, he must begin to believe there is a God, now.

"No thought of money; a mad act committed by mad boys in a dream; money did not enter into it, and yet they tell the doctor and he tells us, on page 106: 'They planned to divide the ten thousand dollars ransom money equally;' and I believe one of our alienists expressed it,—they planned to cut it fifty-fifty.

"I have repeatedly referred to the fact that they tried to create an impression that when the doctors were examining them they were perfectly frank, they co-operated, they did not lie, they did not distort, they did not hold back any evidence, and that is the sworn testimony of the three doctors from the East.

"Let us find out whether that is true or not.

"I suspected and I tried to get them to admit on cross examination that boys of superior education and intellect, boys who could plan a crime of this sort stretching over a period of six months and attend to every minute detail, boys who showed such an abandoned and malignant heart as the facts in this case show that they possessed, might possibly, when caught like rats, lie just a little bit to friendly doctors who were trying to build up a defense for them to save their worthless lives.

"Oh, no, that is impossible.

"Everything they told us was true.

"They withheld nothing. They distorted nothing. They suppressed nothing.

"Well, let's see what they say about it in the report that was intended to be a secret report and was not to fall into your hands or into mine, on page 115, if your Honor please, in a friendly psychiatric examination:

" 'The boy is apparently frank, but is not absolutely so, sometimes distorting his statements, but without anything to indicate it, and sometimes suppresses much data.'

"I wonder, is it possible they did fool old Doc Yak from Washington, and I wonder whether it was necessary to fool him.

"I wonder whether he was not willing to try to fool the court.

"Back to motive again, on page 116:

" 'He had no hatred toward the boy. As the hate of his first planned victim disappeared, the excitement of planning grew, and money developed as an after-thought. Neither he nor his associate would have done it without the money. That extra five thousand dollars would have been his security.'

"And then the doctor, quoting the language of Loeb, says: ' "And five thousand dollars is five thousand dollars." '

"And again, as to whether or not there are any emotions in the defendant, on page 117—I read this morning similar stuff from other sections—: 'He anticipated a few unpleasant minutes in strangling the victim.' Then the doctor comments: 'Facial expression of disgust.' But no interest, no emotion; just mad boys; a feeling of repugnance and disgust at the murder that was not originally contemplated, but was an after-thought because it was necessary to murder in order to remain at large.

"Have they any interest in the money? Follow on page 118, your Honor: 'We anticipated especially the money,' in the language of Loeb, and then the doctor adds in parenthesis: 'Facial expression of interest.'

" 'We thought we had it all so cleverly worked out, and we felt certain of not being caught. We felt certain of not being caught, or we would not have gone into it.'

"Is that the mad talk of a mad man or a mad boy? Or is that the cold-blooded reasoning of a man who is a criminal, with a criminal heart and a superior intelligence and education?

" 'I had considered the possibility of being caught, I was afraid of my father'—more emotion—'a sick man, could not stand the shock.'

"First, if they were not certain they were not going to be caught they would have backed out, their own safety considered.

"Second: 'I had considered the possibility of being caught, and I was afraid my father, a sick man, could not stand the shock, but I felt so certain of not being caught that we went on with it.'

"No emotion. Just a machine. And yet again, on page 118, if your Honor please, the doctor says: 'He expressed remorse.' At what? At his being caught? The only one that he is concerned in, in his scheme of life, is himself.

" 'I asked him if he would go through this plan again if he felt certain he would not be discovered. He replied: "I believe I would." ' Why? Darrow says ten thousand dollars is not the motive, but take it from his own lips: 'I believe I would if I could get the money.' Page 118; not the thrill, not the excitement: 'I believe I would if I could get the money.'

" 'The patient's attention was called to a newspaper account of an interview with Mrs. Franks, the mother of the victim, in which she stated she had no desire to see the boys hanged, but would like to talk to them to know whether the boy suffered in his last moments. The patient was asked whether it would upset him at all to talk with Mrs. Franks. He replied he thought it would upset him a little, and make him feel sad. He said when he read this interview in the paper, "My first feeling was joy." ' Joy at what? ' "That it might help us, her not feeling vindictive." Then a little remorse, not much, perhaps a little bit.' His emotions respond not much when he thinks of the suffering of Mrs. Franks, but when he thinks that her statement might save his neck, he experiences great joy. Emotion! No emotion? These doctors could not find emotion.

" 'The patient stated that although he had no feeling of remorse about the crime, he felt very, very sorry about it for his family's sake, because it might cause them distress. "I would be willing to increase the chance of my hanging to save the family from believing that I was the arch fiend. My folks have probably had the blow softened by blaming him [Leopold], and his folks by blaming me; but before I decide to take the responsibility in order to save my family, I must consult with my older brother first." '

"Everything he said and told the doctors he told it on advice, and repeatedly this report demonstrates that.

"There has been some talk here in order to make him appear to be mad, that he even contemplated killing his little brother Tommy or killing his father.

"The evidence in this case shows that that is just thrown in for good measure. That it has no foundation in fact at all.

"It is another piece of perjury, manufactured in order to build a foundation for a perjured insanity defense.

"On page 120, if your Honor please, when questioned about his attitude toward his family, the questioning was directed toward the possibility of some of them having been considered as the victim of this superior crime.

"It does not emanate from him, and it does not emanate from Leopold.

"The doctor suggested it to him:

" 'The questioning was directed toward the possibility of some of them having been considered. He described having in a joking way proposed that his own younger brother, Tommy, be the victim, and his associate jokingly agreed with it, but they gave up the idea because it was not practical for this reason: that if Tommy had disappeared, the patient would have to be at home and with the family during the period of the hunt and could not be foot loose to carry out the plans of securing the ransom money. "I couldn't have done it because I am tremendously fond of him." '

"Emotion, love.

"After this had been suggested to him, still they thought of money, money, money.

"If they kidnaped one of the fathers—on page 121—he asked, who would furnish the money. They thought again that it was not practicable, that there would be no one to furnish the money.

"Let's see whether they had any thought of money in this kidnaping. Again on page 121, if your Honor please:

" 'He had proposed that with his associate, and with his associate had contemplated using Dick Rubel, a very close friend of the patient and his associate, toward whom neither the patient nor his associate had any ill feeling nor grudge, as a victim.'

"On page 122:

" 'The plan of kidnaping Dick Rubel was given up because Dick Rubel's father was so tight we might not get any money from him.'

"And also another reason. It runs all through. First, the necessity of getting the money, and, second, the necessity of avoiding detection.

" 'And furthermore, they might be suspected because they were such close friends. Therefore, they would be sure to be questioned if Dick Rubel should disappear.'

" 'The patient and his associate were on very intimate terms, but the patient stated that his associate often stated that he would never entirely trust the patient, since the time the associate had found that the patient was taking unfair financial advantage of him.'

"Or, in other words, that he did not have the honor that is supposed to exist among thieves. Loeb was robbing Leopold.

" 'In a way, I have always been sort of afraid of him. He intimidated me by threatening to expose me'—

" 'He intimidated me by threatening to expose me, and I could not stand it.' And on page 123:

" 'Of late the patient, Loeb, had often thought of the possibility of shooting his associate.'

"He was afraid of Leopold.

" 'I could not stand it. I had often thought of the possibility of shooting him.'

"And again on page 123, your Honor:

" 'He often contemplated shooting his associate when they were out together and had the associate's revolver along. He thought of pointing the revolver at his associate and shooting him. He denied ever having thought of hitting him over the head with a chisel. "The idea of murdering a fellow, especially alone,—I don't think I could have done it. If I could have snapped my fingers, and make him pass away in a heart attack, I would have done it." '

"On page 124: 'One reason why he never murdered Leopold'—the report says 'associate'—'was that he felt that he would be suspected, and there was no very safe way of doing it.'

"An innocent boy, doing the killing for a thrill, who did not care what boy he picked out, rich or poor, black or white.

"According to Mr. Darrow, money had nothing to do with it at all.

"I have demonstrated by their own evidence, your Honor, that money was the underlying motive of the whole thing, and a secondary, or an equally pronounced, consideration was that they were not going to kill anybody if they thought there was a possibility of being caught.

"They did not kill the first man they had in mind because he was a larger man than they. They would have backed out at any time if they had thought there was a possibility of being caught. Always that concern about their own precious hides.

"And one reason why he did not kill Leopold was that he knew of no very safe way of doing it and he might have been suspected.

"Well, it might have been a good thing if he could have planned as safe a way to kill Leopold as he did to kill Bobby Franks and then have stopped there; or, he might have carried it a little further and committed suicide, and I think the community—a pall might have settled over them, but I do not think their grief would have lasted long.

" 'In connection with this he had often contemplated murdering his associate and securing a new pal.' Somebody who would have nothing on him.

" 'He states that he had often comtemplated hitting his associate over the head with a pistol, later shooting him, breaking the crystal of his watch, robbing him, leaving things in a way to create the impression that his associate had been robbed, that there had been a struggle, and he had been killed during the struggle.'

"On page 124.

"Money, and his opinion of the power of money. He thought that on account of his millions, or his father's millions that he was above the law. He believed that you cannot hang a million dollars in Cook County, no matter how dastardly the crime.

"Well, I disagree with him. I think the law is superior to money.

"I direct your Honor's attention to page 126:

" 'He contemplated escape from jail, but he does not want to do this, for it would distress his family to have him disappear and be known either as a criminal or an insane person.' 'Before he decides to escape he wanted to discuss this with his older brother, Allan.'

"This is his philosophy, and I don't know whether it was quite a coincidence that one of the books he took to the Morrison Hotel was 'The Influence of Wealth on Imperial Rome,' or not, but get this philosophy here, your honor—

" 'He thinks an escape could be managed by spending a few thousand dollars by bribing the guards at the jail and by some-one giving him a gun. He says this without any swagger, as though it was only a matter of careful, detailed planning, which his mind can do. He has made no plans as to where he would go, should he escape."

"Then the doctors add:

" 'It must be borne in mind that Tommy O'Connor, one of the most desperate and one of the most intelligent criminals Chicago has ever known, did make a successful jail delivery from this jail within the last few years.'

"What a feeling of comfort and security the mothers and fathers of this town would have, with their children going back and forth upon the streets of Chicago to school, and these two mad dogs at large. By God, every mother and father would shudder, and would want to lock their children in the house until they knew that the mad dogs had been captured or killed.

"Let us find out about this superman stuff. Page 127:

" 'He often discussed morals with his associate, who insisted to him that the only wrong he, the patient, can do, is to make a mistake, that anything that gives him pleasure is right for him to do.'

"Let's find out what judgment and credence Loeb paid to that statement. Quoting him literally from 127, he says:

" 'I took this statement with a great big dose of salt. Smile.'

"Well, he knew Leopold, and he knew when Leopold was joking, and he knew when he was in earnest, and when he talked about the superman theory, he says: 'I took it with a great, big dose of salt. Smile?' But the doctors swallowed it as if it was sugar. No emotion?

"Page 128: 'He says he is not sorry for his present predicament.' It reminds me of a fellow who killed his wife, over in jail, some years ago, and when his lawyer went in to talk to him he had no defense on earth.

"At that time these nameless insanity diseases were not thought of, and it looked as if this fellow was going to hang, and he afterwards did, and he told the lawyer, with tears running down his cheeks, 'You know, there isn't anybody in town who feels as bad about this as I do.' There isn't anybody in town that feels as bad as Loeb does about his present predicament.

" 'He says that he is sorry for his present predicament for his family's sake. He says he should be sorrier. He doesn't know what should be done to him. He felt that the law should take its course, unless he could avoid it in some other way.'

"Now, that is probably by escape, by bribing guards, and as he says, that is not out of the question; Tommy O'Connor got out and he is out yet.

"One hurdle at a time is his theory and Darrow's theory, to beat the rope.

"Talk about life imprisonment in the penitentiary.

"Escape if you can, and if you cannot, the same arguments that we made to save your neck we will make to the board of pardons or to the governor and get you out.

"He would repeat, maybe, if he knew he would not be discovered. "Is that mitigation, your Honor?

"All the way through this report runs the statement: 'I would kill again if I thought I could get away with it,' and they offer that in mitigation for the murder.

" 'When he and his associate quarreled in March the patient considered securing another friend for his criminal operations. He actually hinted concerning this to his friend, but as he met with no favorable response he did not press the matter further. As he had considered that he and his associate would be no longer together after June of this year'—that is when Leopold would be in Europe, on page 129—'he had thought of other ways of continuing his career of crime. One idea was to rent a room in a bad neighborhood and hang around poolrooms and meet criminals. He had also considered (on page 130) becoming a clever financial criminal. 'A financial criminal.'

"Money, money, money, not thrill, not excitement. A clever financial criminal after he finished his law course. He stated that he had considered crimes similar to that of Koretz, who had put through a gigantic stock swindle. If Mr. Darrow had read this, I think he would have blamed Koretz for this murder.

"On page 131: 'The patient's intellectual functions are intact; he is obviously of high intelligence. The examination was extensive, but did not show any pathology except the low basal metabolism.'

"That was the only thing that this extensive examination showed, and not a sign of pathology at all.

" 'He is correctly oriented, and in excellent contact with his surroundings. He denies any hallucinatory experiences, and there is no evidence of their presence. He has no feeling that people are against him, or that he is being treated unfairly at the present time. Patient is intensely selfish, and wrapped up in his own thoughts and feelings.'

"Heredity, finally Mr. Darrow says; the family, or some ancestor away back, planted the seed here. Hereditary influence. Well, let us see what their doctors say, on page 139:

" 'There is nothing about the patient's condition to show any evidence of a hereditary nature, and there is not the slightest reason to suppose that a condition of this kind will be transmitted to future generations by any of his siblings or relatives. This condition is acquired within the life history of the individual, and dies out when he dies.'

"It is something of his own construction, and his ancestors are in no degree responsible for it. It will die out when he dies out.

" 'There is nothing elicited from a most careful and painstaking history from all possible sources, to suggest that the family, either by omission or commission, contributed toward his delinquencies in the way they trained this boy.'

"Is your Honor going to be more influenced by an argument of Mr. Darrow that Dickie is not responsible for this, that his family is; that it is due to heredity, and training; or are you going to be more influenced by the statement of their doctors, who say:

" 'After the most extensive investigation, we find nothing in his family history or nothing in his training that contributed in the slightest particular to this crime. It is a matter of his own making, it was born within him and will die within him.'

"Continuing with the Bowman-Hulbert report on page 100, and here the person talking is Leopold and not Loeb:

" 'The reason why they agreed to strangle the victim with a rope, to their mind, was that that would make them equally guilty of the crime. It was not with any idea of close friendship or brotherhood. It was rather the opposite. The patient did not like the idea of strangling the victim and suggested chloroforming him, but his companion would not agree to this.'

"In other words, all this king and slave phantasy is a pure figment of the imagination of the defense. The real tie that binds in this case is that one was a criminal; the other had something on him. He was afraid of exposure; he contemplated murdering him; and the other one blackmailed him in the manner that I have already indicated. Loeb wanted to shut the mouth of Leopold, and then break with him. Leopold had enough on him, and that is why he wanted Leopold to help him choke the life out of little Bobby Franks.

"Again, on page 100: 'Considerable trouble was experienced in perfecting a plan whereby they could secure'—what? The thrill? No. The money. 'Without exposing themselves to too much danger of being apprehended.'

"And again on page 101: 'They wanted to divide the ten thousand dollars ransom money equally.'

"No emotion in the superman Leopold? No, he killed all his emotions before he came into court, on the advice of counsel and the advice of doctors. But on page 102 when he is talking he says:

" 'It was necessary to hit the victim several times over the head and he bled some. This upset the patient a great deal. He said to his companion, "My God, this is awful." '

" 'He experienced a sinking feeling in the pit of his stomach; his hands trembled, he lost some of his self control. His companion, however, laughed and joked, and helped the patient to get back his self control.'

"When they got to the culvert they found the boy had already died and they could not carry out their original scheme of strangling him with the ropes.

"Again on page 108: 'Asked whether he would commit another such a crime if he were certain that he could escape detection, he replied, "I would not commit another such a crime because I realize that no one can ever be sure of escaping detection." '

"He feels that this would be the only reason that would keep him from another such attempt. That there would be no question of remorse or guilt entering into it.

"The desire to save their own worthless hides is the only thing that enters into their thoughts. No emotion, and yet on page 108 before he knew that he would have to chloroform Little Emotion and let Intellect walk into the court alone he stated that he is rather fond of small children. That he always wanted to take a crying child into his arms and comfort it.

"That on such occasions he almost noticed a functioning of his lachrymal glands.

"While in jail the patient has clearly been under considerable emotional tension and is rather irritable at times.

" 'The newspaper report that he is a cold-blooded scientist, with no emotions and entirely unconcerned,' the argument of his counsel, that he is a cold-blooded scientist, with no emotions, and entirely unconcerned, as Drs. Hulbert and Bowman say on page 109:

" 'Is completely wrong.'

" 'The patient ordinarily is able to make a calm, and self-possessed appearance, and before reporters and visitors seems perfectly self-possessed and unconcerned. On the other hand, when he does not feel the need for doing it, and when he is talking frankly with people, and no longer posing, he shows a good deal of irritability and nervous tension.'

"When he is not posing to prepare a defense, based on the fact that he has no emotion, when he is not posing, these doctors say he shows a great deal of emotion.

"He wouldn't lie either.

"Why, your Honor, it really would be too bad if these two young fellows imposed on Old Doc Yak, lied to him.

"I showed to you what Loeb said he would do. I showed to you in this report what he has done. He has lied repeatedly to the doctors.   He has lied under advice of counsel and family. He has suppressed and distorted.

"Let's see what Leopold said he would do. On page 109:

" 'He seems to be reasonably frank during the examinations, particularly with regard to his own feelings and emotions and his estimate of himself. On the other hand, he undoubtedly omits certain data regarding some of his past experiences. He lied rather plausibly at times. Later, when he realized that it was known that he was lying, he appeared perfectly unconcerned. A number of times he inquired whether his story agreed with his companion's, and seemed to show a great deal of concern about this matter.'

"In other words, he wanted to know whether they had both learned their lesson in the same manner from their instructors and whether they were both telling the same story.

" 'In fact, he did this so crudely that it was apparent that he was concerned lest there be some failure of their stories to coincide.'

"In other words, both of them are lying, both of them have lied, both have suppressed things and hid them from their doctors, and they had to do it in order to give a basis of that insanity defense here.

"Both of them had been schooled and trained and instructed as to what to tell these doctors and what not to tell them, and when he is telling his story he is concerned lest there be some failure of their stories to coincide, lest one of them might forget or the other might forget.

"Money!

"The same argument was made by Mr. Darrow with reference to Leopold as was made to Loeb.

"First he began to blame the old German philosopher Nietzsche, although every student in every university for the last twenty-five years has read his philosophy.

"And then I guess he thought that would not do because if reading his philosophy would be an excuse for this crime, how about the countless thousands who have gone before and who are still reading this philosophy who lead decent, honorable lives?

"He did not have a poor old nurse in this case to blame,

and he was not quite satisfied in blaming some remote ancestor, so he blames their parents, respectable, decent law abiding citizens.

"The only unfortunate thing that ever came into their life was to have a snake like Leopold in that decent family. Casting blame where blame was not due, but where sympathy should go out as it does go out from the heart of every person in this community, to the respected families of these men.

"But Darrow says: 'No. Save your sympathy for the boys. Do not place the blame on the boys. Place it on their families. This is the result of heredity.'

"Well, let us see what the doctors say:

" 'However, it might be said that our present degree of knowledge gives us no reason to feel that a mental condition such as the patient's is of an hereditary nature, or that it will appear in future generations. The family has apparently endeavored to do everything possible to bring the patient up in a suitable manner, and there has been no conscious error or neglect on their part.'

"Well, so much for the medical defense in this case. Mr. Darrow has read to you poetry. May I be permitted if your Honor please, for a few moments to read you some prose:

" 'The White House, Washington, D. C.

" 'August 8, 1904.

" 'The application for commutation of sentence of John W. Burley is denied. This man committed the most heinous crime known to our laws. Twice before he has committed crimes of a similar but less horrible character. In my judgment, there is no justification whatever for paying heed to the allegations that he is not of sound mind'—

allegations made after the trial and the conviction, as in this case.

"No person in all this broad land who knew these two defendants ever suspected that they were mentally diseased until after Bachrach and Darrow were retained to defend them, in a case where they had no escape on the facts.

"If I had taken them into custody on the 20th day of May and attempted to have them committed to an insane asylum, Mr. Darrow would have been here, their families would have been here, and all the doctors that they could hire, and there would be only one crazy man in the court room, and that would be the State's Attorney.

" 'Allegations made after the trial and conviction. Nobody would pretend that there has ever been such degree of mental unsoundness shown as would make people even consider sending him to an asylum if he had not committed this crime. Under such circumstances he should certainly be esteemed sane enough to suffer the penalty for his monstrous deed.'

"And the penalty in this case was hanging.

" 'I have scant sympathy with a plea of insanity advanced to save a man from the consequences of crime, when, unless that crime had been committed, it would have been impossible to persuade any reasonable authority to commit him to an asylum as insane.'

"Would it be possible in this case, if this crime had not been committed, to persuade any reasonable authority to commit either one of these men to an insane asylum as insane?

"And I submit, if your honor please, the crime at bar is so revolting that the criminals are not entitled to one particle of sympathy from any human being. I continue the reading:

" 'It is essential that punishment for it should not only be certain, but as swift as possible. The jury in this case did their duty by recommending the infliction of the death penalty. It is to be regretted that we do not have special provision for some more summary dealing with this type of case.'

"That it is to be regretted in this case, if your Honor please, that under the laws as you have found them, we have no more summary manner of dealing with the case at bar. But this is a community of law, and this community will survive or fall as we enforce our laws and respect them.

"I continue the reading:

" 'The more we do what in us lies to secure a certain and swift justice in dealing with these cases, the more effectively do we work against the growth of that lynching spirit which is so full of evil omen for this people, because it seeks to avenge one infamous crime by the commission of another of equal infamy.

" 'The application is denied, and the sentence will be carried into effect.'

"I submit, if your honor please, that it is safer to follow the reasoning of this state document than it is to follow the sophistries of Clarence Darrow. I submit that it is safer to follow the philosophy of Theodore Roosevelt, as he laid it down in this great state paper when he was President of the United States, and was only concerned with the enforcement of the law, than it is to follow the weird and uncanny philosophy of the paid advocate of the defense, whose business it is to make murder safe in Cook County.

"Now, if your Honor please, the other day Mr. Darrow argued that the state had advanced the silly argument that these boys were gamblers, and gambled for high stakes, and he said the only evidence we had to predicate such a charge on was the testimony of Leon Mandel who had played one game of bridge with them, and who said that in that game they played for five or ten cents a point.

"The trouble with Mr. Darrow is that he does not know all the facts in this case. He does not know all the evidence.

"I thank God I am not a great pleader, because I think that sometimes when men are obsessed with the idea that when they open their mouths words of wisdom rush out, that all that is necessary in the trial of a case is to make a wonderful argument, that that is why a great many of them fail in my judgment, because they rely too much upon their oratory; they pay no attention whatever to the facts in the case, and after all I believe that courts and juries are influenced not by oratory, but by hard facts sworn to by witnesses.

"That is why I have paid more attention to the preparation of the evidence in this case than I have to writing a closing speech.

"Now, let us see whether there is any other evidence in this case. Among the letters introduced in evidence we find the following, Allan M. Loeb, 2465 Utah Avenue, Seattle, Washington. Allan Loeb is the generalissimo of the defense. He is the one who is advising young Loeb whether or not he ought to tell the doctors this or whether he ought to tell the lawyers that. This letter was mailed May 19th at 5:30 P. M., 1924, and probably was received by Richard Loeb the day of the murder. Marked 'Personal.'

"'Dear Dick: I wanted to send this letter to you so there would be no possible chance of Dad seeing it. Glad to hear about Sammy Schmaltz, but could that amount have been *possibly* reversed—'

"In other words, as I read this letter, and as your honor will read it after I get all through, he was glad to hear he had won some money, but could that amount have been possibly reversed, could he have lost it instead of winning it?

"'If so, you are *all wrong* in your gambling, and even so'— even if you did win instead of lose—'and even so you must be shooting a little too high. Did you get cash?' Or did he pay on an I. O. U., I suppose.

"'Best love, Allan.'

"Another letter from one of his companions, and it is fair to assume he is a wealthy man or the son of a wealthy man.

"'Robert L. Leopold, 530 Thompson Street, Ann Arbor, Michigan. Dear Dick: Just a line, as I am awfully busy, and I am coming to you for help. I have an exam in history, seventeen, and know nothing about it. Furthermore, my notes are no good. You said last semester that you would let me take your notes in the course. Please send them to me right away if you can. My exam is next Friday and I must study. Please drop me a line and let me know, so I know whether to plan on them or not. I am damn sorry that we couldn't see each other while I was home, but you are always so ——— busy. I guess I am too, while home. But I always feel as though I am intruding when you guys are gambling, because I don't gamble that high. At any rate, better luck next time when home. Thanks in advance for your trouble.

"'Sincerely, Bobby.'

"It is in evidence in this case, if your Honor please, that both of these defendants had a bank account. We put a witness on the stand, an employe of Sears Roebuck, who testified that from time to time she gave checks to the defendant Loeb here. She told about two checks for two hundred and fifty dollars.

"His allowance was two hundred and fifty dollars a month, so they say. The Charleviox bank statement shows that on March 15, 1923, he deposited $141.55; March 25, $125.00; May 16, $345.00; May 31, $300.00—all this was in 1923—

June 28, $683.00; July, $171.40; July 13, $259.00; July 16, $108.00; July 21, $50.00; August 27, $155.00; August 28, $175.00; September 6, $300.00; September 19, $302.75.

"Where did he get it?

"These are not checks for two hundred and fifty dollars from Sears Roebuck.

"Then he had another account at the Hyde Park State Bank. It shows as follows on deposits:

"October 1st, 1923, $485.00; October 16, $50.00; November 1st, $444.50; November 5, $100.00; November 16, $100.00; November 19, $730.00; November 28, $175.00. Business was good that month. December 24, $420.00; January 14, $400.00; February 6th—that is in this year—$425.00; February 14, $230.00; March 14, $137.00; April 16, $350.00; April 25, $100.00; May 15th—the week before the murder—$536.51. And where did he get it? April 16, 1924, $350.00; April 25th, $100.00.

"That is 1924. Where did he get it? He didn't get it from his father in those amounts and at those times.

"When I left off last night, your Honor, I had called your attention to the fact that the defendant Loeb had in the Hyde Park State Bank and the Bank of Charlevoix a sum somewhat over three thousand dollars.

"I read off the deposits, showing that in some months he deposited as high as seven, eight or nine hundred dollars, and the testimony on behalf of the defense is here that he had an allowance of two hundred and fifty dollars a month.

"That can be construed as evidence either in support of the contention of the State that these men gambled for high stakes, higher than their millionaire friends could afford to gamble for, or it may be considered in support of the contention of the State that other crimes committed by the defendant Loeb.

"There has been testimony here that he had bonds, Liberty Bonds, and had not clipped the coupons from them for two or three years.

"Well, if they were the proceeds of a robbery, that was an act of wisdom and discretion.

"Now, if your Honor please, in support of our contention that the motive in this case was first, money; that the original crime planned was the crime of kidnaping; that murder was later decided upon in order to protect them from arrest and punishment, I do not intend to take up your Honor's time by reviewing all the evidence independent of the statements made by these defendants to their doctor that I read to you yesterday from the Bowman-Hulbert report; but I will direct your Honor's attention to the uncomfortable afternoons that they spent along the Illinois Central tracks, the number of times they threw a pad of paper from the car to see where the money would light.

"I will direct your attention again to the ransom letter:

" 'Secure before noon today ten thousand dollars. This money must be composed entirely of old bills.'

"If they merely wanted to get the money and did not want to use it, what difference whether the bills were old; what difference whether they were marked or unmarked if they did not intend to spend them?

"As a final word of warning: 'This is a strictly commercial proposition.' All the way through, if your Honor please, all the way through this most unusual crime runs money, money, money.

"And when it is not money it is blood. I think that we have clearly established the real motive in this case.

"Mr. Darrow relies upon the facts, first he says there was no motive; second, upon the youth of the defendants; and third, upon their mental condition. I strongly suspect that the real defense in this case is not any of those at all. The real defense in this case is Clarence Darrow and his peculiar philosophy of life.

"I quite agree with the senior Bachrach when he was closing, that they brought in a man who was an expert on punishment to instruct your Honor just what punishment you should mete out in this case.

"In other words, the real defense in this case is Clarence Darrow, and those things which he has urged upon your Honor as a defense I would like to take up in detail.

"As I say, I think I have covered completely and have demonstrated beyond the peradventure of a doubt that the only motive, controlling motive in this case, was money, ten thousand dollars and as much more as they could get afterwards.

"Now how about their health. The only thing pathologically about Leopold is that he has a calcified pineal gland.

"Our doctor, Dr. Woodyatt, said that did not mean anything. Nobody knows, and nobody has testified on behalf of the defense, that it did mean anything.

"Glands, they tell us, do not generally calcify until you are about thirty years of age. Now some people develop earlier in life than others. I believe in Africa women are matured at nine years of age and bear children at nine or ten years of age.

"Leopold has developed a little earlier than the average man. He has developed sexually and mentally, and if it means anything at all, it means that he has the intellect and brain and mind of a man thirty years of age and that is all. I read to you last night, report of Drs. Hulbert and Bowman that there was not anything pathological about Loeb except the minus seventeen of his basal metabolism.

"And every doctor who took the stand said that that was within the range of normality.

"That is the only thing that is abnormal, that is the only thing that is diseased, according to their evidence.

"And every expert who took the stand testified that that was normal, assuming it is true.

"Why, your Honor can look at them. You have looked at them. You have observed them. There is nothing the matter with them physically. There is nothing the matter with them mentally. The only fault is the trouble with their moral sense, and that is not a defense in a criminal case.

"I submit, your Honor please, if we can take the power of American manhood, take boys at eighteen years of age and send them to their death in the front line trenches of France in defense of our laws, we have an equal right to take men nineteen years of age and take their lives for violating those laws that these boys gave up their lives to defend.

"Ah, many a boy eighteen years of age lies beneath the poppies in Flanders fields who died to defend the laws of this country. We had no compunction when we did that; why should we have any compunction when we take the lives of men nineteen years of age who want to tear down and destroy the laws that these brave boys died to preserve?

"Mr. Darrow has referred in the case to hanging. Mr. Darrow is a student of criminology; he has written a book on it and he says the criminal age, the time when crimes are committed, is between the age of seventeen and twenty-four.

"And your Honor and I know that the average criminal age is twenty-two.

"If we are going to punish crime and by the punishment stop it, and the criminal age is between seventeen and twenty-four, how can we punish it if the age is a defense?

"Mr. Darrow criticized Mr. Marshall for his quotations from Blackstone, and seemed to be under the impressions that we were trying to try this case under the ancient British law.

"We are trying this case, if your Honor please, under the statutes of the State of Illinois in the year 1924. They say that a boy between ten and fourteen may have sufficient capacity to commit a crime and be answerable for it, but it is the duty of the State to prove beyond a reasonable doubt that he has sufficient capacity.

"The statute that your Honor is bound to enforce in this case, and the statute under which we are trying these defendants further provides that from fourteen years of age up the law assumes that he has the capacity to commit a crime and is entirely and thoroughly responsible for it.

"Let us see at what age some of these men have been hanged. Buff Higgins was hanged at the age of twenty-three. Butch Lyons was twenty-five; Henry Foster, twenty-four; Albert C. Fields, twenty-four; Windreth, twenty-nine; Mannow, twenty-seven; Dan McCarty, twenty-seven; William T. Powers, twenty-three; Chris Murray, twenty-eight; John Drugan, twenty-two; Robert Howard, thirty; Louis P. Peasan, sentenced on a plea of guilty April 15, 1904, by Judge Kersten, was twenty-three; Peter Neidermeyer, twenty-three; Gustav Marks, twenty-one; Harvey Van Dine, twenty-one. These were not the poor sons of multimillionaires; these were the sons of poor men, men who had no advantages in life, men who had no education, men who had been brought up in the gutter and the slums, men who did not develop intellectually at the early age that these men have developed at.

"Richard Ivens, twenty-four; Andrew Williams, twenty-two;

Thomas Jennings, twenty-eight; Thomas Schultz, nineteen; Frank Shiblewski, twenty-two, and his brother hanged the same day; Ewald, twenty-three; Smith, twenty-seven; Lundgren, twenty-five; Dennis Anderson, twenty-one; Lloyd Bopp, twenty-three; Albert Johnson, twenty-five; Earl Dear, twenty-six; Jack O'Brien, twenty-two; Mills, twenty-one; Champion, twenty-two; Zander, twenty-two; Haensel, a man who fought for his country, who was syphilitic, who was hit in the service of his country in the head by a chain weighing a thousand pounds, and who was discharged from further service physically unfit, was hanged in Cook County at the age of twenty-seven; the little songbird from Italy, Viani, seventeen; Brislane, twenty-seven; Sam Ferrari, twenty-six; Oscar McDavit, a colored man who thought that the Lord had appointed him to lead his race back to Africa, twenty-three; George Brown, twenty-nine; Antonio Lopez, twenty-six; Harry Ward, twenty-five; Carl Wanderer, twenty-five; Legrine, twenty-seven; Harvey Church, twenty-three; Pastoni, twenty-six; Dalton, sentenced by your Honor, a colored boy, without any of the advantages that these men had, whose ancestors were slaves, only two or three generations removed from savagery in Africa, and yet he paid the penalty for the violation of the laws. Walter Krauser, sitting in the county jail, marking off the days between now and the day he hangs, twenty-one, Bernard Grant, sitting in the county jail waiting for October seventeenth, when he will pay the penalty upon the gallows, nineteen.

"Oh, but Mr. Darrow says there are only six men who have been hanged on pleas in Cook County.

"Now, your Honor and I are familiar enough with the practice over here not to be fooled by that. What happens when a man gets a guilty client and there is no defense?

"He generally goes to the State's Attorney, and he says: 'If you will waive the death penalty I will plead guilty.'

"If there is in the nature of the case any mitigating circumstances, the State's Attorney says: 'Yes, we will waive the death penalty. Let's go upstairs and plead him guilty, and I will recommend life.' But if the case is of such a nature that the State's Attorney cannot in conscience and in law waive the extreme penalty, he says:

" 'No, that man has got to go to a jury.' And then some-times they do as Walter Stanton did this summer. He went before the State's Attorney and asked him, would he waive the death penalty? The State's Attorney said: 'No, this is a hang-ing case.' Walter Stanton then went in and stated the facts to Judge Steffen, and Judge Steffen said: 'If you plead him guilty I am going to hang him.'

"Walter Stanton then went before another judge, and there apparently was some misunderstanding, because he pleaded the man guilty, and when he got through the judge indicated he was going to sentence him to hang, and then Walter Stanton nearly collapsed and begged the court for God's sake to let him go to a jury.

"The reason that courts do not hang any oftener than they do is because hanging cases always go to juries.

"Where the attorney cannot make an agreement in advance, he says: 'Well, then, I am going to take a chance with twelve men. They can't do any worse than the court can do on a plea, and I am going to give my client a run for his money.'

"Now, your Honor and I know that that is the case, and Mr. Darrow knows it is the case, and everybody who is familiar with procedure in the criminal court knows it is the case.

"It is not because there is one law for the judge and another law for the jury.

"It is not because juries must execute the law to the utter-most, and the court has a right to sit as a friendly father. It is a matter of fact, known to everybody, that when they cannot make an agreement with either the court or the State's Attorney, they go to juries. That is why we only have six hanged on pleas, and so many hanged on verdicts.

"That being the situation, are we going to tell the criminal world, and Mr. Darrow says the criminal world is between seventeen and twenty-four and that the average is twenty-two, the age at which murders are committed, crimes of violence are committed,—are we going to tell them that the new law in-troduced into the statutes of Illinois by Clarence Darrow and approved by the Chief Justice of the Criminal Court makes it perfectly safe for them to murder, or are we going to tell them that the law will be vigorously enforced?

"The law, if your Honor please, is made to protect the innocent, and it is made to protect the innocent by punishing the guilty and in no other way can we protect innocence or protect society.

"I think, if your Honor please, I have now covered the three defenses set forth by Mr. Darrow, their age, lack of motive, and physical and mental condition. When we get all through, Mr. Darrow says that your Honor ought to be merciful and finally, and that is his concluding defense, he appeals to your heart and to your sympathy and not to your mind or your conscience.

"When I was listening to Mr. Darrow plead for sympathy for these two men who showed no sympathy, it reminded me of the story of Abraham Lincoln, about a young boy about their age whose parents were wealthy and he murdered both of them. He was an only child and he did it so that he might inherit their money. His crime was discovered the same as this crime has been discovered, and the court asked him for any reason he might have why sentence of death should not be passed upon him, and he promptly replied, he hoped the court would be lenient to a poor orphan.

"Robert Franks had a right to live. He had a right to the society of his family and his friends and they had a right to his society. These two young law students of superior intelligence, with more intelligence than they have heart, decided that he must die. He was only fourteen. These two law students knew under the law if you had a right to take a life you had a right to take it at fourteen and they thought that they had a right to take his life, and they proceeded to take it.

"Mr. Darrow quoted considerable poetry to you and I would like to again be indulged while I read a little bit of prose.

" 'Crime and criminals. If I looked at jails and crime and prisoners in the way the ordinary person does, I should not speak on this subject to you.'

"This is an address delivered to the prisoners in the county jail, if your Honor please.

" 'The reason I talk to you on the question of crime, its cause and cure, is because I really do not believe the least in crime. There is no such a thing as a crime, as the word is generally understood. I do not believe that there is any sort of distinction between the real moral condition in and out of jail One is just as good as the other. The people here can no more help being here than the people outside can avoid being outside. I do not believe that people are in jail because they deserve to be. They are in jail simply because they cannot avoid it, on account of circumstances which are entirely beyond their control and for which they are in no way responsible.

.   .   .   .

" 'I believe that progress is purely a question of the pleasurable units that we get out of life. The pleasures and pain theory is the only correct theory of morality and the only way of judging life.'

"That is the doctrine of Leopold. That is the doctrine expounded last Sunday in the press of Chicago by Clarence Darrow.

"I want to tell you the real defense in this case, your Honor.

"It is Clarence Darrow's dangerous philosophy of life.

"He said to your Honor that he was not pleading alone for these two young men. He said he was looking to the future, that he was thinking of the ten thousand young boys that in the future would fill the chairs his clients filled, and he wants to soften the law.

"He wants them treated not with the severity that the law of this State prescribes, but it wants them treated with kindness and consideration.

"I want to tell your Honor that it would be much better if God had not caused this crime to be disclosed. It would have been much better if it went unsolved and these men went unwhipped of justice. It would not have done near the harm to this community as will be done if your Honor, as chief justice of this great court, puts your official seal of approval upon the doctrines of anarchy preached by Clarence Darrow as a defense in this case.

"Society can endure, the law can endure, and criminals escape, but if a court such as this court should say that he believes in the doctrine of Darrow, that you ought not to hang when the law says you should, a greater blow has been struck to our institutions than by a hundred, yea, a thousand murders.

"Mr. Darrow has preached in this case that one of the handicaps the defendants are under is that they are rich, the sons of multimillionaires. I have already stated to your Honor that if it was not for their wealth Darrow would not be here and the Bachrachs would not be here.

"If it was not for their wealth we would not have been regaled by all this tommy-rot by the three wise men from the east.

"I don't want to refer to this any more than Mr. Darrow did, but he referred to it and it is in evidence, and he tried to make your Honor believe that somebody lied, that Gortland lied when he talked about a friendly judge.

"On June 10th, 1924, in the Chicago Herald-Examiner—that was before this case had been assigned to anybody; that was when Darrow was announcing and he did announce in this same article, that they were going to plead not guilty—there was an article written by Mr. Slattery, sitting back there, on June 10th:

" 'The friendly judge resort suggested for the defense will be of no avail. It was mentioned as a possibility that a plea of guilty might be entered on the understanding it would result in life sentence. If this becomes an absolute probability, Crowe announced that he will nolle prosse the case and reindict the slayers.'

"Did Gortland lie?

"He gave the name of witness after witness that he told the same story to, as he told it to Slattery, before the case was even assigned.

"He said it was told to him by Leopold. I don't know whether your Honor believes that officer or not, but I want to tell you, if you have observed these two defendants during the trial, if you have observed the conduct of their attorneys and their families with one honorable exception, and that is the old man who sits in sackcloth and ashes and who is entitled to the sympathy of everybody, old Mr. Leopold, with that one honorable exception, everybody connected with the case have laughed and sneered and jeered and if the defendant, Leopold, did not say that he would plead guilty before a friendly judge, his actions demonstrated that he thinks he has got one.

"You have listened with a great deal of patience and kindness and consideration to the state and the defense. I am not going to unduly trespass upon your Honor's time, and I am going to close for the State.

"I believe that the facts and circumstances proven in this case demonstrate that a crime has been committed by these two defendants and that no other punishment except the extreme penalty of the law will fit, and I leave the case with you on behalf of the State of Illinois, and I ask your Honor in the language of Holy Writ to 'Execute justice and righteousness in the land.' "

REMARKS OF THE COURT AT THE CONCLUSION OF THE ARGUMENT OF THE STATE'S ATTORNEY

. . . .

"Before the State rests the court will order stricken from the record the closing remarks of the State's Attorney as being a cowardly and dastardly assault upon the integrity of this court."

"It was not so intended, your Honor."

"And it could not be used for any other purpose except to incite a mob and to try and intimidate this court. It will be stricken from the record."

"If your Honor please, the State's Attorney had no such intention."

"We will go on—"

"I merely want to put my personal feelings plainly before the court. It was not the intention of the State's Attorney."

"The State's Attorney knew that would be heralded all through this country and all over this world, and he knows the court hasn't an opportunity except to do what he did. It was not the proper thing to do."

"It was not the intention."

"This court will not be intimidated by anybody at any time or place as long as he occupies this position.

"Now, in order to fix the date that I will set this case, gentlemen, I want to say there has been a great deal of criticism about the conduct of this case; some of it from well-meaning people who knew no better; others from those who should know better.

"We have been criticized about the delays of justice. The court has been criticized because after a plea of guilty he permitted evidence to be heard, and we have been criticized because of the length of time it takes for an execution after the court passes judgment.

"Permit me to say with reference to the delays of justice, that this trial is one of the speediest trials of a criminal case ever heard in Cook County in which the State asked the death penalty.

"And this could not have been done if it had not been for the able manner in which the State's Attorney of this County investigated and prepared his case and was ready to go to trial when called.

"The defense are to be commended because they made no attempt to delay the trial.

"The murder was committed on May 21st, exactly two months before the trial started. The defendants were arrested on May 31st, ten days after the murder, indicted within a short time thereafter, and within six weeks of the day of the indictment this case was on trial.

"So that it cannot be truthfully said that their wealth or poverty had anything to do with the delay in this case, because there was no delay.

"There were thirty-four murder indictments returned for murders committed in 1924, between January 1st and May 21st, that have not yet been tried; and twenty of them are held without bail in the county jail of Cook County.

"To those who criticize the court for listening to testimony after the defendants pleaded guilty, permit me to call their attention to a section of the statute and to the ruling of the Supreme Court thereon. The Supreme Court has said:

" 'That part of Section 4 of Division 13 of the Criminal Code making it the duty of the Court to examine witnesses as to the aggravation and mitigation of the offense in cases where the party pleads guilty, is mandatory and not discretionary, and it is necessary for the court to make such examination when requested or desired either on the part of the people or of the defendant. It would be reversible error not to do so.'

"As to those who criticize our courts for the delay in execution after judgment, this is because they have been reciting here that in England or some other place they executed them within ten days, I would respectfully call their attention to Section 749, Chapter 38, of our revised statute, which says:

" 'When a defendant is sentenced to death, the date set shall not occur before the 10th day of the term of the Supreme Court occurring next after the pronouncing of the judgment.'

"So that any defendant who was sentenced to death in this county since the date of the indictment of the two defendants in this case, could not be executed before the 17th day of October next, which is the 10th day of the next term of the Supreme Court following the June term.

"A person sentenced to death in the middle of June could not be legally executed sooner than a person sentenced to death between then and October 2nd.

"I am going to take this case under advisement, gentlemen.

"I have nineteen hundred and fifty odd pages, practically two thousand pages of exhibits. When I say exhibits, it is part of the testimony; it is the Bowman-Hulbert report; parts of the confession; some of the testimony that was ready in secret that contained matter that was not fit for publication and should not be heard in the courtroom, and it will take me some little time to do that, and to prepare to decide this matter and render judgment in this case.

"I think I ought to have ten days or so, and I will fix the day at September 10th.

"I will fix the day as September the 10th, at 9:30 o'clock, and I will say to those people who are here now that there will be nobody admitted in this room on that day, except members of the press and members of the family and sheriffs and the State's Attorney's staff.

"If anything occurs whereby I could not be in a position or cannot be in a position to render it on that day, I will notify the press and the authorities at least three days in advance. But there will be nothing to deter me from rendering judgment on that day, gentlemen, unless it is illness.

"We will continue this case now until September the 10th at nine thirty o'clock."

The Decision and Sentence

Not "mitigating circumstances" but "the dictates of enlightened humanity," were the forces which saved the lives of Nathan F. Leopold, Jr., and Richard Loeb, and sent them to the Illinois State Penitentiary at Joliet, to spend the rest of their lives.

Crowds stood about Judge Caverly as he pronounced sentence in the murder of the century, life imprisonment for the murder of Robert Franks and ninety-nine years in the penitentiary as penalty on the kidnaping charge.

When the boys entered the courtroom at nine-thirty the morning of September 10th, each surrounded by guards, they were pale but composed. Loeb sat staring during the Judge's opening remarks, at the base of the Judge's bench, listening to the first judicial words, in an almost sullen mood. Leopold's face was expressionless. The room was tense and silent. Only newspaper reporters, photographers, court officials and attorneys, with the relatives of the boys, were allowed in the room. More than five thousand persons gathered on the outside of the building, but credentials were necessary to gain entrance to the courtroom.

Packed into the few minutes in which Judge Caverly pronounced sentence was the essence of all the drama of the whole trial.

When the boys realized that they were to live, the frozen expressions of their faces broke, and for once they were mere boys. The cool-nerved criminals became at once two boys terribly glad they were not to die. Their pose dropped from them and as they left the courtroom, rushed out by the cordon of guards about them, they laughed and waved to their friends behind them.

Leopold, the mighty Leopold, who does not believe in God and who is a fatalist, too strong to ever show emotion—Leopold cried as he was led down the corridors of the jail. Ashamed he was when the guards noted his tears, but the tears poured from his eyes just the same.

They were rushed away to Joliet the following day. The fear that had prompted the whole army of police guards about Judge Caverly, at the courtroom doors and at every entrance to the criminal court building of Cook County, prompted the hasty removal of the boys back to the jail. Too many cranks had written threatening letters to the judge, threatening to bomb the jail, or to kill the judge, to take chances. Either their courage failed the "cranks," or the police guard was too imposing—but at any rate, no disturbances occurred.

It was not two saddened criminals, faced with life imprisonment who left Chicago, probably for the last time in their lives, but two happy boys, who acted as though they had been freed instead of placed behind bars. The reaction of the tense waiting to know the penalty they were to pay for their crime, was tears, and then laughter. They fairly giggled and pranced because they were to live, even if it were behind prison bars.

At the last they explained why they had cried at the last minute—what it was that had broken their calm exterior. It was the sentence of ninety-nine years. Life imprisonment, they said, they could stand. They were prepared for that. They had prayed for that. But the ninety-nine years the judge tacked on—ninety-nine years to be served, even if they got a parole from the life imprisonment term! That was what brought the tears to Leopold's eyes and made Dick bite his lips and press his hand to his mouth to hide its trembling.

But even the blow of the ninety-nine years, which hung as an added weight to the life sentence, could not keep down their spirits, their animal-like relief from the prospect of death. Forgotten were their boasts that they were not afraid to die, that they were fatalists and prepared for anything. So it was with smiles and a great relief that these two prize students, these two young college men, who were the envy of their classes, turned their backs on college campuses, libraries—turned away from their comfortable homes and their families, toward the prison cells where they will probably live out their lives.

Judge Caverly's decision follows:

"In view of the profound and unusual interest that this case has aroused not only in this community but in the entire country and even beyond its boundaries, the court feels it his duty to state the reasons which have led him to the determination he has reached.

"It is not an uncommon thing that pleas of guilty are entered in criminal cases, but almost without exception in the past such pleas have been the result of a virtual agreement between the defendants and the State's Attorney whereby in consideration of the plea the State's Attorney consents to recommend to the court a sentence deemed appropriate by him, and, in the absence of special reasons to the contrary, it is the practice of the court to follow such recommendations.

"In the present case the situation is a different one. A plea of guilty has been entered by the defense without a previous understanding with the prosecution and without any knowledge whatever on its part. Moreover, the plea of guilty did not in this particular case, as it usually does, render the task of the prosecution easier by substituting the admission of guilt for a possibly difficult and uncertain chain of proof. Here the State was in possession not only of the essential substantiating facts but also of voluntary confessions on the part of the defendants. The plea of guilty, therefore, does not make a special case in favor of the defendant.

"Since both the cases—that, namely, of murder and that of kidnaping for ransom—were of a character which invested the court with discretion as to the extent of the punishment it became his duty under the statute to examine witnesses as to the aggravation and mitigation of the defense. This duty has been fully met. By consent of counsel for the State and for the defendants, the testimony in the murder case has been accepted as equally applicable to the case of kidnaping for ransom. In addition, a prima facie case was made out for the kidnaping case as well.

"The testimony introduced, both by the prosecution and the defense, has been as detailed and elaborate as though the case had been tried before a jury. It has been given the widest publicity and the public is so fully familiar with all its phases that it would serve no useful purpose to restate or analyze the evidence.

"By pleading guilty, the defendants have admitted legal responsibility for their acts; the testimony has satisfied the court that the case is not one in which it would have been possible to set up successfully the defense of insanity as insanity is defined and understood by the established law of this state for the purpose of the administration of criminal justice.

"The court, however, feels impelled to dwell briefly on the mass of data produced as to the physical, mental and moral condition of the two defendants. They have been shown in essential respects to be abnormal; had they been normal they would not have committed the crime. It is beyond the province of this court, as it is beyond the capacity of human kind in its present state of development, to predicate ultimate responsibility for human acts.

"At the same time, the court is willing to recognize that the careful analysis made of the life history of the defendants and of their present mental, emotional and ethical condition has been of extreme interest and is a valuable contribution to criminology. And yet the court feels strongly that similar analyses made of other persons accused of crime will probably reveal similar or different abnormalities. The value of such tests seems to lie in their applicability to crime and criminals in general.

"Since they concern the broad question of human responsibility and legal punishment and are in no wise peculiar to the individual defendants, they may be deserving of legislative but not of judicial consideration. For this reason the court is satisfied that his judgment in the present case cannot be affected thereby.

"The testimony in this case reveals a crime of singular atrocity. It is, in a sense, inexplicable, but is not thereby rendered less inhuman or repulsive. It was deliberately planned and prepared for during a considerable period of time. It was executed with every feature of callousness and cruelty. And here the court will say, not for the purpose of extenuating guilt but merely with the object of dispelling a misapprehension that appears to have found lodgment in the public mind, that he is convinced by conclusive evidence that there was no abuse offered to the body of the victim.

"But it did not need that element to make the crime abhorrent to every instinct of humanity, and the court is satisfied that neither in the act itself, nor in its motives or lack of motives, or in the antecedents of the offenders, can he find any mitigating circumstances.

"For the crime of murder and of kidnaping for ransom the law prescribes different punishments in the alternatives.

"For the crime of murder the statute declares: 'Whoever is guilty of murder shall suffer the punishment of death or imprisonment in the penitentiary for his natural life or for a term not less than fourteen years. If the accused is found guilty by a jury they shall fix the punishment by their verdict; upon a plea of guilty, the punishment shall be fixed by the court.'

"For the crime of kidnaping for ransom the statute reads: 'Whoever is guilty of kidnaping for ransom shall suffer death or be punished by imprisonment in the penitentiary for life, or for any term not less than five years.'

"Under the pleas of guilty, the duty of determining the punishment devolves upon the court, and the law indicates no rule or policy for the guidance of his discretion. In reaching his decision the court would have welcomed the counsel and support of others. In some states the legislature, in its wisdom, has provided for a bench of three judges to determine the penalty in cases such as this. Nevertheless, the court is willing to meet his responsibilities. It would have been the task of least resistance to impose the extreme penalty of the law. In choosing imprisonment instead of death, the court is moved chiefly by the consideration of the age of the defendants, boys of 18 and 19 years.

"It is not for the court to say that he will not, in any case, enforce capital punishment as an alternative, but the court believes it is within his province to decline to impose the sentence of death on persons who are not of full age.

"This determination appears to be in accordance with the progress of criminal law all over the world and with the dictates of enlightened humanity. More than that, it seems to be in accordance with the precedents hitherto observed in this State. The records of Illinois show only two cases of minors who were put to death by legal process . . . . to which number the court does not feel inclined to make an addition.

"Life imprisonment, at the moment, strikes the public imagination as forcibly as would death by hanging, but to the offenders, particularly of the type they are, the prolonged suffering of years of confinement may well be the severest form of retribution and expiation.

"The court feels it proper to add a final word concerning the effect of the parole law upon the punishment of these defendants. In the case of such atrocious crimes it is entirely within the discretion of the department of public welfare, never to admit these defendants to parole.

"To such a policy the court urges them strictly to adhere. If this course is persevered in the punishment of these defendants, it will both satisfy the ends of justice and safeguard the interests of society."

At this point the sentences formally were passed as follows:

"In No. 33,623, indictment for murder, the sentence of the court is that you, Nathan F. Leopold Jr., be confined in the penitentiary at Joliet for the term of your natural life. The court finds that your age is 19.

"In No. 33,623, indictment for murder, the sentence of the court is that you, Richard Loeb, be confined in the penitenitary at Joliet for the term of your natural life. The court finds that your age is 18.

"In 33,624, kidnaping for ransom, it is the sentence of the court that you, Nathan F. Leopold, Jr., be confined in the penitentiary at Joliet for the term of 99 years. The court finds your age at 19.

"In 33,624, kidnaping for ransom, the sentence of the court is that you, Richard Loeb, be confined in the penitentiary at Joliet for the term of 99 years."

This special edition of

THE AMAZING CRIME
AND TRIAL OF
LEOPOLD AND LOEB

By Maureen McKernan

has been privately printed for the members of The Notable Trials Library by Arcata Graphics/Kingsport. The introduction was written for this edition by Alan M. Dershowitz, Professor of Law, Harvard University. Film was prepared from the first American edition of 1924. New type matter was composed by P&M Typesetting, Inc. in Caslon. The text paper was especially made for this edition by the P. H. Glatfelter Company. The volume has been quarter-bound in genuine leather by Arcata Graphics/Sherwood. Endleaves are a specially commissioned original marbled design of Richard J. Wolfe. Edges are gilded; the spine is stamped in 22-karat gold. Cover stampings and design of the edition by Daniel B. Bianchi and Selma Ordewer.